Alts Democratized

Alts Democratized

A Practical Guide to Alternative Mutual Funds and ETFs for Financial Advisors

JESSICA LYNN RABE
ROBERT J. MARTORANA, CFA

WILEY

Library of Congress Cataloging-in-Publication Data is on file.

ISBN 978-1-118-97101-7 (Hardcover)
ISBN 978-1-118-97103-1 (ePDF)
ISBN 978-1-118-97102-4 (ePub)

Printed in the United States of America

10 9 8 7 6 5 4 3 2 1

To my dad, David M. Rabe, for always supporting
me in taking strategic risks and pursuing
unconventional paths

Jessica Lynn Rabe

To the glory of God and to Abraham Samuel,
founder of the Sharon Children's Home
in Andhra Pradesh, India

Robert J. Martorana, CFA

Contents

Foreword

So you've taken the plunge to learn more about alternative funds, or alts. No doubt you feel compelled in some way to find out more about these fascinating and oft-talked-about investments, and you're ready to jump in and start—or maybe not. Maybe you just want a better understanding of the unknown before you find one popping up or, worse yet, blowing up in your portfolio. Let's take a quick look at the potential reasons why you bought this book and now find yourself reading this Foreword:

- You are an avid self-directed investor who wants to know about the latest product innovations.
- You are a well-read advisor seeking to broaden the palette of investment vehicles you use to build your clients' portfolios.
- You employ the services of an advisor and/or you invest in a fund that utilizes multiple asset classes in its investment solutions, and you recently learned that liquid alts were to be part of the mix.
- You keep hearing about these so-called alts on financial media, at cocktail parties, or on the sidelines at your children's soccer games, and want some meaningful fun facts to add to the conversation.
- You're a student, and this is on the syllabus.

All these or any combinations thereof are excellent reasons to read this book. Why am I writing the Foreword, you ask? I will tell you, of course, and I think you'll find my rationale strikes a similar theme across many of the aforementioned scenarios. Like many of you, I lived through the financial crisis of 2008. I also lived through the tech bubble meltdown of 2001 and every other market downdraft dating back to 1987. That doesn't make me either a dinosaur or a neophyte, but it does make me aware of the fact that dynamics in the market have changed over time and the tools used by investors to weather such storms have had varying degrees of success and seemingly less efficacy with each new episode. Time-tested adages such as building diversified portfolios with underlying holdings that zig while others zag have fallen short. And it's not just that market dynamics seem to have evolved over the years; it's also the degree of urgency placed on those in the position of building portfolios to get it right and limit losses.

If you, too, have personally lived through all the market events mentioned—and particularly if you've lived through a few more even further back in time—you are probably not in a position to suffer the impacts of another market meltdown. You're simply too vulnerable at this stage of your savings and investing horizon to sit tight and let the corrections right themselves. You are also likely to be in need of generating income and at least keeping pace with inflation, if not rising health care costs. Stuffing mattresses and rolling over certificates of deposit (CDs) aren't very good options, yet traditional asset allocation across stocks, bonds, and cash also seems insufficient. The most recent market meltdown certainly taught us that when old-guard asset classes "correlated to one and went to zero" (which means the offsetting zigs and zags all zigged or zagged together), substantial losses were seen even in strategically designed asset allocation products incorporating the usually reliable diversification tools wielded by professional managers.

New tools are needed that are almost custom-tailored to behave in a certain way. For example, we as investors would surely benefit from a product that will diversify equity risk during a rocky equity market, or a product that has bondlike characteristics yet is designed not to follow the rest of the bond world down during a rising interest rate environment. At a high level, the implicit usefulness of such products seems too simple and too obvious to ignore. Who wouldn't want to use such vehicles in one's portfolio if—and this is a big *if*—they truly exist and perform as advertised?

Well, the investment management industry is nothing if not resourceful and forever inventive, and it is this zeal to create—or at least repackage—that is bringing investors just such products in an easy-to-access mutual fund form. Liquid alts give the average investor access to sophisticated strategies that had once been reserved exclusively for high-net-worth investors, so mutual funds and exchange-traded funds (ETFs) truly are "democratizing alts." Unfortunately, the fund industry also has a tendency to blithely follow flavor-of-the-month trends in investor demand and to crank out ill-conceived efforts and rushed product designs in order to participate in the next big thing. All they need to do is label it in a compelling way, and investors may blindly buy in (Internet funds, anyone?). This is why you are reading a book like this.

For all of the foregoing reasons, my colleagues at Lipper and I believe that understanding alternatives is an important, if not critical step for investors and advisors who desire to build better diversified portfolios. With the aging demographics of the developed world, such products are a must in order for individuals to build secure retirements and protect their nest eggs. Even younger investors can benefit from products that help navigate market volatilities stemming from such newfound sources as high-frequency trading, derivative-laden structured products, and the massive ebb and flow of herd-mentality asset class gyrations—any of which can cause substantial disruptions to the normally sanguine process of putting aside part of your paycheck for your eventual retirement.

Liquid or registered alternatives are a relatively young corner of the industry and, as mentioned already, not everything that is being marketed out there as an alternative fund is well labeled or well designed. Complicating matters further is the fact that the investment industry loves to wax philosophical and craft sweeping white papers and books with Greek letters, long formulas, and big words to give the appearance that they are incredibly smart and deserving of your money. Any one of these tomes, when read by even sophisticated investors, leaves one with the feeling that this truly is the best product out there and is being run by the smartest people in the industry. An additional complication is that there are many of these products that hail from the once-sacrosanct world of hedge funds. Simply because they are run by a former or current hedge fund manager doesn't mean they have any business in your portfolio. The goal of this book is to take a third-party view of this fast-growing segment of the fund industry. The authors aren't tied to any of the major firms launching and running these funds, and they haven't been involved in any of these product designs. Furthermore, no one involved with the writing of this book stands to gain from sales of alternative investment products as a result of their being profiled in this book.

With conflicts of interest removed, what remains is a factually based reference manual that describes the major categories of what are known as liquid alternative funds with descriptions of what they are, how they are designed and managed, how they perform, and how an advisor or investor might consider using them in a portfolio. This book offers a simple, practical guide that helps investors benefit from their newfound access to advanced strategies. This brings power back to the investor and is the democratization of alternatives.

Robert Jenkins
Global Head of Research at Thomson Reuters Lipper

Acknowledgments

We would like to thank everyone at Lipper, including Robert Jenkins, Global Head of Research; Andrew Clark, Head of Alternatives Research; and Tom Roseen, Head of Research Services. At John Wiley & Sons we thank Tula Batanchiev, Associate Editor, and Judy Howarth, Senior Development Editor, as well as all of the other professionals who helped make this book a reality. We thank Owen Zukovich, Client Service Associate at Morgan Stanley Wealth Management, for data analysis and preparation of the tables and figures.

We also thank all of the interviewees for their time, candor, and insights.

Introduction

The allure of hedge funds has enthralled investors since the pioneering work of Alfred Winslow Jones in 1949. Talented money managers have traditionally emerged from the incubator of large institutions prior to gleaning capital from family and friends as a means to launch their own hedge funds, often in the Big Apple. Distant from the Securities and Exchange Commission (SEC) and largely unregulated, hedge fund managers have often employed obscure and complex strategies to generate alpha (excess return or outperformance relative to their benchmarks), and this has allowed the notoriously lucrative "2 and 20 percent" fee structure. Hedge funds are also notorious for their illiquidity, lack of transparency, and high investment minimums. Nevertheless, hedge funds remain an exclusive club that attracts high-net-worth and institutional clients, while being out of reach for the average investor.

That is, until these sophisticated strategies were democratized in the form of Investment Company Act of 1940 ('40 Act) wrappers (i.e., mutual funds), thereby giving hedge fund managers access to the retail market. For some top-tier managers, small accounts are time-consuming and burdensome, but other managers recognize the opportunity to expand their footprints through retail distribution of their hedge fund strategies. Their efforts are paying off, and this book will explore the rapid growth of the liquid alts space.

Why do we say "democratized"? Because liquid alts have extended access to hedge fund strategies to investors on Main Street. Mutual funds have used leverage and short selling for decades, and these are the same strategies that trailblazer Alfred Winslow Jones used in the first pooled investment vehicle that focused on alternative investment strategies. But recent product innovation has propelled the growth of liquid alts to new heights as these products reach a much broader base of investors. The proliferation of products peaked in the middle of the preceding decade with the launch of dozens of alternative mutual funds. These new products are similar to traditional hedge funds in their use of leverage and the ability to go both long and short in equity, fixed income, currencies, commodities, and derivative instruments. Thus, '40 Act alts democratize access by empowering both high-net-worth and retail investors with sophisticated investment strategies.

In addition to expanding access, liquid alts offer benefits that differ in key ways from traditional hedge funds. The '40 Act products have disclosure requirements that help protect investors and that make the products more transparent. Liquid alts also have lower investment minimums, greater tax efficiency, and lower expense ratios. Thus, these funds offer diversification benefits and potential alpha that had been available only to the upper echelons of the income scale by way of traditional hedge funds.

The democratization of hedge fund strategies starts with access to '40 Act products, but what value is this access if investors are unsure of how to use liquid alts effectively in traditional portfolios? In order for '40 Act liquid alts to truly penetrate the retail market, the education of liquid alts must also be democratized. This is especially challenging given the history of hedge funds, which have historically been abstruse strategies that do not always report underlying positions.

Many of the concepts required to use liquid alts are genuinely new to retail investors, and beyond the scope of traditional educational materials since the analysis of hedge fund strategies has been necessary only for institutional investors. These strategies are complex, and are often further obscured by hyperbole in the marketing materials. If advisors use liquid alts without a proper framework and proper management of expectations, investment results will suffer and clients will be disappointed.

This is where we come in. Our objective is to serve as your guides by arming you as the advisor with the analysis, tools, and, above all, the process that will enable you to incorporate liquid alts within portfolios to reach clients' goals. Liquid alts offer potential alpha and diversification through noncorrelation, thereby creating the potential to push client portfolios further out on the efficient frontier. Advisors' understanding of these products and the underlying strategies will help achieve a more optimal balance of risk and return. Equally important for advisors is the need to relay this information back to clients, so they will understand the underlying strategies and positions of their portfolios. This will help you as an advisor to manage expectations, which will enhance long-term performance as clients will be less apt to panic and bail out at a market trough, and advisors will be less likely to come under pressure from clients to unwind positions at fire-sale prices.

Given the right education, what if you could manage client portfolios like an endowment? Liquid alts act as a vehicle to get you one step closer. Endowments must generate sufficient returns to cover the annual withdrawal for university expenses, in addition to growing the asset base to protect the principal from inflation. They often attain high returns in excess of traditional equity and fixed income indexes. How do they achieve these superior returns? By using the endowment model—most notably at Yale University and Harvard University—which usually allocates a smaller portion of the portfolio to equities and fixed income, and a greater portion to nontraditional assets, such as hedge funds, private equity, venture capital, and real assets (including infrastructure and natural resources).

These alternative assets require substantial minimum investments and are highly illiquid, but they can boost returns significantly.

Granted, the endowment model is more suitable for higher allocations to risky nontraditional assets due to its long investment time horizon afforded by institutions such as pensions and universities. Allocations with tilts of this nature would be imprudent for most clients. Consequently, we created a practical framework for the proper usage of liquid alts by modifying the endowment approach. We call this the Micro-Endowment Model (MEM). Throughout this book, we assign five roles to liquid alts depending on their factor exposures: equity complement, fixed income complement, portfolio diversifier, tactical hedge, and directional bet. These roles supplement the equity and fixed income exposures of a traditional portfolio, and, like the endowment model, include allocations to alternatives (hedge funds and private equity) and real assets, while leaving room for a little cash.

The MEM therefore sports an alternative tilt that is more reasonable for individual investors, providing the portfolio with potential for enhanced returns and alpha generation from a number of sources: diversification through noncorrelation, directional bets, hedging of tail risks, active management of credit and duration risks, and preservation of capital using nontraditional assets. The MEM may not be suitable for all clients, but we describe it as a tool that may help the portfolio construction process.

Bear in mind that the MEM assumes a core/satellite approach, which blends passive and active funds and helps separate beta from alpha. This process can enable customization by focusing the satellite of the portfolio on specific client needs. Meanwhile it limits costs by using passive funds in the core for beta exposure to equity, fixed income, real assets, and certain alternative assets. The customization facilitated by the core/satellite approach helps advisors adapt to the changes in portfolio construction that we outline in Figure 15.2: Rather than targeting a benchmark and sticking with a buy-and-hold strategy, many advisors now use both strategic and tactical approaches to meet client goals.

Another advantage of the core/satellite approach is its focus on cost-effective portfolio construction, which underscores a major headwind for liquid alts: high expense ratios. We acknowledge that fees should be a primary concern at the *portfolio* level since expenses are the only factor known with certainty in advance. However, an investor should not always make fees a primary concern at the *product* level, since a portfolio that combines alpha and beta will have a wide range of expense ratios.

To put these strategies, models, and approaches in perspective, the current macroeconomic environment is one in which investors are scouring the globe for yield as interest rates hover near zero, rising rates are on the horizon, inflation is inching toward the Federal Reserve's 2 percent target, and correlations are normalizing after converging during the financial crisis. These factors encourage investors to seek enhanced income, active management of credit and duration risks, hedging of tail risks, preservation of capital for those worried about inflation, and, most notably, diversification. Liquid alts help achieve these goals.

With that said, liquid alts are by no means ideal, and not all classifications are truly uncorrelated. Many strategies have high equity beta, and others do not comport to their mandates or to what the classification's name suggests. We help advisors sift through each classification as defined by Lipper by evaluating factor exposures and identifying the likely roles of funds within portfolios. But there are natural limits to applying any analytical framework that relies on abstract theoretical assumptions. It may make sense for investors who have a process that is quantitatively rigorous, has significant research resources, and is applied in a disciplined manner over time horizons measured in decades.

This approach may be feasible for institutions, but it is impractical for most individuals. Every client relationship must eventually address a wide variety of random life events that involve money. These include death, divorce, new jobs, retirement, medical issues, sale of the family business, and so on. Adapting to these events is part of what makes investment advice an art, and not a science. We believe that alts democratized can be a useful concept, and our framework aims to help you as the advisor achieve more tactical, customized, transparent, and cost-effective portfolios for your clients. But we leave the application in the hands of the advisor.

Overall, we view liquid alts as a source of psychological alpha: investments that mitigate the consequences of fear-driven and nonproductive asset reallocation that is often triggered by market volatility. Liquid alts provide a sense of security due to their uncorrelated characteristics, which in turn encourage discipline when it is needed most: during bear markets. If markets were rational, equities would be less volatile, and investors would not panic during crashes. In some ways, alternatives act as a form of insurance, and allow investors to take prudent risks with the equity allocations of their portfolios. Investors need stocks for long-term growth, but the volatility is difficult to live with.

Therefore, liquid alts provide a behavioral hedge that makes it easier for investors to tolerate market volatility and reach their long-term investment goals. An allocation to liquid alts enables advisors to hold a greater share of equities, and reduces bail-out risk during declines in the market, as long as clients understand the diversification benefits of alts. Likewise, advisors must also keep clients abreast of the tendency for liquid alts to lag during bull markets: Just as alts keep investors from bailing out of equities at the bottom, investors need to stick with liquid alts even when equities are reaching new highs.

Liquid alts, as a source of psychological alpha, help investors stay in the game.

CHAPTER 1

Definitions and Methodology

Synopsis

This book defines liquid alternatives as hedge fund strategies used in a '40 Act wrapper, and it uses Lipper data to evaluate 11 different alternative classifications. The analysis focuses on the risk and return of each classification, and the 10 largest funds. The methodology uses factor exposures to analyze fund returns, and to identify different roles that liquid alts can play in portfolios. These roles include portfolio diversifier, equity complement, fixed income complement, tactical hedge, and directional bet.

Readers may wish to read this book straight through, skim through the chapter summaries, or use it as a reference tool. Each chapter is written as independently as possible, while adhering to a comprehensive framework for studying liquid alternatives.

DEFINITIONS

Alts Democratized defines liquid alternatives as hedge fund strategies in an Investment Company Act of 1940 ('40 Act) wrapper, such as an exchange-traded fund (ETF) or a mutual fund. This description concurs with the 11 alternative classifications used by Lipper, and the definition emphasizes the investment strategy rather than the legal structure.

The term *hedge fund strategies* includes a broad range of investment vehicles that operate in a different legal structure. Hedge funds are usually pooled vehicles with investments managed in a general partner/limited partner structure, and held by a limited liability company. These funds have fewer restrictions on the investment strategy, manager compensation, and public disclosures than do '40 Act investments.

Traditional hedge funds are designed for accredited investors, and typically have high minimum investments, limited liquidity, and long lockup periods. Investors get K-1 statements that can make tax reporting difficult, and the paperwork and suitability requirements are demanding.

When we mention "traditional alternatives," this refers to single-manager hedge funds, fund-of-funds hedge funds, private equity, and privately held real estate. These traditional alternatives are usually available only to high-net-worth investors, and this gives wide latitude to hedge fund managers.

In contrast, '40 Act investments are meant for the masses, and have strict regulatory requirements, including limits on leverage and illiquid assets. For example, '40 Act funds can have borrowings of no more than one-third of total assets, and this reduces their ability to replicate certain hedge fund strategies that rely on high leverage (credit arbitrage). Also, '40 Act investments limit holdings of illiquid assets and transactions with affiliated persons, which makes it difficult to participate in private equity strategies such as venture capital. And '40 Act funds have strict disclosure requirements about the positions they hold and the compensation paid to investment managers, and these disclosures are made through the filing of the prospectus, annual report, and statement of additional information. These funds usually offer daily liquidity to investors who seek redemptions, though this is not true for closed-end funds or interval funds. There are many other legal nuances that distinguish traditional and liquid alts, but the main differences involve fees, liquidity, transparency, and taxation.

Today the lines between '40 Act funds and limited partnerships are blurring as traditional alternative fund managers enter the '40 Act space in search of broader distribution. The entrance of traditional alternative managers is leading to product innovation and a breadth of new choices for advisors and investors, and this requires new approaches to fund research and deeper levels of fund manager due diligence.

LIPPER CLASSIFICATIONS

This book uses Lipper classifications to define liquid alts, and these classifications exclude certain assets that some investors define as alternative. The Lipper classifications used in this book exclude real assets of all types—commodities, precious metals, master limited partnerships (MLPs), real estate investment trusts (REITs), privately held real estate, infrastructure investments, and Treasury Inflation-Protected Securities (TIPS). These securities are generally considered real assets in the framework used by institutional investors.

THE FUTURE

There is currently no industry standard for exactly what constitutes an "alternative" investment. The definition of liquid alts is continually evolving, and precise classifications are in the eye of the investor.

The future of liquid alts is likely to include some form of private equity, such as leveraged buyouts, mezzanine financing, infrastructure, and venture capital. These are now difficult to package effectively in a '40 Act structure, but strong investor demand suggests that this is a large potential market for product providers that can innovate.

The definition of liquid alts may also expand to include forms of so-called smart beta. Smart beta uses rules-based approaches to define factor exposures, such as indexes that are not weighted by market capitalization, but by equal weights or fundamental factors such as sales, profits, or price-to-book ratios. Smart beta also includes sophisticated algorithms for optimization, such as minimum variance, maximum diversification, and risk-efficient indexes.

The factor exposures discussed in this book may overlap with some forms of smart beta. Chapter 7 discusses Alternative Equity Market Neutral Funds, and includes the PIMCO Fundamental Advantage Absolute Return Strategy Fund (PFATX). This fund has long exposure to a smart beta strategy, a fundamental equity index called the Enhanced Research Affiliates Fundamental Index (Enhanced RAFI 1000). PFATX also has a short exposure to the Standard & Poor's (S&P) 500 index, so the fund seeks to capture the return premium of an index that is weighted according to fundamentals over an index that is weighted according to market capitalization. This is an example where liquid alts and smart beta converge, and there is room for disagreement as to the demarcation between smart beta and liquid alternatives.

Note: This book focuses on the track record of funds through year-end 2013. We occasionally note subsequent events, such as the departure of Bill Gross from PIMCO (see PFIUX in Chapter 9), and the downturn in returns at MainStay Marketfield (see MFLDX in Chapter 10). These events highlight the need for ongoing due diligence of liquid alternatives, especially for funds that give broad discretion to the portfolio manager.

This book focuses on funds that Lipper classifies as alternative, and the underlying factor exposures of these funds. This provides a clear, functional, and comprehensive map of the liquid alts space. These classifications will continue to evolve, and may eventually include smart beta and private equity. The authors believe that the Lipper data provide a useful framework and functional tools for asset allocation and fund selection, and the Lipper classification methodology is among the most practical and accurate systems that are widely available at this point in time.

METHODOLOGY

This book is aimed at financial advisors and sophisticated investors and it assumes familiarity with basic investment concepts. It is meant to be a practical tool, so we stick with a simple framework and we disclose our key assumptions.

How to Use This Book

The chapters in this book can be read independently, and the authors intended each section to serve as a reference tool. Advisors are busy, and may want a quick overview of a classification and the funds in it. Advisors may choose to read the synopsis at the beginning of each chapter, just to get a feel for the key takeaways.

The book does have a comprehensive framework for liquid alts that starts at the 10,000-foot level, and eventually offers granular detail about individual funds. Some advisors may be interested in only a road map for the alternatives space, and how the classifications fit into the investment landscape. Other advisors may want to understand the specific factor exposures and fund selection process for a given Lipper classification, in order to augment their existing due diligence process.

We offer a framework as a guide, mainly to clarify our assumptions and prevent misunderstandings. We are not looking to either encourage or discourage the use of liquid alternatives, and we are not promoting one investment approach over another. We hope that clear definitions and a clearly articulated structure allow for a coherent discussion, even for advisors who operate with a different investment philosophy and a different set of assumptions. We may agree or disagree with other investors about the proper definition, purpose, and role of liquid alternatives. Our main goal is to provide a framework that is internally consistent, and that provides a springboard for advisors who want to put these products to work for their clients.

Or perhaps an advisor will review the data and conclude that liquid alts are not worth their time and energy, given their clients' needs and their firm's resources.

Illustrations, Not Recommendations

This book offers a process for asset allocation and fund selection, and discusses specific ETFs and mutual funds. Any analysis or example in this book is for illustration purposes only, and is not an investment recommendation for any advisor or investor.

All written content is for informational purposes only. Material presented is believed to be from reliable sources, but the authors make no representations as to its accuracy or completeness. Individual investors should discuss all information and ideas in this book in detail with their individual advisor prior to implementation. Investment advisors should note that their parent firm may strictly limit the use of certain funds described in this book. This is especially true for leveraged and inverse ETFs. Both individual investors and investment advisors should note that certain leveraged products may rapidly lose value and are not suitable for all investors.

Legal Disclosures

One of the authors of this book, Robert J. Martorana, CFA, owns a registered investment advisory firm, Right Blend Investing, LLC, in the state of New Jersey. This content shall in no way be construed or interpreted as a solicitation to sell or offer to sell investment advisory services. This is not a complete discussion of the information needed to make a decision to open an account with Right Blend Investing, LLC. There are always risks in making investments, including the investment strategies described.

Right Blend Investing, LLC, may have long positions in the ETFs and mutual funds described, and these positions may change without notice. Mr. Martorana believes that the position sizes at his firm are too small to have a material impact on any fund described in the book.

GUIDE TO CHAPTERS 3 THROUGH 13

Chapters 3 through 13 review each of the 11 Lipper classifications in detail. This analysis forms the core of this book, and the following describes each of the subsections in these chapters. We briefly explain why we used certain data, and some of the pros and cons of our choices.

The authors thank Tom Roseen, Head of Research Services at Lipper, for providing the data used throughout this book.

Synopsis

We offer a synopsis at the beginning of each chapter that covers the highlights and summarizes the key takeaways. This material may overlap with the conclusion of the chapter. But the synopsis is meant as a summary, while the conclusion focuses more on how advisors would use funds, and it presumes that advisors have actually read the chapter.

The synopses can be read as freestanding content, and the advisor should not have to read the entire chapter to get value. *The synopses are written in general language, and may be particularly helpful when advisors are creating talking points for clients.* If the client has follow-up questions, the advisor can be confident that the chapter explains the concepts in detail and offers a supporting rationale for the trends, themes, and investment conclusions.

Definition

We start with the definition of each Lipper classification, supplemented by a working definition derived from the fact sheets and disclosure documents of the most popular funds. These chapters assume a strict adherence to the

Lipper classification system. So while we acknowledge that some funds and strategies may have fuzzy boundaries, we aim first and foremost to explain the funds that each Lipper classification includes.

Total Net Assets and Net Flows

This section examines the history of total assets in each classification and their development over the past 10 years. We evaluate trends in assets, net flows, fund launches, and fund closures. This analysis gives a sense of how investor interest in the classification has waxed and waned in light of market returns and the returns for the classification.

This section also explores the depth and breadth of fund choices for investors. Are there many funds with a variety of strategies? Or is the classification relatively homogeneous, with different flavors of the same basic strategy?

As part of this process, we note any blockbuster funds that dominate the Lipper classification. The dominance of blockbuster funds is critical to understand, since some funds comprise 50 percent or more of the assets and net flows in a classification. This may give a distorted impression of the trends in the classification, since the asset growth may be dominated by a single fund. It can seem that a certain strategy is growing rapidly, and is worthy of deep investigation. The truth may be that a certain fund is popular because of recent investment performance, and the popularity of the classification may rest on the success or failure of a single portfolio manager.

Risk and Return

We discuss the returns of each classification over the past year, three years, five years, and 10 years. Some classifications have a limited history, so the data are absent and there are blank spaces in some of the exhibits.

Our analysis focuses on the overall level of returns and on the dispersion of returns, which may be wide or narrow depending on whether the classification is homogeneous or heterogeneous. We also note when returns tend to cluster around some type of benchmark, reflecting the underlying factor exposures. Some classifications have high beta and high correlations to an index, whereas others are driven by idiosyncratic risks and decisions by the portfolio manager.

When we compare returns in the classification to the underlying factor exposure, we usually offer a comparison to the S&P 500. As a convenience, data on the S&P 500 appears as a table in each chapter, so the reader does not have to flip through the book to find out how the classification compared to the equity market under different market conditions.

We also show measures of risk: Sharpe ratios, Sortino ratios, and maximum drawdowns. There are many measures of risk we could have used, but our experience with these funds showed that returns and drawdowns were generally the most useful. These offer a thumbnail guide to whether the funds are offering an attractive mix of risk and return, though we must offer a major cautionary note: The five-year data coincide with a bull market, and this makes nearly all alternative strategies look poor in comparison to equities. Unfortunately, many of these products have not existed for a complete cycle of bull and bear markets, so it is impossible to definitively say how they might perform in a crisis.

Factor Exposures

This section of each chapter is intended to help advisors understand what drives the risk and return of each Lipper alternative classification. Fund performance can often be explained by equity beta, credit risk, and other factors, and these help determine the role that each fund plays in an investor's portfolio.

This book often refers to analysis by the research staff at Lipper, which has done extensive work on factor exposures. We discuss this in detail in Chapter 3, Absolute Return Funds, and this chapter is the best starting point for a detailed discussion of how factor exposures affect the risk/return profile of alternative mutual funds and ETFs. The authors wish to thank Andrew Clark, PhD, Manager of Alternative Investment Research, for his assistance in helping to understand and interpret Lipper's research in this area.

Asset Allocation and Fund Selection

This section helps the advisor understand the proper role of each fund in a portfolio. It starts with the factor exposures that drive the classification, and it uses these to determine a process for evaluating a fund's track record. We discuss how some funds have stood out from the crowd, and we assess the degree to which this might be explained by top-down factors. Each classification is driven by different factors, so we discuss how to evaluate the effectiveness of funds using different strategies.

This book assumes that alternative funds have different roles in the portfolio: portfolio diversifier, equity complement, fixed income complement, directional bet, or hedging of tail risk. Chapter 18 on fund selection discusses these roles in detail. Chapter 15 discusses the process, and it assumes the same roles for alts in a portfolio.

Top Ten Funds

This section reviews the assets, net flows, and investment performance of the top ten funds in each classification. The authors chose to focus on the top ten funds by assets because we believe this is an objective standard that can be used across classifications.

Each Lipper alternative classification is driven by different factors, and the funds play distinct roles in portfolios. This makes it difficult to use a quantitative ranking method that is both fair and comprehensive. It is difficult for a single book to discuss the complete range of alternative strategies using a single measure of risk and return. For example, if we had ranked funds based on returns we would have favored funds with high equity beta, while a ranking based on low max drawdowns would have favored funds with low equity beta.

The downside to our approach is that we seem to be favoring the largest funds in each category. This was not our intent, and we encourage advisors to use their own due diligence and the processes described in this book to uncover hidden gems in each classification that will help their clients reach their goals.

Blockbuster and Spotlight

This section discusses the largest fund in each classification—the blockbuster. The dominance of certain alternative funds may be a sign of investors chasing the hot performance or a popular fund manager. Or it may be a sign that a fund has earned the top spot because of a sustainable investment process. The analysis of blockbusters also helps in understanding investor demand, and may reveal larger trends about issues such as risk tolerance.

The authors also choose a spotlight fund in each classification to allow a deeper dive into the process of a single fund. This fund may have a particularly impressive track record, or it may simply be a good representative of the strategy and investment process that typifies the Lipper alternative classification. This analysis also offers the opportunity to contrast the approach by the blockbuster fund, and to show how the classification has room for a variety of strategies. The main purpose of the spotlight discussion is to show how an advisor might uncover an attractive fund in the classification, depending on the role of the alternative fund in a portfolio and the goals of a particular investor.

SUMMARY

This book attempts to offer practical information to a wide audience, and is designed to help investors consider how they might use a fund in their portfolios, or to help advisors consider how they might use liquid alts in their practices. Each investor has different goals, and each advisor has a different value proposition. Some readers may be new to liquid alts whereas others may already have an established process. The authors recognize this range of expertise, and show how liquid alts might be used accordingly. We aim for this book to be both a practical tool and an authoritative source of information, and we hope you find it useful.

CHAPTER 2

Road Map for the Liquid Alts Space

Synopsis

Despite a decade of blistering growth in assets, including 10 straight years of positive net flows, liquid alternatives have only a 2 percent share of the mutual fund market. This suggests significant growth potential as liquid alts potentially command a larger share of portfolios. When it comes to risk and return data, we caution against a quick read of aggregate data, since each classification has quirks that can be deceptive. This chapter is best used as a high-level overview, and not as a means of comparing classifications.

LIQUID ALTS IN CONTEXT

The following figure and tables show how the market share of liquid alts compares to traditional alternatives and traditional mutual funds. These data put liquid alts in a broader context, and show the long-term growth potential. Some of this potential rests on investor familiarity, and some of it rests on investment performance. Both of these factors are likely to drive the continued growth of liquid alts, assuming that these funds deliver on their promises, and eventually grab a larger slice of the asset allocation pie.

Liquid Alts versus Traditional Alts

In Figure 2.1, traditional alternative investments include single hedge funds, hedge funds of funds (FOFs), private equity, and private real estate assets that are distributed through the firm's private client or broker/dealer. Liquid alternative investments comprise mutual funds and exchange-traded funds (ETFs) that generate alternative outcomes and are predominately distributed through the firm's broker/dealer by financial advisors. Morningstar

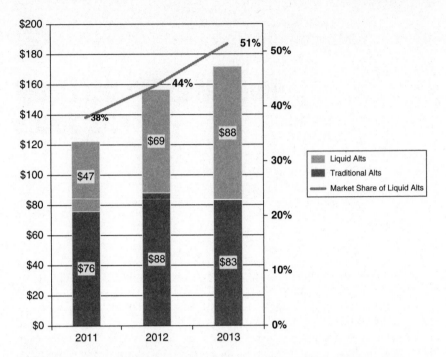

FIGURE 2.1   Assets in Traditional Alternatives versus Liquid Alternative at
Wirehouse Firms ($ Billions)
Source: Distribution of Alternative Investments through Wirehouses, 3rd Issue,
May 2014. Washington, DC: Money Management Institute and Dover Financial
Research.
Note: Data are from Morgan Stanley, Merrill Lynch, Wells Fargo, and UBS.

categories are used to define the universe of liquid alternative investment
strategies. Real estate mutual funds and real estate ETFs are not included.

It is extremely challenging to find data that compare the usage of liquid
alternatives with traditional alternatives. These markets have been historically separate, and the data providers rarely have comparable information about both markets. Fortunately, the Money Management Institute and
Dover Financial Research completed a study in early 2014 that examined
how wirehouse advisors use both traditional and liquid alts.

Figure 2.1 shows wirehouse assets held in both traditional and liquid
alternatives. Liquid alternative assets grew from $47 billion in 2011 to
$88 billion in 2013, due to market appreciation and net inflows. During
the same period, assets held in traditional alternatives have grown more
slowly, and dipped slightly from $88 billion in 2012 to $83 billion in 2013.
The headwinds for traditional alternatives include high fees and the limited

liquidity of hedge funds, private equity, and other strategies held in a limited partnership structure. The year 2013 was also a banner year for equities, and the ongoing rally creates a tough environment for all types of alternative strategies, since bull markets increase risk tolerance and decrease investor preferences for products that diversify or offer downside protection.

Some of the headwinds for traditional alts are tailwinds for liquid alts, which offer better liquidity, transparency, and tax efficiency, and which generally have lower expense ratios. We are careful to avoid any direct comparison between the risk/return benefits of liquid alts versus traditional alts, since liquid alts have restrictions on leverage and liquidity that prevent them from replicating hedge fund strategies. Certain performance data show that these restrictions on liquid alts cause these products to underperform traditional alts when using certain investment strategies. Direct comparisons are muddied by the availability of data, and differences in classification systems. In any case, this evaluation of investment performance is beyond the scope of this book.

Regardless of their structural limitations, liquid alts offer clear benefits that continue to attract investors, and there is potential for significantly more growth. Institutional investors routinely allocate 30 percent or more of their portfolios to hedge fund strategies, while most portfolios managed by wirehouse advisors have an allocation of less than 5 percent. The fund manager research teams recommend a significantly higher weighting to alternative strategies, with most clustering around 10 percent to 15 percent. This suggests significant growth ahead as advisors and investors become more familiar with the products.

Liquid Alts versus Traditional Mutual Funds

Table 2.1 shows Lipper data for total net assets (TNA) of ETFs and open-end mutual funds. These assets totaled $16.3 trillion in 2013, an increase of 17 percent compared to $13.9 trillion in 2012. Much of this growth reflects market appreciation, since the Standard & Poor's (S&P) 500 rose 32 percent in 2013.

The recent growth in the mutual fund industry also reflects organic growth, represented by net inflows, which were $547 billion in 2013. The net flows were concentrated in equity funds, while fixed income funds tended to have outflows.

We highlight two key numbers in Table 2.1 for the liquid alts space. In 2013 liquid alts accounted for 1.9 percent of mutual fund assets, but accounted for 20 percent of net flows. This shows robust investor demand for these products, even during a year when stocks rallied. Since liquid alts still represent a small portion of the overall mutual fund universe, they have the potential to capture significant market share from traditional mutual funds.

TABLE 2.1　Total Net Assets and Estimated Net Flows for Lipper Macro-Classifications

Lipper Macro Classifications	Sum of TNAs 2012 ($Mil)	Sum of TNAs 2013 ($Mil)	Sum of Estimated Net Flows 2012 ($Mil)	Sum of Estimated Net Flows 2013 ($Mil)
Alternatives Fixed Income Funds	$50,516	$96,047	$1,828	$44,696
Alternatives Funds	$144,429	$211,452	$26,012	$64,921
Subtotal	$194,945	$307,499	$27,840	$109,617
Alternatives Subtotal as % of Grand Total	1.4%	1.9%	5%	20%
Commodities Funds	$169,305	$103,285	$12,181	($34,341)
Developed International Markets Funds	$1,292,825	$1,750,641	$974	$169,061
Emerging Markets Funds	$428,400	$436,855	$45,709	$18,223
Large-Cap Funds	$1,439,357	$1,898,339	($88,176)	($13,187)
Long-Term Municipal Debt Funds	$345,951	$279,770	$26,209	($46,934)
Long-Term Taxable Bond Funds	$1,316,394	$1,288,943	$166,795	($32,316)
Mid-Cap Funds	$405,382	$573,148	($8,826)	$27,010
Mixed-Asset Funds	$1,598,393	$1,958,133	$88,175	$108,415
Money Market Funds	$2,312,409	$2,337,732	$9,995	$40,638
Multi-Cap Funds	$870,508	$1,216,747	($3,883)	$63,990
Sector Equity Funds	$350,240	$465,405	$29,128	$62,405
Short-/Intermediate-Term Bond Funds	$1,105,175	$1,060,141	$109,611	($15,807)
Short-/Intermediate-Term Municipal Debt Funds	$250,473	$234,110	$27,737	($11,613)
Small-Cap Funds	$406,367	$589,725	($14,281)	$29,444
Tax-Exempt Money Market Funds	$285,667	$269,686	($146)	($15,539)
U.S. Diversified Equity Funds	$788,528	$1,099,008	$54,331	$63,845
World Sector Equity Funds	$114,750	$139,824	($127)	$5,308
World Taxable Fixed Income Funds	$262,293	$270,128	$37,930	$18,544
Grand Total	$13,937,361	$16,279,118	$521,177	$546,763

Source: Lipper, a Thomson Reuters company. Includes ETFs and conventional mutual funds; excludes closed-end funds.

ASSETS AND NET FLOWS

Table 2.2 shows the historical assets in each of Lipper's 11 classifications of liquid alts. Total assets grew from $18 billion in 2004 to $307 billion in 2013, a compound annual growth rate of 37 percent. The largest classification in 2013 was Alternative Credit Focus Funds with $83 billion in assets, followed by Alternative Long/Short Equity Funds with $44 billion in assets.

It is worth noting that asset growth barely paused during the financial crisis, with assets falling from $58 billion in 2007 to less than $57 billion in 2008, before rebounding to $93 billion in 2009 as markets recovered. We discuss details about the growth of each classification in Chapters 3 through 13.

The historical growth in assets reflects both market appreciation and net flows, which are shown in Table 2.3. Net flows were a mere $5 billion in 2004 and have surged to nearly $110 billion in 2013. As we noted earlier, the net flows in alternative classifications accounted for 20 percent of all net flows for mutual funds last year, demonstrating the strong organic growth. The net flow data reveal considerable cyclicality in demand for some classifications from one year to the next, and Alternative Credit Focus Funds are an excellent example. Net flows in 2012 were less than $5 billion, and this jumped almost tenfold in 2013 to more than $45 billion. The net flows for Alternative Currency Strategies Funds often flip from positive to negative from one year to the next, since most of these funds offer pure beta exposure to non-U.S. dollar currencies.

Finally, we point out that Dedicated Short Bias Funds have disproportionately large net flows relative to total net assets. Funds in this classification depreciate rapidly, and are typically used as short-term trading vehicles. So the net flows in these funds sometimes exceed the assets in these funds.

The key takeaway from this exhibit is that net flows for liquid alts have been consistently positive for 10 straight years, a remarkable testimony to investor appetite for liquid alts.

IPOS AND LIQUIDATIONS

Table 2.4 shows the initial public offerings (IPOs) of liquid alternative funds for all 11 Lipper classifications going back to 1969. These funds were not labeled as alternative back then, but a few funds that exist today have long track records. The data extend through April 22, 2014.

The growth of liquid alts accelerated dramatically in 2005, when there were 25 new products launched in eight different Lipper alternative classifications. This marked a surge of IPO activity as fund providers sought to meet investor demand, and some fund companies simply decided to jump

TABLE 2.2 Alternative Mutual Funds and ETFs: Total Net Assets ($ Millions)

Lipper Classification	2004	2005	2006	2007	2008	2009	2010	2011	2012	2013
Absolute Return Funds	$3,322	$6,252	$8,788	$9,240	$6,697	$9,346	$15,333	$16,015	$23,368	$39,621
Alternative Active Extension Funds	$199	$245	$782	$3,197	$3,724	$6,295	$7,770	$7,884	$8,286	$11,117
Alternative Credit Focus Funds	$2,755	$2,400	$2,876	$3,768	$4,361	$12,320	$23,173	$30,041	$36,685	$83,285
Alternative Currency Strategies Funds	$312	$1,583	$5,242.6	$8,738	$7,166	$11,600	$11,124	$15,842	$13,831	$12,762
Alternative Equity Market Neutral Funds	$4,287	$6,331	$9,898	$10,902	$12,122	$15,920	$19,607	$17,538	$21,673	$26,532
Alternative Event Driven Funds	$2,495	$2,010	$2,469	$2,557	$1,785	$3,776	$8,117	$10,928	$11,468	$13,284
Alternative Global Macro Funds			$0.1	$260	$892	$4,821	$22,770	$23,233	$26,903	$35,398
Alternative Long/Short Equity Funds	$3,283	$5,142	$7,881	$9,060	$7,954	$11,062	$13,660	$15,354	$20,025	$44,016
Alternative Managed Futures Funds				$244	$1,252	$2,330	$4,091	$8,251	$8,468	$10,691
Alternative Multi-Strategy Funds		$228	$734	$1,454	$1,155	$1,495	$2,455	$5,319	$8,739	$15,658
Dedicated Short Bias Funds	$3	$2,135	$3,232	$8,664	$9,581	$14,073	$13,016	$14,684	$15,500	$15,136
Total	$18,120	$26,325	$41,902	$58,084	$56,689	$93,039	$141,114	$165,087	$194,945	$307,499

Source: Lipper, a Thomson Reuters company

TABLE 2.3 Sum of Estimated Net Flows by Mutual Fund Classification ($ Millions)

Mutual Fund Classification	2004	2005	2006	2007	2008	2009	2010	2011	2012	2013
Absolute Return Funds	$1,726	$2,554	$2,054	$442	($1,125)	$1,869	$5,648	$1,017	$6,717	$14,922
Alternative Active Extension Funds	($92)	$32	$461	$2,282	$2,387	$1,087	$561	$500	($704)	$534
Alternative Credit Focus Funds	$705	($398)	$342	$726	$688	$7,260	$9,409	$7,517	$4,506	$45,347
Alternative Currency Strategies Funds	$5	$1,395	$3,264	$2,558	($489)	$3,634	($1,099)	$5,345	($2,678)	($651)
Alternative Equity Market Neutral Funds	$1,119	$1,852	$3,013	$564	$1,841	$3,495	$3,164	($2,203)	$3,444	$4,004
Alternative Event Driven Funds	$396	($546)	$215	$0	($626)	$1,664	$4,150	$2,554	$291	$1,505
Alternative Global Macro Funds				$265	$709	$3,667	$17,501	$649	$2,310	$9,366
Alternative Long/Short Equity Funds	$896	$1,634	$2,325	$847	$1,048	$2,404	$2,656	$1,661	$4,649	$19,869
Alternative Managed Futures Funds				$231	$963	$1,155	$1,775	$4,593	$657	$1,845
Alternative Multi-Strategy Funds		$13	$369	$605	$148	$460	$850	$2,886	$3,147	$5,727
Dedicated Short Bias Funds	$530	$746	$1,917	$5,925	($1,564)	$19,942	$5,632	$5,174	$5,500	$7,150
Total	$5,284	$7,282	$13,961	$14,446	$3,980	$46,638	$50,247	$29,694	$27,840	$109,617

Source: Lipper, a Thomson Reuters company

TABLE 2.4 Alternative Fund IPOs

	ABR	ACF	AED	AGM	AMS	CRX	DSB	ELCC	EMN	LSE	MFF	Grand Total
1969		1										1
1977		1							1			2
1982			1									1
1988						1						1
1989						1						1
1990									1			1
1991										1		1
1992								1				1
1993			1					1				2
1994							1		1			2
1995										1		1
1996		1								1		2
1997		1					3		2	1		7
1998	1						2		3	2		8
1999							1			4		5
2000	1		1				4		1	4		11
2001			1				2			1		4
2002	1	1					2			6		10
2003	2		1				1		1	2		7
2004					1		6		1	1		9
2005	4	1			1	4	3	1	5	6		25
2006	6	3			2	7	17	5	3	6		49
2007	2			3	3	9	33	8		18	1	77
2008	8	3		2	1	14	16	2	4	17		67
2009	4	3	2	1	5	2	14	2	1	14	1	49
2010	14	7	3	1	4	3	26	1	5	19	6	89
2011	18	12	2	3	5	4	17	3	14	16	11	105
2012	29	4	3	2	9	3	7		6	17	9	89
2013	23	13	6	3	9	6	6		6	22	5	99
2014	1	5	1	1	4		4		1	2	2	21
Grand Total	114	56	22	16	44	54	165	24	56	161	35	747

Abbrev	Classification
ABR	Absolute Return Funds
AED	Alternative Event Driven Funds
ELCC	Alternative Active Extension Funds
ACF	Alternative Credit Focus Funds
CRX	Alternative Currency Strategies Funds
EMN	Alternative Equity Market Neutral Funds
AGM	Alternative Global Macro Funds
LSE	Alternative Long/Short Equity Funds
MFF	Alternative Managed Futures Funds
AMS	Alternative Multi-Strategy Funds
DSB	Dedicated Short Bias Funds

Source: Lipper, a Thomson Reuters company

on the alts bandwagon. Product launches peaked in 2011 at 105, with IPOs in all 11 Lipper alternative classifications. This peak in new products coincided with a period of great uncertainty among investors, who were scarred by the crash of 2008, and who actively sought new sources of portfolio diversification.

The history of IPOs gives a snapshot of the depth and breadth of the liquid alts space, and we discuss the details of fund launches in the chapters describing each classification.

Table 2.5 shows fund closures from 2006 to early 2014. Alternative Long/Short Equity Funds and Dedicated Short Bias Funds have had the greatest number of liquidations, which makes sense since these classifications have the most funds. Profitability is usually the driving force behind fund closures, since funds need a certain level of assets to remain viable (though fund families may carry small funds on the books to offer a complete lineup, or for other competitive reasons). Despite robust historical growth, alternative mutual funds and ETFs are not immune to the economics of the mutual fund industry.

TABLE 2.5 Alternative Fund Liquidations

	ABR	ACF	AED	AGM	AMS	CRX	DSB	ELCC	EMN	LSE	MFF	Total
2006										2		2
2007							3		4	4		11
2008							4	3	2	4		13
2009							1	2	2	10		15
2010						2	8	1	1	10		22
2011	4					1	3	1	1	11		21
2012	2					4	18	2	5	10		41
2013	13				1	1	6	3	1	7	2	34
2014	2				1	2				2		7
Total	21	0	0	0	2	10	43	12	16	60	2	166

Abbrev	Classification
ABR	Absolute Return Funds
AED	Alternative Event Driven Funds
ELCC	Alternative Active Extension Funds
ACF	Alternative Credit Focus Funds
CRX	Alternative Currency Strategies Funds
EMN	Alternative Equity Market Neutral Funds
AGM	Alternative Global Macro Funds
LSE	Alternative Long/Short Equity Funds
MFF	Alternative Managed Futures Funds
AMS	Alternative Multi-Strategy Funds
DSB	Dedicated Short Bias Funds

Source: Lipper, a Thomson Reuters company

RISK AND RETURN

Table 2.6 shows the historical returns of Lipper alternative classifications. We did not aggregate the data since it is not meaningful to combine these diverse strategies. For example, Dedicated Short Bias Funds have leveraged short equity beta, whereas Alternative Active Extension Funds have leveraged long equity beta. This explains why the track records of these two categories are outliers.

Aside from Alternative Active Extension Funds, the long-term returns for alternative classifications are typically in the single digits. This lags the

TABLE 2.6 Average Returns by Mutual Fund Classification

Mutual Fund Classification	Average One-Year Return	Average Three-Year Annualized Return	Average Five-Year Annualized Return	Average Ten-Year Annualized Return
Absolute Return Funds	3.9%	1.8%	3.3%	1.1%
Alternative Active Extension Funds	34.0%	15.5%	16.9%	
Alternative Credit Focus Funds	0.9%	3.6%	8.6%	4.5%
Alternative Currency Strategies Funds	−3.0%	−0.9%	2.6%	2.8%
Alternative Equity Market Neutral Funds	3.4%	1.9%	2.0%	2.1%
Alternative Event Driven Funds	6.4%	4.3%	7.1%	4.3%
Alternative Global Macro Funds	2.2%	3.2%	6.2%	
Alternative Long/Short Equity Funds	15.9%	6.4%	8.8%	4.8%
Alternative Managed Futures Funds	0.4%	−3.2%	−4.8%	
Alternative Multi-Strategy Funds	4.9%	3.2%	5.8%	
Dedicated Short Bias Funds	−30.6%	−25.1%	−34.2%	−16.4%
S&P 500	32.4%	16.2%	17.9%	7.4%

Source: Lipper, a Thomson Reuters company

performance of the S&P 500, shown at the bottom of the exhibit. Readers must take this return data with a large grain of salt: During the five years ending in 2013 of the S&P 500 had annualized average returns of 18 percent, and during the ten years ending in 2013 many alternative classifications did not contain enough funds to be statistically significant. We recommend that investors refer to the classification chapters for a more in-depth analysis.

The Sharpe ratios shown in Table 2.7 are potentially more interesting, since these adjust returns for volatility. These Sharpe ratios are calculated by subtracting the risk-free rate from returns, and then dividing the result by the standard deviation of the fund.

The Sharpe ratios for the S&P 500 appear at the bottom of the chart, and only one Lipper alternative classification consistently beats it: Alternative Credit Focus Funds. This classification benefited from fixed

TABLE 2.7 Average Sharpe Ratios by Mutual Fund Classification

Mutual Fund Classification	Average One-Year Sharpe Ratio	Average Three-Year Annualized Sharpe Ratio	Average Five-Year Annualized Sharpe Ratio	Average Ten-Year Annualized Sharpe Ratio
Absolute Return Funds	0.10	0.33	0.75	0.10
Alternative Active Extension Funds	0.36	0.86	0.79	
Alternative Credit Focus Funds	0.07	1.03	1.88	0.66
Alternative Currency Strategies Funds	−0.06	−0.08	0.32	0.15
Alternative Equity Market Neutral Funds	0.12	0.39	0.24	0.07
Alternative Event Driven Funds	0.27	0.80	1.02	0.37
Alternative Global Macro Funds	−0.01	0.59	1.03	
Alternative Long/Short Equity Funds	0.27	0.56	0.64	0.22
Alternative Managed Futures Funds	−0.00	−0.43	−0.56	
Alternative Multi-Strategy Funds	0.14	0.46	0.61	
Dedicated Short Bias Funds	−0.11	−0.58	−0.74	−0.33
S&P 500	0.97	1.24	1.04	0.38

Source: Lipper, a Thomson Reuters company

income beta, since bonds outperformed stocks during most of these periods on a risk-adjusted basis. So even when using Sharpe ratios, it is not easy to make apples-to-apples comparisons. In Chapter 5 covering Alternative Credit Focus Funds we offer data on fixed income indexes, which provide a more appropriate basis for comparison.

This brings us to a critical point about risk and return: It is easy to draw misleading conclusions from the return data, even after adjusting for the riskiness of these funds. The authors address the factor exposures for each Lipper classification in the appropriate chapter, and believe this offers a much more accurate basis for evaluating these funds.

SUMMARY

This overview of liquid alternatives is best used to evaluate the historical growth of the liquid alts space and each classification. This includes a look at assets, net flows, IPOs, and fund liquidations. These measures are often directly comparable to each other, and are less prone to distortion than the risk and return data. Advisors should be careful when comparing liquid alts to traditional mutual funds, and when comparing Lipper alternative classifications to each other. The data do not aggregate in a meaningful way, and each classification has its idiosyncrasies, making it is easy to come to the wrong conclusion.

QUESTIONS

1. What are the key drivers behind the growth of liquid alts?
2. Why is it dangerous to make direct comparisons of risk and return for different Lipper alternative classifications?

CHAPTER 3

Absolute Return Funds

Synopsis

Absolute Return Funds have become tremendously popular in the wake of the 2008 crash as investors seek new forms of diversification. This classification contains a wide variety of strategies, and some funds offer an attractive level of risk and return that is uncorrelated with the market. Such funds are in the minority, however, since most of these strategies have returns that are driven by exposure to equities. Thus, investors need to do their homework, and cannot blithely assume that Absolute Return Funds will deliver what the name suggests.

DEFINITION

> *Funds that aim for positive returns in all market conditions. The funds are not benchmarked against a traditional long-only market index but rather have the aim of outperforming a cash or risk-free benchmark.*
> Definition of the Lipper classification: Absolute Return Funds

Absolute Return Funds are heterogeneous by nature, and like most classifications, the definition continues to evolve. The prospectus-based definition used by Lipper describes an Absolute Return Fund as any fund that aims to provide a positive return over a rolling period, or a 12-month basis, regardless of market conditions. These funds are benchmarked against indexes that are typically positive, such as Treasury bills, the London Interbank Offered Rate (LIBOR), or the consumer price index (CPI) plus 100 to 500 basis points. Broad market indexes, such as the Standard & Poor's (S&P) 500, are not usually used as benchmarks.

Absolute Return Funds use a variety of instruments and tactics to help achieve their goals. These funds may use stocks, bonds, currencies, derivatives, and other securities, as well as short selling and go-anywhere approaches. Many of these strategies are tactical in nature, and are driven by quantitative analysis over a short time horizon; other funds rebalance the asset allocation based on long-term valuations, and target broad diversification across all asset classes. Some funds use subadvisors to manage various strategies, and reallocate assets based on expectations of the risk/return potential for each subadvisor.

Although Absolute Return Funds are considered lower-risk investments, investors are not always protected from adverse swings in the stock or bond markets. A fund may have a negative nominal return despite beating its benchmark, or it may fail to overcome inflation. Since Absolute Return Funds have an extraordinarily demanding objective, the portfolio managers within this classification must have exceptional skill. Ideally, investors would back-test these strategies over multiple market cycles, and may also consider stress-testing these strategies to evaluate how the fund might react to unusual events or extreme market conditions.

TOTAL NET ASSETS AND NET FLOWS

In 2013, Absolute Return Funds had almost $40 billion in total net assets (TNA), or 13 percent of the total assets in Lipper alternative classifications. (See Table 3.1.) Net flows were consistently positive until 2008, when the financial crisis led to negative net flows of $1.1 billion. This classification also experienced market depreciation in 2008, and assets fell from $9.2 billion in 2007 to $6.7 billion in 2008. Assets have skyrocketed since then, reaching $39.6 billion in 2013, aided by dozens of fund launches in recent years.

As for returns, most Absolute Return Funds failed to meet their objectives in 2008, when the average fund in this classification declined 16.3 percent. Consequently, these funds did not offer the downside protection that many investors had expected.

TABLE 3.1   Absolute Return Funds: Historical Overview

	Total Net Assets ($ Millions)	Estimated Net Flows ($ Millions)	Returns	IPOs	Liquidations
2004	$3,322	$1,726	9.1%		
2005	$6,252	$2,554	4.1%	4	
2006	$8,788	$2,054	5.3%	6	
2007	$9,240	$442	4.4%	2	
2008	$6,697	($1,125)	−16.3%	8	
2009	$9,346	$1,869	9.2%	4	
2010	$15,333	$5,648	2.4%	14	
2011	$16,015	$1,017	−2.6%	18	4
2012	$23,368	$6,717	4.4%	29	2
2013	$39,621	$14,922	3.9%	23	13

Source: Lipper, a Thomson Reuters Company.

Despite the failure to generate positive returns during the crash of 2008, this classification has enjoyed strong popularity among investors. The financial crisis left deep scars on investors, who are increasingly hungry for uncorrelated products that help diversify portfolios. Absolute Return Funds can fit the bill, depending on underlying factor exposures and the approach used by the portfolio manager.

The growth in net assets has led to a surge in initial public offerings (IPOs) as fund companies capitalize on strong investor demand, and the number of funds and types of strategies have proliferated at a brisk pace. The sharp rise in fund launches has also led to a marked rise in liquidations, which is a natural by-product of a maturing classification.

RISK AND RETURN

When looking at risk and return, an appropriate place to start for Absolute Return Funds is the latest five-year period, since only seven funds have 10-year track records. During the past five years Absolute Return Funds have had annual returns of 3.3 percent (compared to 17.9 percent for the S&P 500) and a Sharpe ratio of 0.75 (compared to 1.04 for the S&P 500). (See Table 3.2.) These returns and the Sharpe ratio both lag the equity market by a wide margin, which is what one would expect during the past five years, which included the stock market rebound that began in March 2009.

Absolute Return Funds have lagged the S&P 500 more recently as well. Returns over the past one-year and three-year periods were 0.0 percent and 1.8 percent, respectively, compared to 32.4 percent and 16.2 percent for the S&P 500. So even though these funds have a modest correlation to equities, they are not designed with enough equity beta to deliver robust long-term returns.

Granted, Absolute Return Funds have offered a healthy dose of downside protection: The average maximum drawdown for these funds was −33.6 percent, compared to −50.9 percent for the S&P 500. (The maximum

TABLE 3.2 Absolute Return Funds: Average Returns and Risk Ratios as of 12/31/13

	Average Return	Average Sharpe Ratio	Average Sortino Ratio	Average Maximum Drawdown
One-Year	0.0%	0.10	0.10	−5.0%
Annualized Three-Year	1.8%	0.33	0.30	−9.9%
Annualized Five-Year	3.3%	0.75	0.70	−10.5%
Annualized 10-Year	1.1%	0.10	0.07	−33.6%

Source: Lipper, a Thomson Reuters Company.

drawdowns for the S&P 500 are based on monthly total returns; the decline in the S&P 500 from peak to trough was −56.8 percent.) The five-year Sortino ratio for Absolute Return Funds was 0.70, compared to 0.89 for the S&P 500. So these funds did not generate much in the way of returns per unit of risk, whether the risk is measured in terms of maximum drawdown or Sortino ratio. (In subsequent discussions, Andrew Clark noted that Alternative Absolute Return Funds have superior maximum drawdowns when compared to the S&P 500. He suggests using downside deviation in addition to the Sortino ratio, or perhaps even in place of the Sortino ratio.)

In fact, any way you slice it, it is clear that these funds do not capture much equity upside, yet they remain volatile and have significant downside risk. After all, if an investor wanted to limit both volatility and downside, a portfolio of 50 percent stocks and 50 percent cash would have generated a superior risk/return profile compared to the average Absolute Return Fund.

In other words, this classification has struggled to rid itself of systemic risk, and these funds should not be considered market-neutral strategies. As we discuss in our next section, many of these funds underperform because they assume too much market beta relative to their benchmarks, thereby failing to eliminate nonsystemic risk. Some funds have been able to hedge traditional market risks, but most have not been able to generate positive returns during a complete market cycle.

FACTOR EXPOSURES

Andrew Clark, PhD, Manager of Alternative Investment Research at Lipper, has studied factor exposures for Absolute Return Funds. These factor exposures capture both alpha and beta, with alpha defined as market inefficiencies and beta described as market exposures. More specifically, Clark defines beta as risk premiums derived from exposure to asset-based style factors determined by the capital asset pricing model (CAPM). Beta includes a wide variety of factor exposures, and nearly all of these can be replicated by investing in an exchange-traded fund (ETF) or index fund. These beta exposures include:

- The general stock market
- The general bond market
- High-yield bonds
- Value versus growth
- Trend following
- Optionality
- Dynamic hedging (portfolio insurance using the Chicago Board Options Exchange [CBOE] Volatility Index [VIX], etc.)

These beta exposures help explain what factors to focus on, and we now examine correlations, or the depth of the relationship between these betas and the underlying funds. Jeff Tjornehoj, Research Manager at Lipper, has found that the correlation of Absolute Return Funds to the S&P 500 was 0.55 from 2010 through 2013 ("Are Alts Making the Grade?," *Lipper Insight*, November 5, 2013, http://lipperinsight.thomsonreuters .com/2013/11/are-alts-making-the-grade/). Thus, most of the returns of this classification can be explained by stock market exposure.

Clark confirmed this hypothesis in December 2013 when he tested 29 Absolute Return Funds that had been in existence for three years or more. Twenty-four of these 29 funds had similar co-movements to the S&P 500, and any differences were not statistically significant ("Risk Measures for Alternative Investment Funds: Part 2," *Lipper Insight,* December 30, 2013, http://lipperinsight.thomsonreuters.com/2013/12/risk-measures-for-alternative-investment-funds-part-2/).

In addition to identifying the betas and correlations that drive these funds, it is also important to consider tail risk, defined as vulnerability to sudden losses. Although Absolute Return Funds are heterogeneous, value at risk (VaR) can assess tail risk in the event of an abrupt drop in the market. Maximum drawdown is another helpful variable in assessing tail risk, and advisors can compare the fund's drawdown relative to the market, to other Absolute Return Funds, and in the context of the client's portfolio.

ASSET ALLOCATION AND FUND SELECTION

The authors believe that the best role for an Absolute Return Fund is as a portfolio diversifier. In this role, long-term noncorrelation should be the primary driver of the asset allocation decision. Therefore, these funds would be selected to reduce the correlations of the portfolio to the stock and bond markets, and to other asset exposures that could easily be purchased in an index form (real estate, commodities, precious metals, etc.). Fund selection will also emphasize positive returns, of course, though the expectation should be modest for a fund that sticks to its absolute return mandate, and that does not artificially boost returns by hidden exposures to other asset classes.

Most Absolute Return Funds have a high correlation to the S&P 500. Clark found five funds, however, that had low systematic risk and might therefore be useful as portfolio diversifiers:

1. Federated Absolute Return Fund Class A (FMAAX)
2. Parametric Absolute Return Fund Institutional (EOAIX)
3. Metropolitan West Strategic Income Fund Class M (MWSTX)
4. Natixis ASG Diversifying Strategies Fund Class Y (DSFYX)
5. UBS Fixed Income Opportunities Fund Class Y (FNOIX)

The funds from Parametric and UBS had especially low systemic risk (compared to the other three). This process illustrates how investors can screen for products with uncorrelated returns.

As for tail risk, Clark ranked the value at risk (VaR) of the 29 funds with a three-year track record as of December 30, 2013. Three funds came in with low VaR measures:

1. Metropolitan West Strategic Income Fund Class M (MWSTX)
2. Absolute Strategies Fund Institutional (ASFIX)
3. Putnam Absolute Return 100 Fund Class A (PARTX)

The Metropolitan West Strategic Income Fund has both low tail risk and low systematic risk. This process illustrates how investors can screen for funds that offer multiple attributes that enhance the risk/return profile of portfolios.

TOP TEN FUNDS

The Wells Fargo Advantage Absolute Return Fund (WARDX) tops the list in terms of total net assets and estimated net flows for Absolute Return Funds. (See Tables 3.3 through 3.8.) The GMO Benchmark-Free Allocation

TABLE 3.3   Top Ten Absolute Return Funds as of 12/31/13: Total Assets ($ Millions)

	Symbol	Total Net Assets	Estimated Net Flows
Wells Fargo Advantage Absolute Return Fund	WARDX	$8,139	$5,459
GMO Benchmark-Free Allocation Fund	GBMFX	$4,993	$3,543
John Hancock Global Absolute Return Strategy Fund	JHAIX	$4,611	$2,736
Absolute Strategies Fund (Institutional)	ASFIX	$3,270	($879)
Goldman Sachs Absolute Return Tracker Fund	GJRTX	$1,745	$84
John Hancock Absolute Return Currency Fund	JCUAX	$1,314	$194
Natixis Loomis Sayles Strategic Alpha	LASYX	$1,243	$606
Goldman Sachs Dynamic Allocation Fund	GDIFX	$1,039	($302)
Putnam Absolute Return 700 Fund	PDMYX	$1,025	$143
Putnam Absolute Return 300 Fund	PTRNX	$985	$43

Source: Lipper, a Thomson Reuters Company.

TABLE 3.4 Top Ten Absolute Return Funds as of 12/31/13: Historical Returns

	One Year	Three Years Annualized	Five Years Annualized	Ten Years Annualized	Expense Ratio
Wells Fargo Advantage Absolute Return Fund	10.0%				1.5%
GMO Benchmark-Free Allocation Fund	10.7%	8.2%	9.9%	9.4%	0.9%
John Hancock Global Absolute Return Strategy Fund	4.8%				1.5%
Absolute Strategies Fund	−1.0%	0.6%	4.7%		2.5%
Goldman Sachs Absolute Return Tracker Fund	8.3%	2.4%	3.3%		1.2%
John Hancock Absolute Return Currency Fund	3.6%	3.6%			0.9%
Natixis Loomis Sayles Strategic Alpha	1.2%	3.1%			0.9%
Goldman Sachs Dynamic Allocation Fund	5.7%	4.0%			1.0%
Putnam Absolute Return 700 Fund	6.2%	4.9%	6.6%		1.0%
Putnam Absolute Return 300 Fund	4.4%	1.8%	3.3%		0.8%

Source: Lipper, a Thomson Reuters Company.

Fund (GBMFX) follows thereafter, since both funds use the same underlying strategy. WARDX has much lower minimums than GBMFX, and is available through multiple advisor platforms with an initial investment as low as $1,000; GBMFX, in contrast, requires a minimum investment of $10 million.

To some degree, the success of WARDX in gathering assets reflects the reach of the Wells Fargo franchise: WARDX offers essentially the same strategy as GBMFX, though for retail investors. These two funds combined account for almost half of the sector assets in the Absolute Return Fund classification, with total net assets of $13.1 billion.

The blockbuster success of this strategy demonstrates the importance of distribution, as well as the allure of a strategy with a 10-year track record. (At the end of 2013, only six other funds in this classification also had 10-year track records.) The parent company of GBMFX is GMO, LLC, a private partnership that was cofounded in 1977 by Jeremy Grantham. A well-established track record helps attract assets, especially with a

TABLE 3.5　Top Ten Absolute Return Funds as of 12/31/13: Sharpe Ratios

	One Year	Three Years Annualized	Five Years Annualized	Ten Years Annualized	Expense Ratio
Wells Fargo Advantage Absolute Return Fund	10.0%				1.5%
GMO Benchmark-Free Allocation Fund	10.7%	8.2%	9.9%	9.4%	0.9%
John Hancock Global Absolute Return Strategy Fund	4.8%				1.5%
Absolute Strategies Fund	−1.0%	0.6%	4.7%		2.5%
Goldman Sachs Absolute Return Tracker Fund	8.3%	2.4%	3.3%		1.2%
John Hancock Absolute Return Currency Fund	3.6%	3.6%			0.9%
Natixis Loomis Sayles Strategic Alpha	1.2%	3.1%			0.9%
Goldman Sachs Dynamic Allocation Fund	5.7%	4.0%			1.0%
Putnam Absolute Return 700 Fund	6.2%	4.9%	6.6%		1.0%
Putnam Absolute Return 300 Fund	4.4%	1.8%	3.3%		0.8%

Source: Lipper, a Thomson Reuters Company.

complex and unfamiliar strategy such as those used in Absolute Return Funds. Since most investors buy these funds in the quest for uncorrelated returns and low risk, it is easy to understand why GBMFX has become a blockbuster.

Many of the other funds that make the top ten list are from big brand names: John Hancock, Goldman Sachs, and Putnam. Even Natixis, a major player in alternatives, teamed up with Loomis Sayles for their Absolute Return Fund, Natixis Loomis Sayles Strategic Alpha (LASYX). The domination of brand names among the top ten reflects the power of these firms as distributors, though all of these funds have reasonable returns, risk ratios, and expense ratios.

There is one notable exception: the Absolute Strategies Fund (ASFIX), which has had mixed performance over the past three years and that sports an expense ratio of 2.5 percent. This expense ratio is well above its peers,

TABLE 3.6 Top Ten Absolute Return Funds as of 12/31/13: Sortino Ratios

	One Year	Three Years Annualized	Five Years Annualized	Ten Years Annualized
Wells Fargo Advantage Absolute Return Fund	0.19			
GMO Benchmark-Free Allocation Fund	0.20	1.04	1.20	0.91
John Hancock Global Absolute Return Strategy Fund	0.10			
Absolute Strategies Fund	−0.06	0.26	1.19	
Goldman Sachs Absolute Return Tracker Fund	0.21	0.39	0.51	
John Hancock Absolute Return Currency Fund	0.09	0.44		
Natixis Loomis Sayles Strategic Alpha	0.04	0.74		
Goldman Sachs Dynamic Allocation Fund	0.07	0.41		
Putnam Absolute Return 700 Fund	0.13	0.76	1.17	
Putnam Absolute Return 300 Fund	0.25	0.57	1.33	

Source: Lipper, a Thomson Reuters Company.

especially for an institutional share class. In 2013 ASFIX had outflows, and was the only fund among the top ten that lost money.

BLOCKBUSTER AND SPOTLIGHT

The Wells Fargo Advantage Absolute Return Fund (WARDX) has leaped to blockbuster status in a short period of time, since it piggybacks on the track record of its sole holding: the GMO Benchmark-Free Allocation Fund (GBMFX). (See Table 3.9.) Since GBMFX has a 10-year track record, our analysis focuses on this fund, though investors cannot expect the same performance net of fees, taxes, and transaction costs.

Performance and longevity are the primary drivers of this fund's popularity, which also benefits from the visibility and stature of portfolio manager Jeremy Grantham. GBMFX has delivered 10-year performance of 9.8 percent with a Sharpe ratio of 0.98 and a Sortino ratio of 0.91. Granted, many equity index funds have had stronger Sharpe and Sortino ratios, especially

TABLE 3.7 Top Ten Absolute Return Funds as of 12/31/13: Maximum Drawdowns

	One Year	Three Years Annualized	Five Years Annualized	Ten Years Annualized
Wells Fargo Advantage Absolute Return Fund	−5.1%			
GMO Benchmark-Free Allocation Fund	−5.1%	−5.2%	−7.1%	−19.0%
John Hancock Global Absolute Return Strategy Fund	−4.6%			
Absolute Strategies Fund	−3.4%	−3.4%	−7.7%	
Goldman Sachs Absolute Return Tracker Fund	−3.0%	−8.1%	−8.1%	
John Hancock Absolute Return Currency Fund	−4.2%	−13.8%		
Natixis Loomis Sayles Strategic Alpha	−5.2%	−7.2%		
Goldman Sachs Dynamic Allocation Fund	−9.3%	−9.3%		
Putnam Absolute Return 700 Fund	−4.4%	−8.1%	−8.1%	
Putnam Absolute Return 300 Fund	−1.6%	−6.9%	−6.9%	

Source: Lipper, a Thomson Reuters Company.

during the past five years. But GBMFX has had an attractive 10-year maximum drawdown of only −19.0 percent, compared to −50.9 percent for the S&P 500.

GBMFX also appears to have relatively low tail risk compared to its peers. In December 2013, Andrew Clark conducted an analysis of Absolute Return Funds using a conditional beta and VaR at the 5 percent level (http://lipperinsight.thomsonreuters.com/2013/12/risk-measures-for-alternative-investment-funds-part-2/). At that time, GMO's Benchmark-Free Allocation Fund (GBMFX) had a VaR of 2.92, which was low tail risk versus most of its peers.

The investment approach for GBMFX follows the philosophy that current valuations eventually revert back to their long-term averages. Management invests in several GMO funds, thereby gaining exposure to GMO's seven-year asset class forecasts. The portfolio's asset allocation is shifted to capitalize on what the managers believe is attractively priced, and seeks to

TABLE 3.8 S&P 500 Returns and Risk Data
as of 12/31/13

Calendar Year Returns	
2003	28.7%
2004	10.9%
2005	4.9%
2006	15.8%
2007	5.5%
2008	−37.0%
2009	26.5%
2010	15.1%
2011	2.1%
2012	16.0%
2013	32.4%
Rolling Period Returns	
1-Year Returns	32.4%
3-Year Returns	16.2%
5-Year Returns	17.9%
10-Year Returns	7.4%
Sharpe Ratio	
1-Year Sharpe	0.97
3-Year Sharpe	1.24
5-Year Sharpe	1.04
10-Year Sharpe	0.38
Sortino Ratio	
1-Year Sortino	0.72
3-Year Sortino	1.13
5-Year Sortino	0.89
10-Year Sortino	0.31
Maximum Drawdown	
1-Year Maximum Drawdown	−2.9%
3-Year Maximum Drawdown	−16.3%
5-Year Maximum Drawdown	−18.1%
10-Year Maximum Drawdown	−50.9%

Source: Lipper, a Thomson Reuters Company.

TABLE 3.9 Absolute Return Funds as of 12/31/2013: Blockbuster and Spotlight

	Blockbuster: Wells Fargo Advantage Absolute Return	Classification Average	Spotlight: Metropolitan West Strategic Income
Total Net Assets 2013 ($Mil)	$8,139	$140	$254
Estimated Net Flows 2013 ($Mil)	$5,459	$50	$30
One-Year Return	10.0%	3.9%	3.7%
Three-Year Annualized Return		1.8%	5.8%
Five-Year Annualized Return		3.3%	13.0%
Ten-Year Annualized Return		1.1%	4.0%
Expense Ratio	1.5%	1.8%	2.2%

Source: Lipper, a Thomson Reuters Company.

outpace inflation by 5 percent, with 5 to 10 percent total annualized standard deviation.

We now turn to the spotlight among Absolute Return Funds, the Metropolitan West Strategic Income Fund, which has both class M shares (MWSTX) and institutional shares (MWSIX). MWSTX screens well as a portfolio diversifier and as a fixed income complement, since it has a low correlation to stocks and has low tail risk. The fund has also generated returns well above its peers: MWSTX had one-year returns of 3.7 percent, three-year returns of 5.8 percent, five-year returns of 13.0 percent, and 10-year returns of 4.0 percent. These returns compare to 3.9 percent, 1.8 percent, 3.3 percent, and 1.1 percent for the average fund in the Absolute Return Funds classification. MWSTX outperformed its peers in every time period, often by a wide margin.

Not only did MWSTX outperform comparable funds, but it did so with lower risk. We use the five-year period to evaluate risk, since this was the longest period with sufficient funds in the database. MWSTX had a five-year Sharpe ratio of 2.5 (versus classification average of 0.75), a five-year Sortino ratio of 3.3 (versus average of 0.7), and a five-year maximum drawdown of −9.5 percent (versus average of −10.5 percent). Simply put, MWSTX outperformed other Absolute Return Funds while having smaller drawdowns and a higher return for unit of risk.

The portfolio managers are Tad Rivelle, Steve Kane, CFA, and Laird Landmann. All have been members of the team managing the fund since 1996 (they all joined TCW Group in 2009). Metropolitan West has $30 billion in assets and focuses on fixed income portfolio management: The firm manages eight bond funds and one advanced equity index fund. The strategy is available in two share classes: The class M shares have a minimum of $5,000 ($1,000 in an individual retirement account [IRA]) and an expense ratio of 2.16 percent. The institutional shares have a minimum of $3 million and an expense ratio of 1.91 percent.

MWSTX uses a bottom-up approach based on fundamental valuations. The fund has a long-term approach to bond selection, and has portfolio turnover of about 50 percent. Market timing strategies help manage duration over a full economic cycle, and the investment process focuses on real interest rates relative to historical levels.

What does all of this mean for clients? Advisors are always on the lookout for a fund that goes beyond bonds to help diversify portfolios. Most advisors are concerned about a gradual rise in rates that will hurt bonds, and also need assets that offset the volatility in equities.

For investors with these concerns, MWSTX provides an active approach to managing interest rate risk. The returns have been steady and the risk profile makes this fund an attractive portfolio diversifier. This fund makes sense as a spotlight since it exemplifies the ideal attributes of Absolute Return Funds: portfolio diversification via noncorrelation, and attractive returns without excessive risk.

SUMMARY

Absolute Return Funds grew in popularity after the financial crisis, but most of these products have failed to consistently deliver the positive returns and downside protection implied by their mandates. This classification is heterogeneous, so investors have to dig deeply to evaluate the exact exposure of each fund that informs its role as either an equity complement, a fixed income complement, or a portfolio diversifier. These roles determine the appropriate usage in each client's portfolio, and advisors should manage expectations accordingly.

PROBLEMS

1. Absolute Return Funds are sometimes marketed as offering stable returns in any market environment. What is a more appropriate way to guide client expectations?
2. What factor exposures drive the performances of different Absolute Return Funds? How do these factors affect the roles that these funds can play in portfolio construction?

REFERENCES

Clark, Andrew. "Risk Measures for Alternative Investment Funds: Part 2." *Lipper Insight*, December 30, 2013. http://lipperinsight.thomsonreuters.com/2013/12/risk-measures-for-alternative-investment-funds-part-2/

Tjornehoj, Jeff. "Are Alts Making the Grade?" *Lipper Insight*, November 5, 2013. http:// lipperinsight.thomsonreuters.com/2013/11/are-alts-making-the-grade/

CHAPTER 4

Alternative Active Extension Funds

Synopsis

Alternative Active Extension Funds is a homogenous classification with a high correlation to U.S. equities, though leverage creates higher volatility than the large-cap benchmarks that these funds mimic. These funds have a narrow range of returns and have historically had higher drawdowns than the S&P 500. Thus, this classification is less alternative than most other Lipper classifications, and is best suited to the role of equity complement in diversified portfolios. The JPMorgan U.S. Large Cap Core Plus Fund dominates the space with an 86 percent market share of total net assets, making this the most concentrated of Lipper's 11 alternative classifications.

DEFINITION

Funds that combine long and short stock selection to invest in a diversified portfolio of U.S. large-cap equities, with a target net exposure of 100 percent long. Typical strategies vary between 110 percent long and 10 percent short to 160 percent long and 60 percent short.

Definition of the Lipper classification:
Alternative Active Extension Funds

Alternative Active Extension Funds have boomed since 2007, as investors seek exposure to equities with the potential for enhanced returns. These funds hold long and short positions in a diversified portfolio of equities, with varying exposures. The 130/30 funds are the most popular version of this strategy, and the process starts when managers go long $100 in stocks they find attractive, and short $30 in stocks that they believe are overvalued. Since the proceeds from short sales are reinvested, the portfolio manager can invest an additional $30 in long positions in stocks that appear undervalued. In this case the fund would have a net long position of 100 percent, comprised of 130 percent long and 30 percent short. This leverages the investor's assets, enhancing potential returns but also magnifying potential risks.

Although this strategy is leveraged and uses short selling, it does not seek absolute returns relative to the market. Rather, Alternative Active Extension Funds try to outperform an index or benchmark, such as the Standard & Poor's (S&P) 500 index. These funds are typically called beta-one strategies since they have 100 percent net exposure to the market; this contrasts with market-neutral long/short strategies that have zero beta. Thus, products in this classification can combine long-only exposure with limited short selling, which may provide an additional source of alpha to investor portfolios.

TOTAL NET ASSETS AND NET FLOWS

Alternative Active Extension Funds have experienced steady growth in total net assets (TNA) since 2004, picking up more rapidly during the financial crisis in 2007 and thereafter. (See Table 4.1.) The spike in TNA from 2006 to 2009 occurred when other Lipper alternative classifications were still new and uncertain, and may reflect the simplicity of these strategies for investors who were unfamiliar with alternative investments. The classification's return of 17.9 percent in 2006 further solidified its mark in the liquid alternatives space, compared to a 3.2 percent aggregate return for all Lipper alternative classifications. The growth in TNA can be attributed mainly to market appreciation, though much of this growth relies on one fund, as we describe later in the chapter.

Net flows for Alternative Active Extension Funds slowed in 2009, and subsequently dissipated. Though these funds attracted investors for a solid

TABLE 4.1 Alternative Active Extension Funds: Historical Overview

	Total Net Assets ($ Millions)	Estimated Net Flows ($ Millions)	Returns	IPOs	Liquidations
2004	$199	($92)	8.0%		
2005	$245	$32	5.5%	1	
2006	$782	$461	17.9%	5	
2007	$3,197	$2,282	3.6%	8	
2008	$3,724	$2,387	−39.4%	2	3
2009	$6,295	$1,087	22.4%	2	2
2010	$7,770	$561	12.8%	1	1
2011	$7,884	$500	−1.7%	3	1
2012	$8,286	($704)	15.6%		2
2013	$11,117	$534	34.0%		3

Source: Lipper, a Thomson Reuters Company.

four years, this burst of interest faded, and flows have only recently returned to positive territory in 2013. The ebb and flow of interest in these funds probably reflects the strategy's underperformance versus the S&P 500 in most years. In fact, 2013 was the first year that Alternative Active Extension Funds (34.0 percent) outperformed the S&P 500 (32.4 percent) post–financial crisis. In other years, the classification missed the performance of the S&P 500 by a few hundred basis points.

The underlying issue with this classification remains its correlation to the S&P 500 and its fee structure. Since the returns of Alternative Active Extension Funds are similar to those of the S&P 500 and have an average expense ratio of 2.2 percent, investors have been gravitating toward less expensive index funds that track the S&P. Even though the returns of Alternative Active Extension Funds are net of the expense ratio, investors most likely focus on the costs and forgo these funds in favor of products that achieve similar returns with lower costs. In short, the high fee structure of liquid alternatives warrants funds that are more aggressive and sexy, such as long/short equity or global macro, not funds that track a standard benchmark. Consequently, initial public offerings (IPOs) have dried up, while liquidations have picked up; an increase in liquidations can also be explained by the inability of Alternative Active Extension Funds to compete with the blockbuster fund that dominates this exceptionally concentrated classification.

RISK AND RETURN

As noted earlier, the performance of Alternative Active Extension Funds is highly correlated with the S&P 500. Unfortunately, the classification underperformed the S&P 500 for six straight years from 2006 through 2012, including a drop of 1.7 percent in 2011 even as the S&P 500 rose 2.1 percent. After such a lackluster year of performance in 2011, it is not surprising that investors pulled $703 million out of this classification in 2012. Granted, Alternative Active Extension Funds do not seek absolute returns in any market environment. But the consistent failure for most of these funds to beat the S&P 500 may encourage investors to opt for other strategies that are less expensive to execute. The average prospectus net expense ratio for Alternative Active Extension Funds is 2.4 percent, compared to approximately 1.2 percent for U.S. Large-Cap Core Funds, a Lipper equity classification.

In relation to other liquid alternative strategies, Alternative Active Extension Funds have typically led the pack, for better or for worse, due to their high correlation with equities. As noted earlier, 2013 was an exceptional year for the strategy (34 percent), achieving one-year returns that were double its shadow, Long-Short Equity Funds (16 percent) far exceeded the average 2013 one-year annualized return for all Lipper alternative classifications (1.3 percent). The strategy also performed well

TABLE 4.2 Alternative Active Extension Funds: Average Returns and Risk Ratios as of 12/31/13

	Average Return	Average Sharpe Ratio	Average Sortino Ratio	Average Maximum Drawdown
One-Year	34.0%	0.36	0.31	−4.9%
Annualized Three-Year	15.5%	0.86	0.71	−19.0%
Annualized Five-Year	16.9%	0.79	0.68	−24.3%
Annualized 10-Year	Not available			

Source: Lipper, a Thomson Reuters Company.

in 2012, ending up 16 percent, beating the second-best performer (Credit Focus Funds), which gained 8.7 percent, and beating the aggregate one-year return of 0.4 percent for Lipper alternative classifications.

When the market plummets, however, investors cannot expect Alternative Active Extension Funds to limit losses in the way many prospectuses suggest, based on their typical structure of 130/30. In 2008 Alternative Active Extension Funds plunged 39 percent, more than any other Lipper alternative classification. This compares to a decline of 7 percent for all Lipper alternative classifications, and compares to a drop of 29 percent for Long-Short Equity Funds, the second-worst-performing classification among Lipper alternative funds.

To put this in context, the five-year average maximum drawdown is more than 24 percent compared with average five-year returns of just under 17 percent. (See Table 4.2.) The average three-year Sharpe and Sortino ratios are 0.86 and 0.71, with an average three-year return of 15.5 percent. The Sharpe and Sortino ratios of Alternative Active Extension Funds are relatively low, largely due to the classification's unimpressive performance. The one-year Sharpe and Sortino ratios were 0.36 and 0.31, compared to 0.97 and 0.72 for the S&P 500. If a fund underperforms the S&P 500—unless it has very low volatility—the risk ratios are going to lag those of the S&P 500. The one-year, three-year, and five-year average maximum drawdowns for Alternative Active Extension Funds have been consistently worse than the S&P 500: −4.9 versus −2.9 percent for the S&P 500, −19.0 percent versus −16.3 percent, and −24.3 versus −18.1 percent.

FACTOR EXPOSURES

This classification is highly correlated to the S&P 500, and nearly all of the funds are designed to closely mimic a large-cap benchmark. In fact, the names of these funds often include the words "Core Plus," which is an accurate description of the exposures and the investment process. This correlation to equities makes Alternative Active Extension Funds less alternative than other Lipper classifications, though these funds can go short and can generate uncorrelated returns.

Turning to fund design, these funds have a number of commonalities:

- Broadly diversified holdings across sectors and securities
- Small tracking error compared to the benchmark
- Quantitative ranking systems

The emphasis on quantitative analysis is worth describing in detail, since it figures so prominently in these funds. Here are some examples:

- ProShares Large Cap Core Plus (CSM) seeks "to outperform the S&P 500 through enhanced portfolio construction and a rules-based, multifactor stock selection methodology."
- Convergence Core Plus Fund (MARNX) uses a "proprietary dynamic quantitative model" and pursues "consistent alpha."
- MainStay U.S. Equity Opportunities Fund (MYCIX and other share classes) uses "quantitative analysis to identify undervalued securities in an objective, disciplined and broadly applied process while seeking limited exposure to risk."

Not every fund, however, puts quantitative analysis at the center of its investment process. The JPMorgan U.S. Large Cap Core Plus Fund (JLPSX and other share classes) combines fundamental and quantitative analysis, and the fact sheet emphasizes the 55 years of combined experience of its two portfolio managers as well as the reliance on the "expertise of 22 research analysts averaging 18 years' experience." This fund takes large positions in its top holdings, both long and short, and consequently has greater tracking error. The larger position sizes make this fund slightly riskier, since these investments reflect high confidence in the directional bets of its analysts and portfolio managers.

The high equity exposure and low tracking error of Alternative Active Extension Funds is evidenced in the long-term performance of these funds. The average five-year return for this classification is 16.9 percent, compared to 17.9 percent for the S&P 500. Among the top ten funds, the five-year annualized returns range from a low of 15.4 percent to a high of 19.3 percent. This is a remarkably narrow range of returns for funds using an alternative strategy.

Looking more broadly, there are 19 share classes in this classification that have a five-year track record. (We included all share classes in this calculation to fully capture the dispersion of fund returns, since these share classes include a wide range of expense ratios.) During the five years ending in 2013 the annualized returns range from a low of 14.2 percent to a high of 19.5 percent. This low dispersion of returns is evidence of its high correlation to the S&P 500, which had five-year returns of 17.9 percent. *Thus, the worst fund lagged the S&P 500 by 3.7 percent and the best fund beat the S&P 500 by 1.6 percent.*

What about risk? The maximum drawdowns for these funds over the five years ending in 2013 averaged −24.3 percent, and ranged from a low of −22.8 percent to a high of −29.2 percent. These maximum drawdowns are all greater than the maximum drawdown for the S&P 500, which was −18.1 percent. All of these funds had higher risk relative to the S&P 500 as measured by their five-year maximum drawdowns, so these funds add risk relative to an equity benchmark.

This is to be expected, however, since a 130/30 fund can use leverage, and at times it may have higher beta than its equity benchmark. Unless the fund strictly limits equity exposure to 100 percent long, it is inevitable that the fund will, at some point, have higher beta and higher risk than the equity benchmark. There may be other factors at play that contribute to high drawdowns compared to the S&P 500, though this is beyond the scope of this analysis.

Finally, it is worth looking at Sharpe and Sortino ratios, since these combine risk and return. These funds in aggregate have lower returns than the S&P 500 and higher maximum drawdowns, so one would expect the Sharpe and Sortino ratios to lag the S&P 500. As we shall see, this is exactly what we find.

The five-year Sharpe ratio for Alternative Active Extension Funds is 0.79, compared to 1.04 for the S&P 500. The five-year Sortino ratio is 0.68 compared to 0.89 for the S&P 500. So whether we look at Sharpe ratios, Sortino ratios, or maximum drawdowns, these funds have higher risk than the S&P 500. It is possible that the recent five years are an anomaly, since equity returns were unusually strong. Unfortunately, there is insufficient data to test these funds through a full market cycle, since there are no funds with 10-year track records.

Based on the data we have, we can conclude that Alternative Active Extension Funds generate lower returns per unit of risk than the S&P 500, and we will now explore how this affects the usage of these funds in a portfolio.

ASSET ALLOCATION AND FUND SELECTION

This section is brief, since Alternative Active Extension Funds are not particularly alternative compared to other funds that Lipper classifies as alternative. As noted in the factor exposures section, these funds are quite homogeneous, and are unambiguously well suited to play the role of an equity complement in a portfolio. In fact, they could be considered a substitute for U.S. equity exposure.

The companies that market these funds generally embrace the role of equity complement. The following is a sample of how one fund company describes the potential use of its product in a portfolio:

> ProShares Large Cap Core Plus (CSM) is an alternative for large cap allocations. The fund offers the potential to outperform traditional large cap index funds, plus the transparency and cost effectiveness of an ETF. CSM is designed to help diversify large cap strategies within a portfolio, increase large cap holdings or replace underperforming large cap investments.

This description is typical, and makes it clear that these funds should be used to fill the role of large-cap stocks. Based on the factor exposures of these funds, the authors agree with this assessment. We offer the caveat, however, that these funds add risk to the portfolio, since they have higher volatility than the S&P 500 or other equity benchmarks. This suggests that Alternative Active Extension Funds cannot fully substitute for an investor's exposure to U.S. equities, and advisors need to keep this in mind throughout the portfolio construction process.

TOP TEN FUNDS

This classification is extremely concentrated, and it would not be wrong for investors to pause and wonder why this is even a classification—similar to Absolute Return Funds. The JPMorgan U.S. Large Cap Core Plus Fund (JLPSX) overshadows all other Alternative Active Extension Funds, comprising 86.4 percent of the classification's TNA at $9.6 billion as of 2013. (See Tables 4.3 through 4.8.) To put this in perspective, MainStay U.S. Equity Opportunities Fund (MYCIX)—whose sister MainStay Marketfield (MFLDX) reaped the strongest net flows of any mutual fund in 2013—comes in second with TNA of $437 million. Not to mention, MFLDX had negative net flows, while JLPSX had inflows of $530 million, or more than MFLDX's total TNA. Other funds in the top ten maintain TNA lower than $300 million, with the last four bringing in under $50 million. The smallest funds, JPMorgan U.S. Research Equity Plus Fund (JEPAX) and American Century Disciplined Growth Plus Fund (ACDQX), top out at a mere $18 million and $15 million. By looking at the top ten funds, advisors can recognize that many fund names allude to large-cap exposure, and the classification itself used to be called Large Cap Core.

The JPMorgan U.S. Large Cap Core Plus Fund (JLPSX) is a blockbuster comprising 86.4 percent of the classification's TNA. The year 2007 was a strong one for JLPSX (+14 percent), beating the S&P 500 by 850 basis points, which explains the surge of interest in the classification heading into

TABLE 4.3 Top Ten Alternative Active Extension Funds as of 12/31/13: Total Assets ($ Millions)

	Symbol	Total Net Assets	Estimated Net Flows
JPMorgan U.S. Large Cap Core Plus Fund	JLPSX	$9,605	$530
MainStay U.S. Equity Opportunities Fund	MYCIX	$437	($209)
Convergence Core Plus Fund	MARNX	$299	$158
JPMorgan U.S. Dynamic Plus Fund	JILSX	$261	$61
ProShares Large Cap Core Plus	CSM	$229	$108
American Century Core Equity Plus Fund	ACPQX	$142	$4
BlackRock Large Cap Core Plus Fund	BILPX	$46	$2
Glenmede Total Market Portfolio	GTTMX	$37	($21)
JPMorgan U.S. Research Equity Plus Fund	JEPAX	$18	$1
American Century Disciplined Growth Plus Fund	ACDQX	$15	$8

Source: Lipper, a Thomson Reuters Company.

TABLE 4.4 Top Ten Alternative Active Extension Funds as of 12/31/13: Historical Returns

	One Year	Three Years Annualized	Five Years Annualized	Ten Years Annualized	Expense Ratio
JPMorgan U.S. Large Cap Core Plus Fund	36.9%	15.8%	19.3%	*Not available*	1.98%
MainStay U.S. Equity Opportunities Fund	40.6%	18.6%	17.8%		2.36%
Convergence Core Plus Fund	31.3%	18.1%			2.21%
JPMorgan U.S. Dynamic Plus Fund	34.2%	15.3%	16.6%		1.75%
ProShares Large Cap Core Plus	35.8%	16.7%			0.45%
American Century Core Equity Plus Fund	35.1%				2.12%
BlackRock Large Cap Core Plus Fund	32.3%	16.4%	15.4%		2.10%
Glenmede Total Market Portfolio	39.5%	16.3%	17.5%		1.94%
JPMorgan U.S. Research Equity Plus Fund	33.1%	15.1%			2.52%
American Century Disciplined Growth Plus Fund	35.6%				2.12%

Source: Lipper, a Thomson Reuters Company.

TABLE 4.5 Top Ten Alternative Active Extension Funds as of 12/31/13: Sharpe Ratios

	One Year	Three Years Annualized	Five Years Annualized	Ten Years Annualized
JPMorgan U.S. Large Cap Core Plus Fund	0.38	0.87	0.89	
MainStay U.S. Equity Opportunities Fund	0.39	1.04	0.88	
Convergence Core Plus Fund	0.34	1.00		
JPMorgan U.S. Dynamic Plus Fund	0.33	0.85	0.79	
ProShares Large Cap Core Plus	0.41	0.97		
American Century Core Equity Plus Fund	0.39			*Not available*
BlackRock Large Cap Core Plus Fund	0.33	0.85	0.73	
Glenmede Total Market Portfolio	0.38	0.83	0.80	
JPMorgan U.S. Research Equity Plus Fund	0.35	0.85		
American Century Disciplined Growth Plus Fund	0.38			

Source: Lipper, a Thomson Reuters Company.

TABLE 4.6 Top Ten Alternative Active Extension Funds as of 12/31/13: Sortino Ratios

	One Year	Three Years Annualized	Five Years Annualized	Ten Years Annualized
JPMorgan U.S. Large Cap Core Plus Fund	0.34	0.71	0.76	
MainStay U.S. Equity Opportunities Fund	0.33	0.87	0.77	*Not available*
Convergence Core Plus Fund	0.29	0.81		
JPMorgan U.S. Dynamic Plus Fund	0.25	0.7	0.69	
ProShares Large Cap Core Plus	0.36	0.82		
American Century Core Equity Plus Fund	0.33			
BlackRock Large Cap Core Plus Fund	0.29	0.69	0.62	
Glenmede Total Market Portfolio	0.35	0.67	0.68	
JPMorgan U.S. Research Equity Plus Fund	0.34	0.71		
American Century Disciplined Growth Plus Fund	0.31			

Source: Lipper, a Thomson Reuters Company.

TABLE 4.7 Top Ten Alternative Active Extension Funds as of 12/31/13: Maximum Drawdowns

	One Year	Three Years Annualized	Five Years Annualized	Ten Years Annualized
JPMorgan U.S. Large Cap Core Plus Fund	−4.6%	−18.6%	−22.9%	
MainStay U.S. Equity Opportunities Fund	−5.1%	−16.5%	−23.3%	
Convergence Core Plus Fund	−4.4%	−19.5%		
JPMorgan U.S. Dynamic Plus Fund	−5.7%	−16.5%	−23.8%	
ProShares Large Cap Core Plus	−4.5%	−18.0%		*Not*
American Century Core Equity Plus Fund	−4.4%			*available*
BlackRock Large Cap Core Plus Fund	−5.7%	−23.5%	−23.6%	
Glenmede Total Market Portfolio	−5.1%	−21.4%	−24.9%	
JPMorgan U.S. Research Equity Plus Fund	−4.9%	−18.5%		
American Century Disciplined Growth Plus Fund	−5.2%			

Source: Lipper, a Thomson Reuters Company.

the financial crisis. JLPSX performed well from 2006 to 2009, with the exception of 2008 (−34.6 percent, though better than the S&P 500 at −37 percent). However, 2011 was a down year (−3.9 percent), which is not surprising as these funds have high beta, and this may explain the outflows for the classification in 2012 (−$703 million). Performance came roaring back in 2012 and 2013, up 18 percent and 37 percent—mostly due to the bull market—and naturally, the classification's net flows as a whole have been rebounding.

BLOCKBUSTER AND SPOTLIGHT

JLPSX uses the typical 130/30 strategy that "seeks to offer more flexibility and return potential than long-only equity investments." The managers believe this approach allows them to capitalize on both sides of a trade, while paring losses in down markets by using short positions. This fund highlights its experienced team: Its portfolio managers, Tom Luddy and Susan Bao, have combined industry experience of 55 years, and its research analysts have an average of 18 years. The fund also credits its stock ranking process that it uses to identify long and short opportunities.

The fund's performance generally stands out relative to the other top ten funds. (See Table 4.9.) Investors could argue MYCIX is giving JLPSX a run for its money, since its one-year and three-year annualized returns surpass the other funds in the top ten. With that said, JLPSX's five-year annualized return tops 19 percent, which is 150 basis points above that of MYCIX. JLPSX was the first fund to exist in this space, and its solid

TABLE 4.8 S&P 500 Returns and Risk Data as of 12/31/13

Calendar Year Returns	
2003	28.7%
2004	10.9%
2005	4.9%
2006	15.8%
2007	5.5%
2008	−37.0%
2009	26.5%
2010	15.1%
2011	2.1%
2012	16.0%
2013	32.4%
Rolling Period Returns	
1-Year Returns	32.4%
3-Year Returns	16.2%
5-Year Returns	17.9%
10-Year Returns	7.4%
Sharpe Ratio	
1-Year Sharpe	0.97
3-Year Sharpe	1.24
5-Year Sharpe	1.04
10-Year Sharpe	0.38
Sortino Ratio	
1-Year Sortino	0.72
3-Year Sortino	1.13
5-Year Sortino	0.89
10-Year Sortino	0.31
Maximum Drawdown	
1-Year Maximum Drawdown	−2.9%
3-Year Maximum Drawdown	−16.3%
5-Year Maximum Drawdown	−18.1%
10-Year Maximum Drawdown	−50.9%

Source: Lipper, a Thomson Reuters Company.

long-term performance and brand name have enabled the fund to gather assets like no other product within this Lipper classification.

JLPSX's expense ratio is also relatively cheap at 1.98 percent, compared to the classification average of 2.16 percent. ProShares Large Cap Core Plus Fund (CSM) has the lowest expense ratio of 0.45 percent because it is an ETF. Otherwise, Glenmede Total Market Portfolio (GTTMX) and the

TABLE 4.9 Alternative Active Extension Funds as of 12/31/13: Blockbuster and Spotlight

	Blockbuster: JPMorgan U.S. Large Cap Core Plus Fund	Classification Average	Spotlight: MainStay U.S. Equity Opportunities Fund
Total Net Assets 2013 ($Mil)	$9,605	$285	$437
Estimated Net Flows 2013 ($Mil)	$530	$10	($209)
One-Year Return	36.9%	34.0%	40.6%
Three-Year Annualized Return	15.8%	15.5%	18.6%
Five-Year Annualized Return	19.3%	16.9%	17.8%
Ten-Year Annualized Return	*Not available*		
Expense Ratio	1.98%	2.16%	2.36%

Source: Lipper, a Thomson Reuters Company.

JPMorgan U.S. Dynamic Plus Fund (JILSX) have slightly lower expense ratios of 1.94 percent and 1.75 percent. Although returns are net of fees, GTTMX's lower expense ratio and better one-year (39.5 percent) and three-year (16.3 percent) returns relative to JLPSX may cause investors to opt for the smaller, lesser-known fund; its TNA is $37 million.

In regard to risk ratios, JLPSX has solid three-year and five-year Sharpe ratios of 0.87 and 0.89, just under MYCIX and CSM's three-year Sharpe ratios of 1.04 and 0.97, and just inching above MYCIX's five-year Sharpe ratio of 0.88. JLPSX's three-year and five-year Sortino ratios of 0.71 and 0.76 lag MYCIX's 0.87 and 0.77, but the fund remains in the middle of the pack for the three-year Sortino ratio, and comes in second during the most recent five-year period. JLPSX's five-year maximum drawdown of −22.9 percent also slightly beat MYCIX's −23.3 percent, and its five-year downside deviation places first relative to the other funds within the top ten. Overall, JLPSX has earned its blockbuster status with an impressive long-term risk/return profile.

Turning to the spotlight, the MainStay U.S. Equity Opportunities Fund (MYCIX) seeks long-term growth of capital, according to its prospectus. The fund holds long positions up to 140 percent of the fund's net assets, and short positions up to 40 percent of the fund's assets, according to quantitative analysis that signals whether certain opportunities will potentially outperform the Russell 1000 index.

MYCIX has both excellent return and risk ratios. The fund's one-year and three-year returns of 40.5 percent and 18.6 percent exceed the other funds' returns within the top ten, and its five-year annualized return of 17.8 percent is just shy of that of the JPMorgan U.S. Large Cap Core Plus

Fund (JLPSX) at 19 percent. However, advisors should note the fund's high expense ratio of 2.36 percent, above the classification's average of 2.16 percent and second behind the classification's most expensive fund, JPMorgan U.S. Research Equity Plus Fund (JEPAX), at 2.52 percent.

MYCIX's three-year annualized Sharpe ratio leaves the other funds in the dust at 1.04, and its one-year and five-year annualized Sharpe ratios compete with the leaders at 0.39 and 0.88. Similarly, its three-year and five-year annualized Sortino ratios lead at 0.87 and 0.77. Its three-year maximum drawdown goes toe-to-toe with the JPMorgan U.S. Dynamic Plus Fund with −16.5 percent versus −16.5 percent, and its three-year and five-year downside deviation is in the middle. Summing up, the fund's risk ratios exceed those of most funds in this classification, and the fund has also delivered superior returns.

SUMMARY

Alternative Active Extension Funds are best used to fill the role of equity complement, or even the role of large-cap U.S. equities. The use of leverage means that these funds add systematic risk to the portfolio, though the low dispersion of returns means that fund selection is not as critical as it is in other Lipper alternative classifications. Given this classification's high correlation to the S&P 500, advisors will find that these funds can serve as an ideal gateway product for investors who are unfamiliar with alternatives.

PROBLEMS

1. Alternative Active Extension Funds have a high correlation to U.S. equities, and are best used as equity complements. The fund selection process is similar to the process used for equity mutual funds. Since these funds use leverage, however, should they be excluded from conservative portfolios?
2. How does the leverage of these funds affect allocation during the portfolio construction process? Should positions be smaller due to the additional equity beta? Is this sufficient to mitigate risk? If so, how should advisors manage client expectations?
3. Successful equity managers often expand into Alternative Active Extension Funds. Should an investor assume that a long-only manager will also be successful using a long/short equity strategy?
4. Some of these funds have concentrated positions. How will this affect tracking error? Should these high-conviction strategies also use high leverage?

CHAPTER 5

Alternative Credit Focus Funds

Synopsis

Booming demand for Alternative Credit Focus Funds has driven assets to record levels as investors search for enhanced yields and active management of interest rate risk. This classification employs a variety of approaches to achieve these goals, ranging from high-risk funds with wide latitude in the search for total returns to low-risk approaches that tread carefully and focus on capital preservation. Our analysis of risk and return shows that many of these funds are attractive as bond complements that will enhance the fixed income allocation of a portfolio, so advisors who do their homework are not searching in vain.

DEFINITION

Funds that, by prospectus language, invest in a wide range of credit-structured vehicles by using either fundamental credit research analysis or quantitative credit portfolio modeling trying to benefit from any changes in credit quality, credit spreads, and market liquidity.

Definition of the Lipper classification:
Alternative Credit Focus Funds

Investors have had a steady appetite for Alternative Credit Focus Funds since 2006, and this appetite became voracious in 2013. This recent boom reflects many factors: today's environment of low interest rates, a desire for enhanced income among retirees, and demand for active management of interest rate risk from advisors who are concerned about rising rates. These factors, combined with the retirement of baby boomers, create a bright future for the innovative strategies used by Alternative Credit Focus Funds.

This classification employs relative value strategies by allocating across investment-grade corporate bonds, mortgage-backed securities, bank loans, emerging market debt, and Treasuries. Most Alternative Credit Focus Funds aim to maximize returns while minimizing volatility, though the priorities of the funds vary from aggressive to conservative.

Generally speaking, Alternative Credit Focus Funds have a low correlation to long-only bond funds that enables these funds to limit losses during bear markets. Andrew Clark of Lipper summarizes it: "A well-constructed return-enhancing credit fund should perform no worse than, and at least nominally better than, a long-only bond fund in a declining bond market." As interest rates rise from near-zero levels, this classification has provided a viable option for investors to find products with potential capital appreciation, a scarce feature in an environment of persistently low rates and high volatility. As we discuss later in the chapter, our analysis shows that many Alternative Credit Focus Funds achieve their goal of protecting capital during a rising interest rate environment. This feature makes many of these funds attractive additions to the fixed income portion of portfolios.

TOTAL NET ASSETS AND NET FLOWS

Alternative Credit Focus Funds comprise the largest Lipper alternative classification, with total net assets (TNA) of $83.3 billion as of 2013, or 27 percent of aggregate net assets in all of Lipper's alternative classifications. (See Table 5.1.) This $83 billion is nearly double the TNA of the second largest Lipper classification: Alternative Long/Short Equity Funds, which had $44.0 billion of TNA in 2013.

While Alternative Credit Focus Funds have grown steadily since 2004— with the exception of 2005—their dominance first became evident in 2010, and exploded in 2013. The year 2009 was a breakout year, as TNA tripled to $12.3 billion from $4.4 billion in 2008. Although the classification

TABLE 5.1 Alternative Credit Focus Funds: Historical Overview

	Total Net Assets ($ Millions)	Estimated Net Flows ($ Millions)	Returns	IPOs	Liquidations
2004	$2,755	$705	6.5%		
2005	$2,400	($398)	2.0%	1	
2006	$2,876	$342	5.9%	3	
2007	$3,768	$726	4.4%		
2008	$4,361	$688	−11.7%	3	*No liquidations*
2009	$12,320	$7,260	23.9%	3	
2010	$23,173	$9,409	8.1%	7	
2011	$30,041	$7,517	1.5%	12	
2012	$36,685	$4,506	8.7%	4	
2013	$83,285	$45,347	0.9%	13	

Source: Lipper, a Thomson Reuters Company.

had negative returns of 11.7 percent in 2008, the financial crash caused investors to flee from equities in search of safety, stability, and better investment solutions.

Hence, investors flocked to fixed income products in droves, and this classification saw net flows balloon from $688 million in 2008 to $7.3 billion in 2009. Net flows remained positive thereafter, with a noticeable dip in 2012 to $4.5 billion. This fall in positive net flows is understandable given the classification's performance in 2011 of 1.5 percent after 8.1 percent in 2010, and a noteworthy 23.9 percent in 2009.

The staggering growth in net flows for these funds in 2013 is larger than the TNA for any other Lipper alternative classification, and more than doubled the size of this classification from 2012 levels.

To be fair, this classification had returns of 8.7 percent in 2012, and this may have drawn investors into these funds in 2013, though net flows of this magnitude are unprecedented. In short, advisors with 60/40 port-folios have sought to catch the bull market in equities over the past few years, but also needed fixed income exposure. With interest rates at near-zero levels, advisors have looked to unconstrained bond funds to complement their long-only fixed income allocation in order to move beyond bonds. Additionally, an environment of rising interest rates is more conducive to unconstrained bond funds.

RISK AND RETURN

The returns for this classification are attractive compared to the iShares Core U.S. Aggregate Bond ETF (AGG) from Barclays. Alternative Credit Focus Funds have outperformed the AGG by a comfortable margin: The 2013 return of 0.9 percent was positive in a year when the AGG fell 2 percent. (See Table 5.2.) The annualized five-year return for Alternative Credit Focus Funds was 8.6 percent, almost double the 4.4 percent return for the AGG

TABLE 5.2 Alternative Credit Focus Funds: Average Returns and Risk Ratios as of 12/31/13

	Average Return	Average Sharpe Ratio	Average Sortino Ratio	Average Maximum Drawdown
One-Year	0.9%	0.07	0.06	−4.23%
Annualized Three-Year	3.6%	1.03	0.91	−6.49%
Annualized Five-Year	8.6%	1.88	1.76	−6.94%
Annualized 10-Year	4.5%	0.66	0.61	−16.50%

Source: Lipper, a Thomson Reuters Company.

over the same period. Meanwhile, this classification had a 10-year annualized return of 4.5 percent, identical to 4.5 percent for the AGG.

Alternative Credit Focus Funds had three-year and 10-year annualized Sharpe and Sortino ratios that slightly trailed the AGG, but its risk ratios were solid overall. The classification's one-year Sharpe and Sortino ratios were positive at 0.07 and 0.06, compared to negative Sharpe and Sortino ratios for the AGG of −0.19 and −0.15. (The negative risk ratios reflect the loss of 2.0 percent for the AGG in 2013.)

FACTOR EXPOSURES

As one might expect, Alternative Credit Focus Funds have a high correlation to fixed income markets. All of the funds in the Alternative Credit Focus Funds classification display lower volatility and lower returns compared to equities for most time periods.

Andrew Clark examined the factor exposures for this classification in an article published on March 26, 2014: "Alternative-Investment Mutual Funds, Part 2: Sources of Return." Clark found that 80 percent of the variance in returns of Alternative Credit Focus Funds can be explained by exposures to bond market factors (such as the term structure of interest rates) and alternative factors (such as trend following). This classification has exposures that reflect the directional bets of an unconstrained bond fund, such as exposures to the yield curve and credit spreads. This may seem obvious for funds classified as Alternative Credit Focus Funds, though readers should know by now that they cannot assume that the name of an alternative mutual fund will explain its investment characteristics.

The design of most Alternative Credit Focus Funds is intended to reduce losses during periods of rising interest rates, and this may be the single most important factor that distinguishes this classification from a long-only bond fund. These funds may also seek enhanced returns by a go-anywhere approach in their search for yield, and in the quest for total returns.

Unfortunately, the precise definitions of these funds are not easy to capture, since the prospectus descriptions offer generalized explanations that may or may not reflect the process that the portfolio manager actually uses. The authors have observed that prospectus explanations increasingly use boilerplate language and blanket coverage to refer to any strategy and any risk that may apply—past, present, or future. To some degree, this is a challenge for all mutual funds, since fund companies are increasingly using legalistic language to file the prospectus, which may include dozens of funds in a single document. This approach may save on compliance costs, but it certainly does not promote transparency or convenience.

Another way to evaluate Alternative Credit Focus Funds is to look at the goals listed on the fund fact sheets. The fact sheets of the top ten funds include the following objectives and approaches:

- An absolute return orientation, seeking positive returns in any market environment
- Potential for positive returns despite movements in interest rates, and active management of interest rate risk
- A flexible mandate that allows broad changes to exposures depending on the market cycle and expected risk/return trade-offs
- Total returns over a long time horizon
- Preservation of capital

Thus, the Alternative Credit Focus Funds classification shares characteristics of both Absolute Return Funds and Alternative Global Macro Funds, which also give wide latitude to the portfolio manager in the pursuit of risk and return. This ambiguity requires advisors to examine the fact sheets, holdings, and track record for each fund, and make a best-efforts evaluation of the risk/return characteristics of the fund. For example, a fund that puts emphasis on preservation of capital should have low volatility and small maximum drawdowns. A fund that has a total return mandate, in turn, would have higher expected volatility and lower correlation to bond market factors. Sometimes the track record aligns with the fund's goals, and sometimes it does not; it is up to the advisor to check.

It may also be helpful to consider Lipper's analysis of these funds. On April 11, 2014, Andrew Clark ranked the funds in terms of maximum drawdowns and returns compared to the iShares Core U.S. Aggregate Bond ETF (AGG). The test period was the 18 months ending on April 7, 2014, a period that included substantial volatility in interest rates.

We recognize that this is a short time period to back-test, but it does include the "taper tantrum" of 2013. An analysis of Alternative Credit Focus Funds would use a full market cycle of risk and return, or perhaps multiple cycles. The reality, however, is that most of these funds have not been in existence for a full interest rate cycle (depending on how we define that).

Clark evaluated 39 funds in this classification that had 18 months or more of history, and found that 11 had superior maximum drawdowns compared to the AGG. (The maximum drawdown for the AGG was 4 percent for the 18-month period.) In addition, Clark examined the Sharpe and Sortino ratios for the same 39 funds, and found that 11 also outperformed the AGG. These were many of the same 11 funds, since the AGG fell almost 4 percent during this period, so the return analysis was dominated by bear market measures. Therefore, the fund's Sharpe and Sortino ratios coincided with the funds that had small maximum drawdowns.

In the accompanying tables we look at the same risk and return measures for longer time periods. As always, advisors should evaluate these ratios in light of the goal of the fund. For example, a fund that emphasizes capital preservation would naturally be expected to have lower volatility and lower returns.

Andrew Clark has pointed out that historical risk and return analysis cannot capture what an unconstrained fund may do in the future. This includes the potential for these funds to make negative duration bets during an extended period of rising interest rates. This aggressively active management of interest rate risk would certainly help reduce exposure to rising interest rates, a key concern for retirees.

The factor analysis of Alternative Credit Focus Funds shows that the flood of money into this classification has often generated attractive risk/return benefits for investors. Perhaps this reflects the fact that the bond market is broad and deep, and can easily absorb the influx of money. This is not true of many alternative strategies, which have limited capacity that may dilute returns as the fund grows.

ASSET ALLOCATION AND FUND SELECTION

The factor exposures for Alternative Credit Focus Funds serve these roles within a portfolio:

- *Diversification:* Long-term noncorrelation with stocks and bonds; includes funds with a goal of absolute returns.
- *Bond complement:* High correlation with bonds, with similar risk/return profile.
- *Alpha:* Potential outperformance compared to benchmark.

The ideal role for Alternative Credit Focus Funds, however, is as a bond complement. Advisors may allocate a portion of their fixed income exposure to the funds in this classification with high confidence that they are actually correlated with bonds. Many of the funds also offer management of interest rate risk, which is especially attractive in today's environment of near-zero rates. After rates normalize, these funds still have flexibility to manage duration and credit risk to remain relevant.

These funds have attracted a tsunami of capital as investors seek to move beyond bonds in their search for income and capital preservation. This demand for uncorrelated fixed income strategies is likely to remain strong for the foreseeable future, since the U.S. bond market has had a tailwind from falling interest rates since the early 1980s, leaving investors concerned about the future. So while retirees are eager for income, they are also cautious about an eventual normalization of interest rates and a potential rise in inflation, both of which can be devastating to fixed income portfolios.

Alternative Credit Focus Funds have another important role that does not garner much attention: volatility management. Retirees need volatility management, since a pure equity portfolio has too much volatility to generate lifetime income with a high degree of confidence. A bear market early in retirement is a major headwind to a portfolio in distribution. After all, money that is withdrawn during a bear market can never rebound or recover. This is the sequence of returns problem, and it is a vexing issue for retirees.

Funds within this classification can help address the volatility of portfolio returns in retirement. When these funds are used as a bond complement, they may offer the noncorrelation benefits of bonds without the interest rate risk of bonds. This benefit assumes that the portfolio manager has skill in managing interest rate risk, of course. Many advisors are turning to these funds because the alternative is worse: Owning the AGG generated losses of 2 percent in 2013, which demonstrates the danger of interest rate risk that is not hedged, managed, or mitigated. Retiree portfolios would be severely impacted if this decline in bonds coincided with a bear market for stocks. The authors believe that unconstrained fixed income strategies have a bright future, and they expect continued strong interest in this classification.

TOP TEN FUNDS

The Alternative Credit Focus Funds classification is less concentrated than other Lipper alternative classifications, such as Absolute Return Funds and Alternative Active Extension Funds, where the top one or two funds reign supreme. Alternative Credit Focus Funds have healthy competition among the top ten funds, with the JPMorgan Strategic Income Opportunities Fund (JSOSX) leading at $24.3 billion in 2013. (See Tables 5.3 through 5.8.) The Goldman Sachs Strategic Income Fund (GSZIX) has significantly lower total net assets than JSOSX, but its estimated net flows of $11.5 billion exceeded JSOSX's $10.3 billion in 2013. The BlackRock Strategic Income Fund (BSIIX) follows close behind with total net assets of $11.2 billion and estimated net flows of $7.3 billion in 2013. The last seven funds comprise between $5.2 billion and $1.7 billion in total net assets. Hence, this classification's top ten funds consist of a variety of large funds from big brand names.

This classification more than doubled its assets in 2013, as did many of its top ten funds. Since these funds were already huge, this development is extraordinary.

The best-performing fund among the top ten in 2013 was the Goldman Sachs Strategic Income Fund (GSZIX), which had a one-year return of 6.4 percent, more than double the top ten funds' average one-year return of 3 percent. GSZIX also had a solid three-year annualized return of 5.8 percent,

TABLE 5.3 Top Ten Alternative Credit Focus Funds as of 12/31/13: Total Assets ($ Millions)

	Symbol	Total Net Assets	Estimated Net Flows
JPMorgan Strategic Income Opportunities Fund	JSOSX	$24,283	$10,307
Goldman Sachs Strategic Income Fund	GSZIX	$14,431	$11,544
BlackRock Strategic Income Opportunities Fund	BSIIX	$11,237	$7,308
FPA New Income Fund	FPNIX	$5,176	$150
BlackRock Global Long/Short Credit Fund	BGCIX	$4,653	$4,131
Driehaus Active Income Fund	LCMAX	$4,600	$1,645
PIMCO Credit Absolute Return Fund	PCARX	$2,468	$1,935
Scout Unconstrained Bond Fund	SUBFX	$1,972	$1,848
Prudential Absolute Return Bond Fund	PADZX	$1,941	$1,560
JPMorgan Multi-Sector Income Fund	JSISX	$1,668	$418

Source: Lipper, a Thomson Reuters Company.

TABLE 5.4 Top Ten Alternative Credit Focus Funds as of 12/31/13: Historical Returns

	One Year	Three Years Annualized	Five Years Annualized	Ten Years Annualized	Expense Ratio
JPMorgan Strategic Income Opportunities Fund	3.0%	3.7%	6.9%		0.84%
Goldman Sachs Strategic Income Fund	6.4%	5.8%			0.65%
BlackRock Strategic Income Opportunities Fund	3.3%	4.1%	9.9%		0.88%
FPA New Income Fund	0.7%	1.7%	2.2%	3.0%	0.58%
BlackRock Global Long/Short Credit Fund	3.7%				1.62%
Driehaus Active Income Fund	3.0%	2.1%	6.4%		1.31%
PIMCO Credit Absolute Return Fund	1.1%				0.90%
Scout Unconstrained Bond Fund	3.7%				0.50%
Prudential Absolute Return Bond Fund	1.7%				0.90%
JPMorgan Multi-Sector Income Fund	3.3%	4.0%			0.79%

Source: Lipper, a Thomson Reuters Company.

TABLE 5.5 Top Ten Alternative Credit Focus Funds as of 12/31/2013: Sharpe Ratios

	One Year	Three Years Annualized	Five Years Annualized	Ten Years Annualized
JPMorgan Strategic Income Opportunities Fund	0.31	1.13	1.87	
Goldman Sachs Strategic Income Fund	0.30	1.64		
BlackRock Strategic Income Opportunities Fund	0.19	1.72	3.05	
FPA New Income Fund	0.06	1.67	2.21	1.31
BlackRock Global Long/Short Credit Fund	0.30			
Driehaus Active Income Fund	0.32	0.40	1.38	
PIMCO Credit Absolute Return Fund	0.06			
Scout Unconstrained Bond Fund	0.22			
Prudential Absolute Return Bond Fund	0.09			
JPMorgan Multi-Sector Income Fund	0.13	1.21		

Source: Lipper, a Thomson Reuters Company.

TABLE 5.6 Top Ten Alternative Credit Focus Funds as of 12/31/13: Sortino Ratios

	One Year	Three Years Annualized	Five Years Annualized	Ten Years Annualized
JPMorgan Strategic Income Opportunities Fund	0.11	1.05	1.69	
Goldman Sachs Strategic Income Fund	0.31	1.39		
BlackRock Strategic Income Opportunities Fund	0.13	1.35	2.86	
FPA New Income Fund	0.06	1.76	2.48	1.42
BlackRock Global Long/Short Credit Fund	0.22			
Driehaus Active Income Fund	0.42	0.34	1.19	
PIMCO Credit Absolute Return Fund	0.05			
Scout Unconstrained Bond Fund	0.21			
Prudential Absolute Return Bond Fund	0.08			
JPMorgan Multi-Sector Income Fund	0.11	1.05		

Source: Lipper, a Thomson Reuters Company.

TABLE 5.7   Top Ten Alternative Credit Focus Funds as of 12/31/13: Maximum Drawdowns

	One Year	Three Years Annualized	Five Years Annualized	Ten Years Annualized
JPMorgan Strategic Income Opportunities Fund	−1.2%	−6.4%	−6.4%	
Goldman Sachs Strategic Income Fund	−2.7%	−5.2%		
BlackRock Strategic Income Opportunities Fund	−3.0%	−3.5%	−3.5%	
FPA New Income Fund	−1.0%	−1.0%	−1.0%	−1.0%
BlackRock Global Long/Short Credit Fund	−1.7%			
Driehaus Active Income Fund	−1.0%	−10.4%	−10.4%	
PIMCO Credit Absolute Return Fund	−3.4%			
Scout Unconstrained Bond Fund	−1.5%			
Prudential Absolute Return Bond Fund	−2.9%			
JPMorgan Multi-Sector Income Fund	−4.2%	−4.2%		

Source: Lipper, a Thomson Reuters Company.

though it has existed only since June 2010. As for the top fund by assets, JSOSX, its one-year and three-year returns have lagged. But this fund has been around since October 2008, and its five-year annualized return of 6.9 percent outperformed the AGG's 4.4 percent returns.

BSIIX's five-year annualized return of 9.9 percent far exceeds the other top ten funds, and the classification average (8.6 percent). BSIIX also has attractive returns for other periods: It had a one-year return of 3.3 percent compared to 0.9 percent for the classification and −2 percent for the AGG, and it had a three-year return of 4.1 percent compared to 3.6 percent for the classification and 3.3 percent for the AGG.

The oldest Alternative Credit Focus Fund, FPA New Income Fund (FPNIX), entered the scene in April 1969, when Lipper classified it as a bond fund. (Lipper's current alternative classifications were introduced in September 2013.) While FPNIX has a long track record, its returns are low: Its one-year return is 0.7 percent and its five-year annualized return is 3 percent. This makes sense, however, given the fund's focus on capital preservation.

Outside of the four funds just mentioned, the other six funds among the top ten have short track records and unexceptional returns.

BSIIX's Sharpe and Sortino ratios stand out among the top ten funds, due to the fund's outperformance over the past few years. The fund has the best three-year and five-year annualized Sharpe ratios of 1.72 and 3.05, respectively. The fund also has impressive three-year and five-year annualized Sortino ratios of 1.35 and 2.86.

TABLE 5.8 Barclays U.S. Aggregate Bond
Total Returns as of 12/31/13

Calendar Year Returns	
2003	4.1%
2004	4.3%
2005	2.4%
2006	4.3%
2007	7.0%
2008	5.2%
2009	5.9%
2010	6.5%
2011	7.8%
2012	4.2%
2013	−2.0%
Rolling Period Returns	
1yr Returns	−2.0%
3yr Returns	3.3%
5yr Returns	4.4%
10yr Returns	4.5%
Sharpe Ratio	
1yr Sharpe	−0.19
3yr Sharpe	1.15
5yr Sharpe	1.49
10yr Sharpe	0.87
Sortino Ratio	
1yr Sortino	−0.15
3yr Sortino	1.07
5yr Sortino	1.41
10yr Sortino	0.85
Max Drawdown	
1yr Max Drawdown	−3.7%
3yr Max Drawdown	−3.7%
5yr Max Drawdown	−3.7%
10yr Max Drawdown	−3.8%

Source: Lipper, a Thomson Reuters company.

Meanwhile, FPNIX has healthy three-year, five-year, and 10-year annualized Sharpe and Sortino ratios, hovering near the top of the list. Although the fund does not generate high returns, its low volatility helps give it appealing risk-adjusted returns. For example, FPNIX has 10-year annualized returns of 3.0 percent, which is below the 4.5 percent returns for the AGG and 4.5 percent returns for the classification. But FPNIX has a 10-year maximum drawdown of only −1.0 percent, an incredible feat for any fund. Only cash or money market funds are likely to have smaller maximum drawdowns for such an extended period of time.

GSZIX's one-year and three-year annualized Sharpe and Sortino ratios also surpassed most of the top ten funds: Its three-year annualized Sharpe ratio of 1.64 beat the top ten funds' average three-year annualized Sharpe ratio of 1.3, and its three-year annualized Sortino ratio of 1.39 exceeded the top ten funds' average three-year annualized Sortino ratio of 1.16. JSOSX's one-year Sharpe ratio of 0.31 falls just short of the Driehaus Active Income Fund (LCMAX), which had the best one-year Sharpe ratio of 0.32 among the top ten funds; LCMAX also had the best one-year Sortino ratio of 0.42, though it had the worst three-year Sharp and Sortino ratios. The remaining top ten funds' Sharpe and Sortino ratios were decent, but as mentioned before, these funds do not have long track records.

Alternative Credit Focus Funds have terrific maximum drawdowns. For the top ten funds in existence five years ago, the worst five-year annualized maximum drawdown was −10.4 percent for the LCMAX, and the JSOSX's five-year annualized maximum drawdown was −6.4 percent. The five-year annualized maximum drawdown of the BlackRock Strategic Income Opportunities Fund (BSIIX) was only −3.5 percent, which matched its three-year annualized maximum drawdown of −3.5 percent and closely mirrored its one-year maximum drawdown of −3 percent. For comparison purposes, the AGG had a five-year maximum drawdown of −3.7 percent, while the S&P 500 had a five-year maximum drawdown of −18.1 percent.

The one-year maximum drawdown of the JPMorgan Multi-Sector Income Fund (JSISX) was −4.2 percent, but the other nine top funds remained above that threshold, and averaged −2 percent. It is worth noting that not only did the FPA New Income Fund (FPNIX) have the lowest one-year maximum drawdown of −1 percent, but the fund maintained this level for its three-year, five-year, and 10-year annualized maximum drawdowns.

BLOCKBUSTER AND SPOTLIGHT

Launched in October 2008, the JPMorgan Strategic Income Opportunities Fund (JSOSX) seeks absolute returns, while limiting systemic risk. The fund manager, Bill Eigen, Head of Absolute Return and Opportunistic Fixed Income Strategies for JPMorgan Asset Management, mainly invests in high-yield corporate bonds, swaps, and loans, and holds a large cash stake. Consequently, JSOSX has achieved returns akin to the high-yield bond market, but with significant less volatility; the fund is also uncorrelated to the AGG. (See Table 5.9.)

TABLE 5.9 Alternative Credit Focus Funds as of 12/31/13: Blockbuster and Spotlight

	Blockbuster: JPMorgan Strategic Income Opportunities Fund	Classification Average	Spotlight: Iron Strategic Income Fund
Total Net Assets 2013 ($Mil)	$24,283	$458	$441
Estimated Net Flows 2013 ($Mil)	$10,307	$253	($13)
One-Year Return	3.0%	0.9%	6.3%
Three-Year Annualized Return	3.7%	3.6%	5.0%
Five-Year Annualized Return	6.9%	8.6%	11.6%
Ten-Year Annualized Return		4.5%	
Expense Ratio	0.84%	1.53%	1.65%

Source: Lipper, a Thomson Reuters Company.

JSOSX's assets of $24.3 billion comprised 35 percent of the TNA for the top ten funds, and its net flows of $10.3 billion accounted for 25 percent of the top ten funds' net flows in 2013. The average assets for the Alternative Credit Focus Fund classification were $458 million, and average net flows were $253 million.

The fund's five-year annualized return of 6.9 percent underperforms the classification's 8.6 percent, though it exceeds the AGG's return (4.4 percent). The three-year annualized return of 3.7 percent beats the classification's three-year annualized average of 3.6 percent, and it beats the 3.3 percent for the AGG. JSOSX had a one-year return of 3 percent, well above the classification's average of 0.9 percent and compared to the 2 percent loss for the AGG.

JSOSX's one-year and three-year annualized Sortino ratios and three-year Sharpe ratio were lower among the top ten funds, but its one-year Sharpe ratio of 0.31 came in second among the top ten funds. JSOSX's expense ratio of 0.84 percent is below the classification by 69 basis points.

Similar to JSOSX, the Iron Strategic Income Fund (IFUNX) aims to "maximize total returns by strategically adjusting the portfolio's exposure to the high yield market." More specifically, the fund seeks to achieve superior risk-adjusted returns against the Merrill Lynch High Yield Master II Index over the full credit market cycle. IFUNX's portfolio managers are Aaron B. Izenstark, cofounder and chief investment officer, and Daniel L. Sternberg, who has been responsible for investment research, trading, and portfolio management on the fund since its inception in October 2006. These managers invest in individual bonds, exchange-traded funds (ETFs), mutual funds, and credit default swaps, while allocating to cash and credit derivatives as a means to maintain credit exposure and hedge against potential credit and liquidity risks. The total net assets for IFUNX were $441 million in 2013, just shy of the classification average of $458 million.

More important, IFUNX's one-year, three-year, and five-year annualized returns exceeded both the blockbuster and classification average. Its five-year annualized return of 11.6 percent outperformed JSOSX's 6.9 percent and the classification's 8.6 percent, and its one-year return of 6.3 percent more than doubled JSOSX's one-year return of 3.0 percent, and shattered the classification average of 0.9 percent. All of these returns are above those of the AGG, as well, which returned −2.0 percent in 2013, 3.3 percent over the past three years, and 4.4 percent over the past five years.

In addition to stellar returns relative to the classification, IFUNX's risk measures challenge the top ten funds. Its five-year annualized Sharpe and Sortino ratios of 2.55 come in second relative to the top ten funds, with the BlackRock Strategic Income Fund (BSIIX) topping the list at 3.05 and 2.86. IFUNX's one-year Sharpe and Sortino ratios of 0.31 also rival the best Sharpe and Sortino ratios among the top ten funds. The spotlight's three-year and five-year maximum drawdown of −8.2 percent is less impressive, and falls at the lower end of the spectrum among the top ten funds.

It is worth pausing a moment to put the risk ratios of IFUNX in perspective. Given the fund's strong returns, its credit exposure, and its focus on total returns, it should not be surprising that it has maximum drawdown above those of the AGG and other funds in its classification. The five-year maximum drawdown of −8.2 percent for IFUNX is still well below the −18.1 percent figure for the S&P 500. Advisors must recognize the trade-off between risk and return, and we do not want to overly penalize this fund for the volatility it has realized in its quest for total returns.

At first glance, the fund's least attractive feature is its expense ratio of 1.65 percent, almost double JSOSX's expense ratio of 0.84 percent, and above the classification average of 1.53 percent. We note, however, that the latest annual report for this fund shows an expense ratio of 1.13 percent, which is well below the prospectus expense ratio. Returns for this fund are net of expenses, and alternative funds are usually a satellite holding in a client's portfolio. Therefore, we do not emphasize expense ratios heavily in our analysis of alternative risk and return, and we would certainly not disqualify this fund as a spotlight because of the expense ratio reported in the prospectus. Advisors should always check the fund fact sheet for the latest information on expense ratios, which may note fee waivers for limited periods and share classes.

SUMMARY

The retirements of baby boomers and the search for yield in a low-return environment have led to an explosion of interest in Alternative Credit Focus Funds. These funds have a high correlation to fixed income markets, and they achieve this using a wide variety of investment approaches. The key issues for advisors will be the proper assessment of client goals, a disciplined evaluation of risk and return, and the selection of funds that fit within the advisor's portfolio construction process. The risk/return profile of the funds within this classification suggests that it offers fruitful hunting grounds.

PROBLEMS

1. If a fund is benchmarked against the AGG, is it reasonable to expect low volatility?
2. If the client's goal is total returns, should the advisor consider funds with high volatility and high maximum drawdowns compared to the AGG?
3. If a client wants preservation of capital over the long term, what risk and return measures are most relevant?
4. Assume that a client's goal is lifetime income and the portfolio has a significant allocation to equities. How can a bond complement in this classification help achieve the client's goal?
5. How can a specific Alternative Credit Focus Fund increase the potential for risk and return? How can it reduce it?
6. Advisors need to manage expectations properly, so clients are less likely to bail out at the bottom when the strategy is out of favor. What should clients expect from these funds? How can advisors manage these expectations?

REFERENCES

Clark, Andrew. "Alternative-Investment Mutual Funds, Part 2: Sources of Return." *Lipper Insight*, March 26, 2014. http://lipperinsight.thomsonreuters.com/2014/03/alternative-investment-mutual-funds-part-2-sources-return/

Clark, Andrew. "The Risk in Liquid Alternative Credit Funds." *Lipper Insight*, April 11, 2014. http://lipperinsight.thomsonreuters.com/2014/04/risk-liquid-alternative-credit-funds/

CHAPTER 6

Alternative Currency Strategies Funds

Synopsis

Alternative Currency Strategies Funds offer more beta and less alpha than most Lipper alternative classifications, since the risks and returns rely almost entirely on exchange rates. The management styles vary, and most of these funds have a track record of low returns and high volatility. These funds are mainly used for tactical hedging and targeted bets, so most of the value added for clients reflects decisions made by the advisor.

DEFINITION

Funds that invest in global currencies through the use of short-term money market instruments, derivatives (forwards, options, swaps), and cash deposits.

Definition of the Lipper classification:
Alternative Currency Strategies Funds

As indicated in the Lipper definition, Alternative Currency Strategies Funds invest in global currencies, using money market vehicles or derivatives with short durations. Some products also use short-term sovereign debt to achieve the desired currency exposure. Most of these funds enable advisors and investors to bet against the U.S. dollar, though some offer leveraged exposure that represents a bullish bet on the U.S. dollar.

In 2004 a large drop in the U.S. dollar helped propel the returns of this classification, since these products offered investors the ability to hedge with foreign currencies. These funds provide naked beta, enabling directional bets based on the discretion of the advisor or investor. As such, these funds are not strategic diversifiers.

TOTAL NET ASSETS AND NET FLOWS

The Alternative Currency Strategies Funds' total net assets climbed steadily from 2004 to 2007, and have proved choppy thereafter, mirroring their volatile returns and uneven net flows. (See Table 6.1.) This classification is relatively small compared to other Lipper alternative classifications; it had total net assets of $12.8 billion in 2013, which accounts for 4 percent of aggregate assets in alternatives. At its peak, total net assets grew to $15.8 billion in 2011, which is a substantial increase from the base of $312 million in 2004.

Prior to 2008, stable net flows into this classification suggest that investors were not chasing performance. Strong returns in 2009 and 2010 attracted $5.3 billion of net flows in 2011, which reversed in 2012 to the tune of $2.7 billion of outflows after negative returns in 2011. Other factors may have driven flows, as the years following the crash of 2008 were marked by high anxiety about federal budget agreements and the outlook for the U.S. dollar.

We should note at the outset that currencies do not, in the aggregate, generate returns, since exchange rates balance out after allowing for interest rate differentials. The short-term and long-term drivers of currencies are subject to plenty of academic analysis, and we will steer clear of the debate.

Having said that, the losses in 2011 may have caught investors by surprise given the pessimism about the economic situation in the United States and the perceived fragility of the euro. This underperformance in 2011 likely contributed to the outflows of $2.7 billion in 2012. Overall, after experiencing strong inflows and initial public offerings (IPOs) up until 2008, this classification seems to have transitioned to a more mature and cyclical stage in recent years.

TABLE 6.1 Alternative Currency Strategies Funds: Historical Overview

	Total Net Assets ($ Millions)	Estimated Net Flows ($ Millions)	Returns	IPOs	Liquidations
2004	$312	$5	8.0%		
2005	$1,583	$1,395	−5.3%	4	
2006	$5,243	$3,264	6.9%	7	
2007	$8,738	$2,558	8.3%	9	
2008	$7,166	($489)	−6.4%	14	
2009	$11,600	$3,634	9.3%	2	
2010	$11,124	($1,099)	5.8%	3	2
2011	$15,842	$5,345	−3.3%	4	1
2012	$13,831	($2,678)	3.9%	3	4
2013	$12,762	($651)	−3.0%	6	1

Source: Lipper, a Thomson Reuters Company.

Turning our attention to fund launches, this classification has had nine straight years of healthy IPOs from 2005 to 2013. Fund liquidations began in 2010, but have remained surprisingly light given the slow growth in assets and the proliferation of funds since 2005. (Bear in mind that mutual fund economics necessitate fund assets of roughly $50 million for long-term viability.) A certain number of liquidations are normal for any classification, and the burst of six IPOs in 2013 signals potential resurgence in investor interest.

RISK AND RETURN

Alternative Currency Strategies Funds have an unattractive risk/return profile relative to most other Lipper alternative classifications. These funds generated average annualized five-year and 10-year returns of only 2.6 percent and 2.8 percent. (See Table 6.2.) Performance more recently has been even worse, with an average one-year return of −3.0 percent and annualized three-year return of −0.9 percent.

Given negative returns, it is no surprise that the strategy also has negative one-year and three-year Sharpe and Sortino ratios. The final insult for investors is the classification's average maximum drawdowns. The 10-year maximum drawdown was −21.6 percent, and the one-year maximum drawdown was −8.1 percent. Given the low level of absolute returns this strategy has generated, these maximum drawdowns appear excessive.

Low returns, high drawdowns, and occasionally negative Sharpe and Sortino ratios demonstrate that these funds are not meant as buy-and-hold investments. Instead, these exchange-traded funds (ETFs) are suitable for trading and directional bets by the advisor. In other words, these funds are not strategic diversifiers, but serve as a tactical hedge, as we further explain in the asset allocation section.

TABLE 6.2 Alternative Currency Strategies Funds: Average Returns and Risk Ratios as of 12/31/13

	Average Return	Average Sharpe Ratio	Average Sortino Ratio	Average Maximum Drawdown
One-Year	−3.0%	−0.06	−0.06	−8.06%
Annualized Three-Year	−0.9%	−0.08	−0.07	−12.87%
Annualized Five-Year	2.6%	0.32	0.32	−14.12%
Annualized 10-Year	2.8%	0.15	0.15	−21.55%

Source: Lipper, a Thomson Reuters Company.

FACTOR EXPOSURES

For the most part, the performance of Alternative Currency Strategies Funds tracks the performance of currencies against the U.S. dollar. (In other words, these are bearish bets on the U.S. dollar.) These funds may have exposure to multiple currencies outside of the United States, so exchange rates drive the risk/return profile. Funds can also assume bullish positions on the U.S. dollar: The PowerShares DB US Dollar Index Bullish Fund (UUP) is a long bet on the U.S. dollar against a basket of six major currencies (euro, yen, pound, Swiss franc, Swedish krona, and Canadian dollar).

Andrew Clark, PhD, Manager of Alternative Investment Research at Lipper, has studied factor exposures for Alternative Currency Strategies Funds. Clark found that only 10 to 15 percent of the funds had downside risk measures that qualified them as effective portfolio diversifiers. The few funds that did perform well from a risk standpoint did not have attractive Sharpe and Sortino ratios. Conversely, the funds that had attractive Sharpe and Sortino ratios did not screen well for downside risk. Clark concludes that these funds may enhance a portfolio's return, though fund selection is critical.

Only two funds in the top ten have a 10-year track record: the Lord Abbett Emerging Markets Currency Fund (LDMAX) and the Franklin Templeton Hard Currency Fund (ICPHX). These funds have 10-year annualized returns of 2.8 percent and 3.4 percent, respectively, and both have high exposures to currencies in emerging markets. So both of these funds benefited from the 5.3 percent return from the MSCI Emerging Markets Currency Index over the past 10 years.

Fifty-two IPOs have joined the space since 2005, as shown in Table 6.1. These funds have many approaches to portfolio management, and include varying degrees of passive and active management:

- The JPMorgan International Currency Income Fund (JCISX) began as a bond fund, and is now benchmarked against a trade-weighted currency index. The fund aims for minimal tracking error versus its index, though it does use fundamental input from JPMorgan's research team.
- PIMCO Emerging Markets Currency Fund (PLMIX) buys local short-term debt and currency forwards in emerging markets, and targets a portfolio's overall duration below one year. The fund is actively managed using PIMCO's expertise in global economics, and is conservatively positioned at the time of this publication, favoring countries with strong credit fundamentals and positive real yields.
- Eaton Vance Diversified Currency Income Fund (EAIIX) is managed more aggressively than many of its peers, and includes a large chunk

of frontier market currencies. EAIIX is not focused on either developing or emerging markets, so the factor exposure will evolve depending on the macroeconomic views of the fund and its allocations across global sovereign debt markets.

Even though funds in this classification have a broad range of management styles, the risk/return characteristics of these funds are still driven by currency allocations and movements. This risk/return profile affects how these funds are used in portfolios, which is mainly for hedging and directional bets.

ASSET ALLOCATION AND FUND SELECTION

The authors believe that the best role for an Alternative Currency Strategies Fund is as a hedge against erosion in the U.S. dollar in either the short run or the long run. As a hedge, we think of using these funds as a satellite position to reduce risk in a core position, whether in stocks, bonds, or some other asset that generates returns above the risk-free rate. These funds may also prove useful for thematic plays by the advisor based on macroeconomics, political risks, technical trends, and so on. These uses may have diversification benefits, too, even though the main goal centers on hedging risk or trading directionally.

Advisors may make a long-term strategic bet on the direction of a specific currency, though this is less common. Our analysis assumes that currencies are not an asset class that generates significant risk-adjusted returns. The exchange rate of global currencies must net to zero, and cannot appreciate in the aggregate over the long term beyond the risk-free rate earned by cash. This return profile is not true for stocks and bonds, which have a legal claim on the cash flows and assets of a corporation or a sovereign nation. Currencies may be uncorrelated to the other holdings in a portfolio, a characteristic they share with commodities and precious metals. But we believe that currency funds are best used to hedge and to make speculative trades, and not as long-term passive holdings.

What about diversification? Many Alternative Currency Strategies Funds advertise the benefits of diversification. This may be true when using an approach to asset allocation that monitors the correlation of currencies and actively manages these correlations relative to other holdings in the portfolio. For most advisors, however, the low returns and high volatility of most Alternative Currency Strategies Funds disqualify them from a potential role as a portfolio diversifier.

Returns have been positive in recent years: The 10-year annualized returns of this classification are 2.8 percent, but this period coincides with a decline in the U.S. dollar that began in 2002. The 10-year maximum drawdown for the classification is −33.6 percent, and maximum drawdowns for the seven funds with 10-year track records range from −19.0 to −70.5 percent. Consequently, given the historical low returns and high volatility, we believe it would be quite unusual for an advisor to use or recommend a currency fund for a long-term strategic holding.

This is not to say that advisors cannot add value for clients by using these funds. An advisor may have a top-down strategy that calls for a weak U.S. dollar over the short term or over the long term. Alternatively, an advisor may wish to hedge the currency exposure of a client's non-U.S. stock and bond positions. Given this outlook, an advisor might use currency funds to hedge, generate alpha, or preserve purchasing power in the country in which the client is domiciled. In these examples, the *advisor* is adding value, and not the fund; the same could be said for Dedicated Short Bias Funds.

Taxes and K-1s

Finally, advisors should note that at least one alternative exchange-traded fund (ETF) in this classification is structured as a limited partnership: Power-Shares DB US Dollar Index Bullish Fund (UUP). Investors will receive a K-1 at the end of the year, which complicates tax reporting and may frustrate clients. In addition, 40 percent of the gains on UUP are taxed as short-term capital gains (the rest are long-term).

Investors may also encounter K-1s for commodity ETFs, leveraged ETFs, dedicated short ETFs, and master limited partnerships (MLPs). Not only is the K-1 inconvenient, but it may also require the investor to file returns in multiple states if the MLP generates oil income from multiple states. Using a limited partnership in a tax-deferred account can help avoid these issues, but the investor may still have to file a Form 990-T if the investment in the partnership generates more than $1,000 of unrelated business taxable income (UBTI).

TOP TEN FUNDS

The PIMCO Emerging Markets Currency Fund (PLMIX) is the blockbuster fund within the Alternative Currency Strategies Funds classification. (See Tables 6.3 through 6.8.) At $6.4 billion in total net assets, PLMIX dwarfs other funds in the top ten, whose assets reach only to the hundreds of millions. The next largest fund, Eaton Vance Diversified Currency Income Fund (EAIIX), had $734 million total net assets in 2013, followed by PowerShares DB US Dollar Index Bullish Fund (UUP) at $667 million.

TABLE 6.3 Top Ten Alternative Currency Strategies Funds as of 12/31/13: Total
Assets ($ Millions)

	Symbol	Total Net Assets	Estimated Net Flows
PIMCO Emerging Markets Currency Fund	PLMIX	$6,394	($55)
Eaton Vance Diversified Currency Income Fund	EAIIX	$734	$146
PowerShares DB US Dollar Index Bullish Fund	UUP	$667	($3)
JPMorgan International Currency Income Fund	JCISX	$607	($578)
WisdomTree Brazilian Real Strategy Fund	BZF	$519	$482
Lord Abbett Emerging Markets Currency Fund	LDMAX	$397	($23)
Guggenheim CurrencyShares Australian Dollar Trust	FXA	$354	($166)
Merk Hard Currency Fund	MERKX	$339	($179)
Franklin Templeton Hard Currency Fund	ICPHX	$316	($121)
Guggenheim CurrencyShares Canadian Dollar Trust	FXC	$309	($165)

Source: Lipper, a Thomson Reuters Company.

TABLE 6.4 Top Ten Alternative Currency Strategies Funds as of 12/31/13:
Historical Returns

	One Year	Three Years Annualized	Five Years Annualized	Ten Years Annualized	Expense Ratio
PIMCO Emerging Markets Currency Fund	−2.5%	0.2%	5.7%		0.85%
Eaton Vance Diversified Currency Income Fund	−2.4%	1.6%	1.6%		1.10%
PowerShares DB US Dollar Index Bullish Fund	−1.3%	−1.9%	−2.7%		0.80%
JPMorgan International Currency Income Fund	0.6%	0.6%	3.1%		0.63%
WisdomTree Brazilian Real Strategy Fund	−8.1%	−5.4%	6.8%		0.45%
Lord Abbett Emerging Markets Currency Fund	1.0%	0.3%	5.2%	2.8%	1.01%
Guggenheim CurrencyShares Australian Dollar Trust	−12.2%	−1.7%	8.2%		0.40%
Merk Hard Currency Fund	−2.8%	0.2%	3.7%		1.30%
Franklin Templeton Hard Currency Fund	−3.3%	−0.1%	2.1%	3.4%	1.13%
Guggenheim CurrencyShares Canadian Dollar Trust	−6.1%	−2.1%	3.1%		0.40%

Source: Lipper, a Thomson Reuters Company.

TABLE 6.5 Top Ten Alternative Currency Strategies Funds as of 12/31/13: Sharpe Ratios

	One Year	Three Years Annualized	Five Years Annualized	Ten Years Annualized
PIMCO Emerging Markets Currency Fund	−0.06	0.02	0.64	
Eaton Vance Diversified Currency Income Fund	−0.10	0.38	0.70	
PowerShares DB US Dollar Index Bullish Fund	−0.03	−0.27	−0.37	
JPMorgan International Currency Income Fund	−0.05	0.15	0.61	
WisdomTree Brazilian Real Strategy Fund	−0.10	−0.44	0.40	
Lord Abbett Emerging Markets Currency Fund	−0.07	0.02	0.55	0.14
Guggenheim CurrencyShares Australian Dollar Trust	−0.19	−0.10	0.52	
Merk Hard Currency Fund	−0.05	0.06	0.42	
Franklin Templeton Hard Currency Fund	−0.09	−0.01	0.32	0.25
Guggenheim CurrencyShares Canadian Dollar Trust	−0.14	−0.27	0.19	

Source: Lipper, a Thomson Reuters Company.

Even more telling for the classification as a whole, eight out of the 10 top funds had net outflows in 2013. Investors redeemed half of their assets in some of these funds, representing a massive migration. For example, the JPMorgan International Currency Income Fund (JCISX) had net outflows of $578 million, approximately 95 percent of total net assets for JCISX in 2013.

Eight out of the top ten funds had negative returns, leading to substantial outflows in aggregate. One exception, EAIIX, had net inflows of $146 million, even after generating a one-year return of −2.4 percent. The worst one-year performer was the Guggenheim CurrencyShares Australian Dollar Trust (FXA), down 12.2 percent; outflows in 2013 were $166 million, or 47 percent of its total net assets.

The best one-year performer was the Lord Abbett Emerging Markets Currency Fund (LDMAX), up 1.0 percent. In fact, LDMAX is the only fund in the top ten to earn positive one-year, three-year, five-year, and 10-year annualized returns. LDMAX's three-year annualized return of 5.2 percent was third best out of the top ten funds, and came in second at 2.8 percent after the Franklin Templeton Hard Currency Fund (ICPHX) at 3.4 percent.

TABLE 6.6 Top Ten Alternative Currency Strategies Funds as of 12/31/13: Sortino Ratios

	One Year	Three Years Annualized	Five Years Annualized	Ten Years Annualized
PIMCO Emerging Markets Currency Fund	−0.06	0.02	0.63	
Eaton Vance Diversified Currency Income Fund	−0.09	0.35	0.68	
PowerShares DB US Dollar Index Bullish Fund	−0.03	−0.27	−0.37	
JPMorgan International Currency Income Fund	−0.05	0.14	0.62	
WisdomTree Brazilian Real Strategy Fund	−0.10	−0.42	0.40	
Lord Abbett Emerging Markets Currency Fund	−0.07	0.02	0.53	0.12
Guggenheim CurrencyShares Australian Dollar Trust	−0.15	−0.09	0.50	
Merk Hard Currency Fund	−0.06	0.06	0.42	
Franklin Templeton Hard Currency Fund	−0.09	−0.01	0.33	0.24
Guggenheim CurrencyShares Canadian Dollar Trust	−0.13	−0.25	0.19	

Source: Lipper, a Thomson Reuters Company.

Only two funds in the top ten have a 10-year track record: the Lord Abbett Emerging Markets Currency Fund (LDMAX) and the Franklin Templeton Hard Currency Fund (ICPHX). LDMAX had 10-year annualized returns of 2.8 percent while ICPHX had 10-year returns of 3.4 percent. These compare to the classification average of 2.8 percent, which is 460 basis points below the 10-year performance of the Standard & Poor's (S&P) 500 Index (7.4 percent). LDMAX had a 10-year maximum drawdown of −25.7 percent compared to ICPHX (−13.0 percent) and the S&P 500 (−50.9 percent).

This suggests that ICPHX is attractive, but it also coincides with a 10-year bull market for emerging market currencies. The MSCI Emerging Markets Currency Index rose at an annualized rate of 5.3 percent for the 10 years ending 12/31/13, and at an annualized rate of 4.4 percent for the five years ending 12/31/13. Thus, the appreciation in emerging market currencies was a tremendous tailwind for funds in this classification.

When looking at the historical returns in Table 6.4, it is worth noting that the expense ratios are low relative to funds in other Lipper alternative

TABLE 6.7 Top Ten Alternative Currency Strategies Funds as of 12/31/13: Maximum Drawdowns

	One Year	Three Years Annualized	Five Years Annualized	Ten Years Annualized
PIMCO Emerging Markets Currency Fund	−7.7%	−11.2%	−11.2%	
Eaton Vance Diversified Currency Income Fund	−5.4%	−5.6%	−7.9%	
PowerShares DB US Dollar Index Bullish Fund	−6.9%	−10.2%	−21.7%	
JPMorgan International Currency Income Fund	−4.0%	−6.5%	−6.8%	
WisdomTree Brazilian Real Strategy Fund	−16.5%	−27.9%	−27.9%	
Lord Abbett Emerging Markets Currency Fund	−8.6%	−12.3%	−12.3%	−25.7%
Guggenheim CurrencyShares Australian Dollar Trust	−14.3%	−14.3%	−14.3%	
Merk Hard Currency Fund	−8.3%	−11.1%	−11.6%	
Franklin Templeton Hard Currency Fund	−6.0%	−9.8%	−11.1%	−13.0%
Guggenheim CurrencyShares Canadian Dollar Trust	−7.5%	−11.2%	−11.2%	

Source: Lipper, a Thomson Reuters Company.

classifications. Most Alternative Currency Strategies Funds are ETFs, which have low management fees and overall expense ratios.

Due to the muted returns throughout the classification, the top ten funds have unappealing Sharpe and Sortino ratios, and many are even negative. JCISX had the most attractive three-year and five-year annualized Sharpe ratios of 0.15 and 0.61, with three-year and five-year annualized Sortino ratios of 0.14 and 0.62. The EAIIX's three-year and five-year annualized Sortino ratios also outperformed at 0.35 and 0.68, in addition to its three-year annualized Sharpe ratio of 0.38. Although these risk measures and returns were competitive compared to the other top ten funds, they remain unimpressive, which is reflected in EAIIX's net outflows and JCISX's low net inflows in 2013.

Even more alarming are the high maximum drawdowns among the top ten funds. The least favorable, WisdomTree Brazilian Real Strategy Fund, had a one-year maximum drawdown of −16.5 percent and three-year and

TABLE 6.8 S&P 500 Returns and Risk Data as of 12/31/13

Calendar Year Returns	
2003	28.7%
2004	10.9%
2005	4.9%
2006	15.8%
2007	5.5%
2008	−37.0%
2009	26.5%
2010	15.1%
2011	2.1%
2012	16.0%
2013	32.4%
Rolling Period Returns	
1-Year Returns	32.4%
3-Year Returns	16.2%
5-Year Returns	17.9%
10-Year Returns	7.4%
Sharpe Ratio	
1-Year Sharpe	0.97
3-Year Sharpe	1.24
5-Year Sharpe	1.04
10-Year Sharpe	0.38
Sortino Ratio	
1-Year Sortino	0.72
3-Year Sortino	1.13
5-Year Sortino	0.89
10-Year Sortino	0.31
Maximum Drawdown	
1-Year Maximum Drawdown	−2.9%
3-Year Maximum Drawdown	−16.3%
5-Year Maximum Drawdown	−18.1%
10-Year Maximum Drawdown	−50.9%

Source: Lipper, a Thomson Reuters Company.

five-year maximum drawdowns of −27.9 percent. Despite LDMAX's superior returns over the top ten funds, investors should note its three-year and five-year annualized maximum drawdown of −12.3 percent and 10-year maximum drawdown of −25.7 percent.

Overall, the poor risk/return profiles of the top ten funds help explain the recent outflows for the classification as investors lost patience with such poor performance. Andrew Clark nails it when he says: "Good risk-adjusted performance is tied to good non-risk-adjusted return, not to good values of downside risk." The classification's low returns do not justify its high volatility: Investors will opt to put money in the S&P 500, which also has high volatility, but which has offered much better returns during the bull market of the past five years.

BLOCKBUSTER AND SPOTLIGHT

The PIMCO Emerging Markets Currency Fund INSTL (PLMIX)—launched in May 2005—is managed by Michael Gomez, the co-head of PIMCO's emerging markets team. The fund invests in non-U.S. currencies or fixed income securities that have an average duration of two years or less.

PLMIX had net outflows of $55 million in 2013 compared to the classification's net outflows of $8 million. (See Table 6.9.) On the plus side, the one-year return of PLMIX was −2.5 percent, which came in a hair better than the −3.0 percent for the classification. The fund's five-year annualized return of 5.7 percent was third best out of the top ten funds, though its three-year annualized return was only 0.2 percent. PLMIX's five-year annualized Sharpe and Sortino ratios of 0.64 and 0.63 are among the best of the top ten funds, but its one-year maximum drawdown of −7.6 percent and three-year and five-year annualized maximum drawdowns of −11.2 percent lag its peers. PLMIX's expense ratio of 0.85 percent is 30 basis points below the classification average.

TABLE 6.9   Alternative Currency Strategies Funds as of 12/31/13: Blockbuster

	Blockbuster: PIMCO Emerging Markets Currency Fund	Classification Average	Spotlight: None
Total Net Assets 2013 ($Mil)	$6,394	$160	*Not applicable*
Estimated Net Flows 2013 ($Mil)	($55)	($8)	
One-Year Return	−2.5%	−3.0%	
Three-Year Annualized Return	0.2%	−0.9%	
Five-Year Annualized Return	5.7%	2.6%	
Ten-Year Annualized Return		2.8%	
Expense Ratio	0.85%	1.15%	

Source: Lipper, a Thomson Reuters Company.

In sum, PLMIX's returns are driven by trends in emerging market currencies, since the fund invests in short-term debt instruments and currency forwards with an overall duration of less than one year. Thus, this fund is more of a directional hedge, and not a strategic diversifier.

Note: The authors did not believe that it was appropriate to choose a Spotlight: No fund stood out as a good representative of the classification, and no fund stood out as attractive in terms of its risk/return profile.

SUMMARY

These funds offer beta in the form of currency exposures rather than alpha in the form of excess return generation. The historical risk/return profiles of these funds make them unsuitable for most buy-and-hold investors. Advisors will find these funds most useful for hedging, and for tactical and strategic bets on the direction of a currency relative to the U.S. dollar.

PROBLEMS

1. Why do the authors say that these funds offer "more beta and less alpha"?
2. Products in this classification are typically used to hedge specific client risks, perhaps for non-U.S. residents or those with large legacy positions in non-dollar-denominated securities. This implies customized portfolio construction: What types of situations would make these funds suitable for clients? How would you monitor these positions as client needs evolve, capital markets change, and new hedging tools emerge?
3. These funds are often used for tactical bets on a currency. What kind of research support will the advisor need to effectively design and monitor these tactical bets?

REFERENCE

Clark, Andrew. "Currency Alternative Funds: Diversifiers or Enhancers of Returns?" *Lipper Insight*, June 29, 2013. http://lipperinsight.thomsonreuters.com/2013/06/ currency-alternative-funds-diversifers-or-enhancers-of-return/

CHAPTER 7

Alternative Equity Market Neutral Funds

Synopsis

Alternative Equity Market Neutral Funds are a collection of low-risk, low-return strategies. As a whole, these funds are the most stable of all Lipper alternative classifications. Investors lose interest in low-volatility strategies when the stock market is doing well, but for long-term investors with the right set of expectations, these funds live up to their name and can make a great portfolio diversifier.

DEFINITION

Funds that employ portfolio strategies generating consistent returns in both up and down markets by selecting positions with a total net market exposure of zero.

Definition of the Lipper classification:
Alternative Equity Market Neutral Funds

Alternative Equity Market Neutral Funds use diverse strategies that have low volatility and low correlation to equity markets. By definition, these funds try to neutralize beta. This strategy hedges market risks by going long and short equities in the same sector, industry, country, style, and market capitalization, aiming to offset gains and losses that are driven by top-down market exposure.

Due to these funds' diverse strategies, it is important for advisors to understand what they are functionally buying. The funds' factor exposures vary widely, and advisors must undertake bottom-up research or rely on third-party research for due diligence.

The returns of these funds have low volatility so investors have a lower potential for losses compared to other Lipper alternative classifications. This classification tends to protect returns in bear markets. As will be

TABLE 7.1   Alternative Equity Market Neutral Funds: Historical Overview

	Total Net Assets ($ Millions)	Estimated Net Flows ($ Millions)	Returns	IPOs	Liquidations
2004	$4,287	$1,119	2.9%	1	
2005	$6,331	$1,852	3.1%	5	
2006	$9,898	$3,013	6.1%	3	
2007	$10,902	$564	3.0%		4
2008	$12,122	$1,841	−2.4%	4	2
2009	$15,920	$3,495	1.5%	1	2
2010	$19,607	$3,164	0.5%	5	1
2011	$17,538	($2,203)	0.4%	14	1
2012	$21,673	$3,444	1.4%	6	5
2013	$26,532	$4,004	3.4%	6	1

Source: Lipper, a Thomson Reuters Company.

discussed in the asset allocation section, this strategy can be either an equity or a fixed income substitute, depending on the underlying strategy and factor exposures.

TOTAL NET ASSETS AND NET FLOWS

With the exception of 2011, the total net assets (TNA) in Alternative Equity Market Neutral Funds have steadily increased since 2004, an unusual trend among Lipper alternative classifications. (See Table 7.1.) Total net assets have grown from less than $4.3 billion in 2004 to more than $26.5 billion in 2013, accounting for 9 percent of aggregate assets in Lipper alternative classifications. This strategy suffered a dip in 2011 after a burst of enthusiasm in 2010, reflected by the 14 initial public offerings (IPOs) in 2011. The classification returned only 0.5 percent during 2010, a year when the Standard & Poor's (S&P) 500 index gained 15.1 percent, contributing to outflows of $2.2 billion in the following year. Flows rebounded in 2012 to $3.4 billion, even though the classification returned only 0.4 percent, perhaps because total returns for the S&P 500 were only 2.1 percent in 2011, making this classification look more attractive in comparison. Strong flows in 2012 and 2013 drove total net assets from $17.5 billion in 2011 to $26.5 billion in 2013.

RISK AND RETURN

This classification earns returns similar to cash, but with higher volatility. (We use returns for the three-month Treasury bill as a proxy for

TABLE 7.2 Alternative Equity Market Neutral Funds: Average Returns and Risk Ratios as of 12/31/13

	Average Return	Average Sharpe Ratio	Average Sortino Ratio	Average Maximum Drawdown
One-Year	3.4%	0.12	0.13	−2.9%
Annualized Three-Year	1.9%	0.39	0.39	−6.5%
Annualized Five-Year	2.0%	0.24	0.21	−10.4%
Annualized 10-Year	2.1%	0.07	0.06	−16.0%

Source: Lipper, a Thomson Reuters Company.

cash returns.) The annualized return for the three-month Treasury bill was 1.6 percent from 2004 to 2013, while Alternative Equity Market Neutral Funds returned an annualized 2.1 percent. (See Table 7.2.) Thus, the classification outperformed cash by a small margin. This margin increased over the past five years, when this classification earned 2.0 percent compared to just 0.1 percent for three-month Treasury bills.

To put this in perspective, it might help to compare Alternative Equity Market Neutral Funds to a classification with a similar objective: Absolute Return Funds. Alternative Equity Market Neutral funds returned 2.1 percent compared to 1.1 percent for Absolute Return Funds. The strategies used by equity market neutral managers earned higher returns over this period.

What about volatility? Alternative Equity Market Neutral Funds had a maximum drawdown of −16 percent over the past 10 years, compared to −33.6 percent for Alternative Absolute Return Funds and −50.9 percent for the S&P 500. On average, Alternative Equity Market Neutral Funds had lower maximum drawdowns than the market and lower drawdowns compared to Absolute Return Funds. This is generally true for shorter time frames as well, though not always: The one-year maximum drawdown of 2.9 percent is the same for the S&P 500 and for this classification. Advisors should not generalize about the riskiness of this classification versus the market, since different funds have different exposures, and the volatility varies over time.

Nevertheless, the returns of Alternative Equity Market Neutral Funds during the financial crisis were impressive: −2.4 percent versus a −37.0 percent for the S&P 500. Only two alternative classifications fared better, and one does not really count: Dedicated Short Bias Funds rose 35.5 percent in 2008, which is what one would expect from funds that bet against the market. The only other classification that outperformed in 2008 was Alternative Managed Futures Funds, which rose 8.3 percent. (As we discuss in Chapter 11 on this classification, it tends to do well during periods of high volatility and pronounced trends, both of which were evident in 2008.)

To sum up the performance of Alternative Equity Market Neutral Funds during downturns, it is clear that it compares well against that of the market and against those of other alternative classifications during a crisis, due to the consistently low beta of the strategy.

Looking at the Sharpe and Sortino ratios, we see small, positive numbers throughout this classification. This is to be expected since the returns are low, and returns are the numerator for these ratios. Alternative classifications with low returns can be expected to generate low Sharpe and Sortino ratios, even when volatility is low.

For Alternative Equity Market Neutral Funds, the annualized three-year Sharpe and Sortino ratios were both 0.39. These measures compare to the S&P 500's Sharpe ratio of 1.24 and Sortino ratio of 1.13. As for maximum drawdowns, Alternative Equity Market Neutral Funds had much lower drawdowns than the S&P 500, especially over the past 10 years: Alternative Equity Market Neutral Funds at −16.04 percent versus S&P 500 at −50.9 percent.

The funds in this classification have generally lived up to their name, which cannot be said for every Lipper alternative classification. This is a low-risk, low-return strategy, and advisors should set investor expectations accordingly.

FACTOR EXPOSURES

The biggest challenge of reviewing funds in this classification is that the funds use many investment processes. They do not lend themselves to quantitative analysis based on any particular factor exposure; instead, a bottom-up approach to analysis is more prudent. These funds also have a wide variety of risk characteristics, reflecting exposures to stocks, credit spreads, optionality, and market capitalization. The following examples illustrate this variety:

- *Gateway Fund (GATEX).* The fund provides exposure to equities with an option collar on risk and return. GATEX sells index call options and buys puts, which combines the income benefits of a buy-write strategy with the hedging benefits of put protection. Gateway harvests gain on individual securities, which adds a level of tax efficiency. The fund has the best 10-year annualized returns in the classification: 4.1 percent versus 2.1 percent for the classification average (and versus 3.7 percent for Calamos, discussed next). The returns of GATEX are driven partly by optionality, and partly by long exposure to equities, though its risk/return profile still makes it a bona fide equity market neutral strategy.
- *Calamos Market Neutral Income Fund (CVSIX).* This fund combines covered call writing (44 percent of portfolio as of March 31, 2014)

with convertible arbitrage (49 percent). Convertible arbitrage involves buying bonds and shorting the underlying stock. CVSIX also uses an opportunistic sleeve with a long/short equity allocation. Calamos added this strategy to CVSIX in January 2013, and allocated 7 percent of assets to the opportunistic sleeve as of March 31, 2014. The convertible arbitrage strategy used by CVSIX benefits from exposure to corporate bonds, so it does have some credit and duration risk. The fund's covered call writing has exposure to market volatility, and affects the premiums received for selling calls, as well as the hedging costs of buying puts. CVSIX has the best 10-year Sortino ratio of all funds in this classification, and its 10-year returns of 3.7 percent are well above the classification average of 2.1 percent. Our biggest caveat is that this fund's convertible bond exposure makes it somewhat less of an equity market neutral fund. In some ways it combines elements of Alternative Credit Focus Funds with aspects of Alternative Equity Market Neutral Funds.

- *PIMCO Fundamental Advantage Absolute Return Strategy Fund (PFATX).* This fund has long exposure to a fundamental equity index called the Enhanced Research Affiliates Fundamental Index (Enhanced RAFI 1000). PFATX also has a short exposure to the S&P 500, so the fund seeks to capture the return premium of an index that is weighted according to fundamentals over an index that is weighted according to market capitalization. The fund makes active bets in its fixed income portfolio in the pursuit of absolute returns. This complex interplay of bets is not easy to characterize, and much of the potential alpha relies on PIMCO's expertise. This fund does not have a 10-year track record, but it has the best five-year annualized returns in the classification: 8 percent annualized versus 2 percent for the average Alternative Equity Market Neutral Fund.

  Considering how high these returns are compared to those of peers, PFATX has healthy results for five-year maximum drawdowns at −11.4 percent versus −10.4 percent for the average fund in this classification, and −18.1 percent for the S&P 500. The knock against this fund is that the active management of fixed income exposure adds an unrelated element of risk and return that is really more suitable for a global macro fund than for an equity market neutral fund.

- *JPMorgan Research Market Neutral Fund (JPMNX).* This fund uses a mixture of quantitative and fundamental analysis to build a diversified long/short portfolio of U.S. equities. It aims for broad diversification, sector neutrality, and beta neutrality, and this low-risk, low-return approach makes JPMNX the epitome of a market neutral fund. This fund has the lowest 10-year maximum drawdown of all funds in the classification at −8.6 percent, but it also has the lowest 10-year annualized returns of 2.2 percent.

ASSET ALLOCATION AND FUND SELECTION

Alternative Equity Market Neutral Funds can serve as an effective portfolio diversifier. Looking at the four funds highlighted in the factor exposures section, it is clear that some are run more aggressively than others. For example, the PIMCO Fundamental Advantage Absolute Return Strategy Fund (PFATX) has higher expected risk and returns than the JPMorgan Research Market Neutral Fund (JPMNX). Assuming that the advisor is using these funds as portfolio diversifiers, PFATX would be more suitable for aggressive investors, or might be used for conservative investors but with a lower weighting. JPMNX, in turn, would be suitable for conservative investors, and would generally be appropriate for a higher weighting in portfolios.

Advisors may use these funds in radically different ways, depending on their investment philosophy, their investment process, and the goals of their clients. An advisor might consider both PFATX and JPMNX as a means of enhancing returns on cash, assuming a long time frame. The advisor might have other ways to diversify or enhance returns using more aggressive means, making these funds seem tame by comparison.

We do not assume that all funds in this classification are diversifiers: CVSIX has exposure to fixed income, and JPMNX has exposure to equities. The usage of these funds will depend on the factor exposures, as well as the investment approach used by each advisor.

TOP TEN FUNDS

The top ten funds by total net assets for the Alternative Equity Market Neutral Funds classification are heterogeneous. The Gateway Fund (GATEX) towers above rivals at $8.2 billion, though the four subsequent funds all top $3 billion. (See Tables 7.3 through 7.8.) Launched in November 2012, the PIMCO Worldwide Fundamental Advantage Absolute Return Strategy Fund (PWWIX) follows GATEX at $3.5 billion. PWWIX's total net assets reflect a surge in net flows after its recent launch. The popularity of PWWIX probably reflects PIMCO's brand power, since it earned one-year returns of only 0.1 percent. PWWIX's one-year maximum drawdown of −5.0 percent trailed all of the top ten funds. The fund's low one-year returns explains its one-year Sharpe and Sortino ratios of 0.0.

Conversely, the Calamos Market Neutral Fund (CVSIX) has existed for more than 20 years, having been launched in September 1990. This fund has one of the best long-term track records within the top ten funds: CVSIX earned a five-year annualized return of 6.5 percent and a three-year annualized return of 4.7 percent. Over the past couple of years, CVSIX yielded

TABLE 7.3 Top Ten Alternative Equity Market Neutral Funds as of 12/31/13: Total Assets ($ Millions)

	Symbol	Total Net Assets	Estimated Net Flows
Gateway Fund	GATEX	$8,191	$616
PIMCO Worldwide Fundamental Advantage Absolute Return Strategy Fund	PWWIX	$3,579	$3,067
Calamos Market Neutral Income Fund	CVSIX	$3,455	$841
GMO Alpha Only Fund	GGHEX	$3,316	$251
PIMCO Fundamental Advantage Absolute Return Strategy Fund	PFATX	$3,147	($214)
TFS Market Neutral Fund	TFSMX	$1,471	($367)
JPMorgan Research Market Neutral Fund	JPMNX	$744	($24)
John Hancock Redwood Fund	JTRAX	$470	($23)
JPMorgan Multi-Cap Market Neutral Fund	OGNAX	$422	($86)
Palmer Square SSI Alternative Income Fund	PSCIX	$384	$190

Source: Lipper, a Thomson Reuters Company.

TABLE 7.4 Top Ten Alternative Equity Market Neutral Funds as of 12/31/13: Historical Returns

	One Year	Three Years Annualized	Five Years Annualized	Ten Years Annualized	Expense Ratio
Gateway Fund	8.4%	5.3%	5.4%	4.1%	0.94%
PIMCO Worldwide Fundamental Advantage Absolute Return Strategy Fund	0.1%				0.99%
Calamos Market Neutral Income Fund	5.9%	4.7%	6.5%	3.4%	1.28%
GMO Alpha Only Fund	−1.4%	0.7%	−2.1%	1.9%	0.66%
PIMCO Fundamental Advantage Absolute Return Strategy Fund	3.6%	4.5%	8.0%		0.89%
TFS Market Neutral Fund	1.4%	3.1%	6.3%		2.41%
JPMorgan Research Market Neutral Fund	2.3%	−0.2%	1.6%	2.3%	3.76%
John Hancock Redwood Fund	6.7%				1.14%
JPMorgan Multi-Cap Market Neutral Fund	4.1%	1.2%	−0.3%	1.0%	3.14%
Palmer Square SSI Alternative Income Fund	2.3%				2.45%

Source: Lipper, a Thomson Reuters Company.

TABLE 7.5 Top Ten Alternative Equity Market Neutral Funds as of 12/31/13: Sharpe Ratios

	One Year	Three Years Annualized	Five Years Annualized	Ten Years Annualized
Gateway Fund	0.31	0.89	0.66	0.32
PIMCO Worldwide Fundamental Advantage Absolute Return Strategy Fund	0.00			
Calamos Market Neutral Income Fund	0.27	0.95	1.02	0.31
GMO Alpha Only Fund	−0.13	0.18	−0.40	0.07
PIMCO Fundamental Advantage Absolute Return Strategy Fund	0.13	1.10	1.18	
TFS Market Neutral Fund	0.04	0.46	0.78	
JPMorgan Research Market Neutral Fund	0.12	−0.12	0.42	0.23
John Hancock Redwood Fund	0.30			
JPMorgan Multi-Cap Market Neutral Fund	0.21	0.38	−0.20	−0.15
Palmer Square SSI Alternative Income Fund	0.21			

Source: Lipper, a Thomson Reuters Company.

consistent returns of 5.8 percent in 2012 and 5.9 percent in 2013, which explains its increase in net flows of $841 million in 2013. This fund also has some of the best Sharpe and Sortino ratios within the top ten funds: Its three-year annualized Sharpe ratio (0.95) and Sortino ratio (0.89) exceed those of all of the other top ten funds. Likewise, CVSIX's 10-year annualized Sharpe ratio of 0.31 falls just short of the Gateway Fund's 0.32, but its Sortino ratio of 0.27 exceeds the Gateway Fund's 0.26. The fund's maximum drawdowns remain in the upper tier relative to the top ten funds. CVSIX's three-year and five-year maximum drawdowns of −5.0 percent and −8.2 percent were trumped by the JPMorgan Multi-Cap Market Neutral Fund's −3.7 percent and −7.4 percent, but its returns were superior.

Although the total net assets of the GMO Alpha Only Fund (GGHEX) slightly lag CVSIX at $3.3 billion (following flows of $251 million in 2013), its long-term track record significantly trails CVSIX. GGHEX was the only fund out of the top ten to lose money in 2013, down 1.4 percent; the fund's five-year return was −2.1 percent. (During this period CVSIX was up 6.5 percent annually, while PWWIX returned 8 percent.) Consequently, the 10-year

TABLE 7.6 Top Ten Alternative Equity Market Neutral Funds as of 12/31/13: Sortino Ratios

	One Year	Three Years Annualized	Five Years Annualized	Ten Years Annualized
Gateway Fund	0.25	0.75	0.54	0.26
PIMCO Worldwide Fundamental Advantage Absolute Return Strategy Fund	0.00			
Calamos Market Neutral Income Fund	0.25	0.89	0.90	0.27
GMO Alpha Only Fund	−0.14	0.21	−0.41	0.07
PIMCO Fundamental Advantage Absolute Return Strategy Fund	0.15	1.11	1.12	
TFS Market Neutral Fund	0.04	0.43	0.74	
JPMorgan Research Market Neutral Fund	0.12	−0.12	0.45	0.23
John Hancock Redwood Fund	0.29			
JPMorgan Multi-Cap Market Neutral Fund	0.22	0.45	−0.23	−0.16
Palmer Square SSI Alternative Income Fund	0.23			

Source: Lipper, a Thomson Reuters Company.

annualized return for GGHEX was only 1.9 percent, the second worst out of the top ten funds. GGHEX has an attractive expense ratio of 0.66 percent compared to the top ten funds' average of 1.77 percent. Yet even with such a low fee, its returns (which are net of the expense ratio) underperform most of the top ten funds.

Looking at other funds among the top ten ranked by TNA, we see widespread outflows. In fact, five out of the bottom six funds experienced net outflows in 2013, as weak returns led investors to abandon these funds. Liquid alts struggle in bull markets, and the S&P 500 has boomed over the past five years, up 16.0 percent in 2012 and 32.4 percent in 2013. This equity rally likely caused investors to pull their assets out of funds with low equity exposure. In a sense, this is routine performance chasing, since the top ten funds in the Alternative Equity Market Neutral Funds classification netted a one-year return of only 3.3 percent. For example, the TFS Market Neutral Fund (TFSMX) rose 7.8 percent in 2012, but was up only 1.4 percent in 2013. This drop contributed to the fund's net outflows of $367 million in 2013 during a great year for equity returns. Likewise, PFATX rose

TABLE 7.7   Top Ten Alternative Equity Market Neutral Funds as of 12/31/13: Maximum Drawdowns

	One Year	Three Years Annualized	Five Years Annualized	Ten Years Annualized
Gateway Fund	−1.9%	−6.1%	−15.1%	−26.3%
PIMCO Worldwide Fundamental Advantage Absolute Return Strategy Fund	−5.0%			
Calamos Market Neutral Income Fund	−1.7%	−5.0%	−8.2%	−19.6%
GMO Alpha Only Fund	−2.3%	−3.8%	−5.4%	−15.4%
PIMCO Fundamental Advantage Absolute Return Strategy Fund	−3.1%	−6.3%	−11.4%	
TFS Market Neutral Fund	−4.6%	−10.9%	−10.9%	
JPMorgan Research Market Neutral Fund	−1.8%	−8.1%	−8.6%	−8.6%
John Hancock Redwood Fund	−1.1%			
JPMorgan Multi-Cap Market Neutral Fund	−1.9%	−3.7%	−7.4%	−10.8%
Palmer Square SSI Alternative Income Fund	−1.6%			

Source: Lipper, a Thomson Reuters Company.

10.8 percent in 2012, but only 3.6 percent in 2013. Again, investors piled in during an outstanding year in 2012, and were impatient with less stellar returns in 2013.

BLOCKBUSTER AND SPOTLIGHT

The Gateway Fund (GATEX), launched in December 1977, has a long history of exceptional returns, even better than the Calamos Market Neutral Income Fund (CVSIX). The fund hedges, but has higher equity beta than the top ten funds, which explains its outperformance. GATEX sells calls and buys puts, providing exposure to the S&P 500, but with a collar on risk and return. This process is similar to a buy-write strategy, and Gateway manages it in a tax-efficient manner. (See Table 7.9.)

The Gateway Fund's $8.2 billion in total net assets exceeds the next largest fund by $4.6 billion, and GATEX garnered a respectable $616 million in net flows in 2013. The steady performance of GATEX is likely driving flows, since its one-year return was 8.4 percent, the three-year annualized return was 5.3 percent, and the 10-year annualized return

TABLE 7.8 S&P 500 Returns and Risk Data as of 12/31/13

Calendar Year Returns	
2003	28.7%
2004	10.9%
2005	4.9%
2006	15.8%
2007	5.5%
2008	−37.0%
2009	26.5%
2010	15.1%
2011	2.1%
2012	16.0%
2013	32.4%
Rolling Period Returns	
1-Year Returns	32.4%
3-Year Returns	16.2%
5-Year Returns	17.9%
10-Year Returns	7.4%
Sharpe Ratio	
1-Year Sharpe	0.97
3-Year Sharpe	1.24
5-Year Sharpe	1.04
10-Year Sharpe	0.38
Sortino Ratio	
1-Year Sortino	0.72
3-Year Sortino	1.13
5-Year Sortino	0.89
10-Year Sortino	0.31
Maximum Drawdown	
1-Year Maximum Drawdown	−2.9%
3-Year Maximum Drawdown	−16.3%
5-Year Maximum Drawdown	−18.1%
10-Year Maximum Drawdown	−50.9%

Source: Lipper, a Thomson Reuters Company.

was 4.1 percent. These returns beat the other top ten funds and the classification averages. The Gateway Fund's five-year annualized return did underperform three of the other top ten funds, but GATEX still generated a healthy 5.4 percent return, compared to a classification average of just 2 percent. GATEX's one-year and 10-year Sharpe ratios proved superior to the other top ten funds at 0.31 and 0.32. Additionally, GATEX's three-year

TABLE 7.9 Alternative Equity Market Neutral Funds as of 12/31/13: Blockbuster and Spotlight

	Blockbuster: Gateway Fund	Classification Average	Spotlight: JPMorgan Research Market Neutral Fund
Total Net Assets 2013 ($Mil)	$8,191	$223	$744
Estimated Net Flows 2013 ($Mil)	$616	$33	($24)
One-Year Return	8.4%	3.4%	2.3%
Three-Year Annualized Return	5.3%	1.9%	−0.2%
Five-Year Annualized Return	5.4%	2.0%	1.6%
Ten-Year Annualized Return	4.1%	2.1%	2.3%
Expense Ratio	0.94%	2.87%	3.76%

Source: Lipper, a Thomson Reuters Company.

Sharpe ratio of 0.89 rivaled the top two funds in the classification for this period: the three-year Sharpe ratio of 0.95 by the Calamos Market Neutral Income Fund (CVSIX) and the three-year Sharpe ratio of 1.1 by the PIMCO Fundamental Advantage Absolute Return Strategy Fund (PFATX). GATEX's five-year and 10-year maximum drawdowns trailed the classification averages, reflecting the fund's high equity exposure. But GATEX's one-year maximum drawdown of −1.9 percent and three-year maximum drawdown of −6.1 percent were middle tier. Last, the fund's 0.94 percent expense ratio may appeal to investors in a classification that has an average prospectus expense ratio of 2.87 percent.

The spotlight fund, JPMorgan Research Market Neutral Fund (JPMNX), was launched on December 31, 1998, and the fund uses a quantitative and fundamental approach based on input from 26 analysts at JPMorgan. The portfolio manager, Terance Chen, announced he would leave JPMorgan by the end of 2014 after managing the fund since 2006. Chen will be replaced by Steven Lee, who is the fund's former autos and transports analyst and has worked at JPMorgan since 2004.

The departure of a fund manager is typically a red flag for the continuity of a fund. This is less of an issue with JPMNX, however, given its disciplined process, its quantitative emphasis, and the extensive involvement of the research team. This leads to greater consistency in performance, for better or worse, and should make the departure of Chen less concerning for investors.

In some ways, JPMNX is an exemplar of an Alternative Equity Market Neutral Fund. The fund has tight restrictions on sector bets, holds about 160 long and 160 short positions, and limits each position to a maximum of 3 percent of fund assets. Since there are three portfolio managers and 26 analysts involved, the process does not depend on any particular superstar. Instead, given the rigorous risk management, the returns of this fund rely almost exclusively on stock selection.

The key to using this fund correctly, in our opinion, is the management of client expectations. This fund consistently posts low volatility and low maximum drawdowns, but it also generates low returns. JPMNX is especially suitable as a portfolio diversifier for conservative clients, given its low equity exposure.

Advisors could also use these funds within this classification for aggressive clients as part of the fixed income portfolio. The role in the portfolio would be volatility management, to hedge the equity exposure without taking on undesirable risks of bonds (credit risk and duration risk). This assumes that the Alternative Equity Market Neutral Fund is truly uncorrelated with stocks, and is being used as a defensive asset with low expectations for returns. These funds have low volatility: If an advisor had to unexpectedly liquidate a position, the low maximum drawdowns suggest that the client would not suffer a catastrophic loss.

Pivoting back to JPMNX specifically, investors should note that the expense ratios shown are from the fund prospectus. JPMNX has a prospectus expense ratio of 3.76 percent, but the actual expense ratio from the 2013 annual report is 0.99 percent. This includes waivers of certain fees and expenses that will last through February 28, 2015, at least. This practice is common, and it would be highly unusual for the fund to raise the expense ratio from 99 basis points to 376 basis points without ample notice.

SUMMARY

Assuming that the advisor has done his or her homework, it is not difficult to find a fund in this classification that will add value to a portfolio. Once the advisor understands the drivers of performance, these funds can be positioned as portfolio diversifiers, depending on the client's goals and the advisor's approach to portfolio construction. The key to success is understanding the factor exposures, using the products appropriately in portfolios, and managing client expectations accordingly.

PROBLEMS

1. Why does this classification have such low volatility?
2. What is the best role of these funds in a portfolio?
3. If a client is aggressive, could these funds be used as part of the fixed income allocation of a portfolio?
4. What type of return expectations should a client have when using these funds?
5. How can an advisor explain the value of a fund with low returns and low volatility?

CHAPTER **8**

Alternative Event-
Driven Funds

Synopsis

Alternative Event Driven Funds typically involve merger arbitrage strategies, and are affected by cyclical changes in deal flow and merger premiums. Most funds offer uncorrelated returns that can diversify portfolios, while other funds may be suitable as equity complements. The risk/return profile for these funds is driven partially by exposure to equities and credit spreads, depending on how the fund is managed. Bottom-up research will help advisors identify the factors driving each fund, and identify the managers who have the skills and process to invest successfully based on the outcomes of corporate mergers, acquisitions, and other corporate events.

DEFINITION

Funds that, by prospectus language, seek to exploit pricing inefficiencies that may occur before or after a corporate event, such as a bankruptcy, merger, acquisition, or spinoff. Event Driven funds can invest in equities, fixed income instruments (investment grade, high yield, bank debt, convertible debt and distressed), options and other derivatives.

Definition of the Lipper classification:
Alternative Event Driven Funds

The Alternative Event Driven Funds classification exploits pricing inefficiencies around corporate events, enabling hedge fund managers to capitalize on mergers and acquisitions, bankruptcies, spin-offs, and corporate reorganization deals. Funds in this classification use a range of strategies to capitalize on corporate events, and merger arbitrage is the most prominent. Merger arbitrage involves long and short positions in the stocks and bonds of acquiring firms and target firms. There are many ways to execute merger arbitrage, depending on the fund manager's approach, the probability of the merger, and the discounts and premiums on the security prices.

This strategy offers exposure to equity or credit arbitrage, which reduces volatility in many asset classes. Event-driven strategies can act as portfolio diversifiers, though these funds bear some tail risk. Alternative Event Driven Funds are driven primarily by equity beta and secondarily by credit spreads, depending on the type of arbitrage strategy. Following the financial crisis, these funds have encountered reduced deal flow, which, along with near-zero interest rates, has narrowed merger spreads (resulting in fewer opportunities for these strategies). Nevertheless, an improving economy and higher interest rates should spur more corporate activity.

TOTAL NET ASSETS AND NET FLOWS

Alternative Event Driven Funds is a niche strategy, reflected in its position as the second smallest liquid alternative classification, behind Alternative Currency Strategies Funds. These funds have grown steadily in total net assets, but at $13.3 billion, they account for only 4 percent of aggregate assets in Lipper alternative classifications. (See Table 8.1.) This strategy has grown more slowly than other classifications, and has not experienced explosive periods of growth. The year 2010 did see inflows of $4.2 billion and 10 initial public offerings (IPOs), signaling growing interest, but these inflows dissipated over the subsequent two years. The burst of 18 IPOs in 2013 is well above most alternative classifications, and is difficult to explain given the limited assets and the history of slow growth for Alternative Event Driven Funds. Perhaps the recent IPO activity reflects inroads made

TABLE 8.1   Alternative Event Driven Funds: Historical Overview

	Total Net Assets ($ Millions)	Estimated Net Flows ($ Millions)	Returns	IPOs	Liquidations
2004	$2,495	$396	6.4%		*None*
2005	$2,010	($546)	3.96%		
2006	$2,469	$215	11.8%		
2007	$2,557	$0.34	3.6%	1	
2008	$1,785	($626)	−14.2%		
2009	$3,776	$1,664	17.0%	3	
2010	$8,117	$4,150	4.9%	10	
2011	$10,928	$2,554	0.3%	5	
2012	$11,468	$291	4.5%	7	
2013	$13,284	$1,505	6.4%	18	

Source: Lipper, a Thomson Reuters Company.

by education about the strategy, as well as two years of healthy returns in 2012 and 2013.

RISK AND RETURN

While Alternative Event Driven Funds have reaped solid returns over the past 10 years, it is difficult to disentangle alpha and beta. The two standout years for the classification were 2006 (11.8 percent) and 2009 (17.0 percent), when the Standard & Poor's (S&P) 500 index was up 15.8 percent and 26.5 percent, respectively. The classification's second weakest year over the past 10 occurred in 2011 (0.3 percent), when the S&P 500 gained just 2.1 percent. Not only are returns for this strategy correlated with equities, but returns often lag. This underperformance evidences the importance of bottom-up research among these funds to find clean forms of alpha; otherwise, investors might as well opt for cheaper index products that mimic equity indexes.

This classification shielded investors from the S&P 500's dramatic loss of −37.0 percent in 2008, having posted a smaller loss of −14.2 percent. This downside protection is one of the key benefits of alternatives, and of Alternative Event Driven Funds. The emphasis on return or risk depends on each fund: Like any alternative strategy, Alternative Event Driven Funds can be run aggressively or conservatively, with an emphasis on upside capture or downside risk.

The average five-year annualized return for this Lipper classification is a solid 7.1 percent, and its returns were 4.3 percent for both the three-year and the 10-year periods. (See Table 8.2.) These returns outpace many Lipper alternative classifications, and can make these funds appealing, assuming that the maximum drawdowns are also well managed. If so, this would give the fund an enticing risk/return profile, as evidenced in its Sortino ratio.

TABLE 8.2 Alternative Event Driven Funds: Average Returns and Risk Ratios as of 12/31/13

	Average Return	Average Sharpe Ratio	Average Sortino Ratio	Average Maximum Drawdown
One-Year	6.4%	0.27	0.29	−1.77%
Annualized Three-Year	4.3%	0.80	0.71	−7.85%
Annualized Five-Year	7.1%	1.02	0.93	−13.88%
Annualized 10-Year	4.3%	0.37	0.32	−28.88%

Source: Lipper, a Thomson Reuters Company.

Alternative Event Driven Funds do in fact have superior maximum drawdowns relative to the S&P 500. The classification's average maximum drawdown of −28.9 percent is much lower than the S&P 500's −50.9 percent, and its annualized three-year average maximum drawdown of −7.9 percent is about half of the S&P 500's three-year maximum drawdown of −16.3 percent. The S&P 500 does have better Sharpe and Sortino ratios, but this classification does not trail too far behind. Alternative Event Driven Funds' annualized five-year Sharpe and Sortino ratios of 1.02 and 0.93 rival the S&P 500's 1.04 and 0.89. Although the S&P 500 may outperform these funds, this strategy has historically generated healthy returns with less risk, depending on the fund.

FACTOR EXPOSURES

In its simplest form, a merger arbitrage strategy buys the stock of an acquisition target and it shorts the stock of the acquirer. Some firms also use options to hedge downside risk. This strategy can generate returns that have little or no correlation to stocks or bonds. Merger arbitrage returns are sensitive to merger spreads, however, and to the boom/bust cycle of deal flow, since these are both factors that create investable opportunities. Performance for the HFRI Merger Arbitrage Index has historically tracked Treasury bills, though returns have been in the low single digits from 2009 through 2013, a period when the Federal Reserve instituted a policy of near-zero interest rates.

The following three funds offer merger arbitrage strategies in its classic form. They may not be pure plays in merger arbitrage, but they generally represent the strategy in the Investment Company Act of 1940 ('40 Act) space:

1. The Merger Fund (MERFX) had $5.0 billion in assets as of March 31, 2014. The fund's 10-year returns through year-end 2013 were 3.5 percent. The fund's average position size is 1 percent of assets, and its 10 largest holdings were 29 percent of assets, making the Merger Fund much less concentrated than the Arbitrage Fund. The fund has had a correlation of 0.21 to the S&P 500 since its inception in 2000, and a beta of 0.16. The fund's short positions were 12 percent of assets as of March 31, 2014. The fund gets kudos for showing both winning and losing positions in its quarterly statistical summary.
2. The Arbitrage Fund (ARBFX) from Water Island Capital had $2.6 billion in assets as of March 31, 2014. This included a net long exposure of just over 60 percent, which helps dampen volatility. Through the end of 2013,

ARBFX had 10-year returns of 2.9 percent compared to 7.4 percent for the S&P 500. The fund has a correlation of just 0.25 to the S&P 500, based on the three years ending March 31, 2014. Most impressively of all, perhaps, is the fund's performance in 2008, when it lost only −0.6 percent, versus −37 percent for the S&P 500. The fund is quite concentrated, however, with 54 percent of assets in the 10 largest holdings.

3. The Gabelli ABC Fund (GABCX) had $1.2 billion in assets as of March 31, 2014. The fund's 10-year returns were 4.5 percent through year-end 2013, and its 10-year maximum drawdown was an impressive −7.6 percent (compared to −50.9 percent for the S&P 500). Equally impressive, GABCX has had only one year of losses since 1993: In 2008 the fund had returns of −2.6 percent. The fund is well diversified, with 20 percent of assets in its 10 largest positions as of March 31, 2014.

The following three funds offer other types of event-driven approaches, and typically have higher correlations to equities and higher maximum drawdowns:

1. *The Gabelli Enterprise Mergers & Acquisitions Fund (EMAAX)* had $264 million in assets as of March 31, 2014, and its 10 largest holdings were 22 percent of assets. The fund had 10-year returns of 4.8 percent through year-end 2013, slightly better than the 4.5 percent generated by the Gabelli ABC Fund. EMAAX is more volatile, since it invests in takeover targets and the fund's primary goal is capital appreciation. This higher-risk approach is evidenced in the 10-year maximum drawdown of −46.7 percent (versus −50.9 percent for the S&P 500).
2. *The Quaker Event Arbitrage Fund (QEAAX)* had assets of $90 million at year-end 2013, and 10-year returns of 6.1 percent, better than most of its peers. But QEAAX also has a correlation of 0.71 to the S&P 500 from December 1, 2003, through March 31, 2014. This high correlation makes the fund more volatile: It lost −25.7 percent in 2008 and the 10-year maximum drawdown was −34.4 percent. QEAAX uses six event-driven strategies, ranging from classic merger arbitrage to distressed securities, and management does not always hedge positions. This explains much of the fund's volatility, which resembles that of a long-only stock fund.
3. *Guggenheim Event Driven and Distressed Strategies (RYDTX)* had $15 million in assets as of March 31, 2014. This fund was launched in June 2010, and has three-year returns of 6.1 percent through March 31, 2014, compared to 16.2 percent for the S&P 500. The maximum drawdown was −13.3 percent, compared to −18.1 percent for the S&P 500. RYDTX invests in far more than merger arbitrage, and the fund seeks to replicate the returns of an event-driven hedge fund. The fund uses an algorithm to

determine weightings in six factors, and it uses derivatives to get exposure to these factors. The factors are:

1. Small cap equities
2. Distressed equities
3. High-yield bonds
4. Credit
5. Merger arbitrage
6. An illiquidity premium (to represent the risk premium for holding illiquid securities)

Generally speaking, the funds that stick to classic merger arbitrage have lower returns and lower correlations to the S&P 500. These merger arbitrage funds are true alternative funds, and make a better complement to the equity portion of a portfolio.

Some investors may prefer the higher-risk/higher-return approach of the other event-driven types, and may have no problem with the accompanying volatility. If an investor holds these types of event-driven funds, the allocation should probably be considered part of the equity allocation, since that is a more accurate description of the risk/return profile. We are not saying that either approach is right or wrong, but the distinction is important, and will affect the asset allocation decision and the proper role of the fund in client portfolios.

ASSET ALLOCATION AND FUND SELECTION

Alternative Event Driven Funds can serve as a portfolio diversifier due to their low correlation with stocks and bonds, assuming that the fund adheres to a mandate of classic merger arbitrage.

Based on data from the HFRI Merger Arbitrage Index, an investor could add different percentages of this index to a 100 percent stock or 100 percent bond portfolio. For example, an investor could add merger arbitrage to the Barclays iShares Core U.S. Aggregate Bond ETF (AGG), and the mix should generate higher returns and lower volatility. Adding the strategy to a 100 percent stock portfolio slightly reduces returns, but also reduces volatility. For both stocks and bonds, the new blends generate an efficient frontier and show how these funds can be portfolio diversifiers.

Alternative Event Driven Funds have been one of the few bright spots among liquid alternative funds during the past decade. Ten-year returns for the classification were 4.5 percent (versus 7.4 percent for the S&P 500), and five-year returns were 7.1 percent (versus 7.4 percent). These returns should be seen in light of the drawdowns for the classification: The five-year maximum drawdown was −13.9 percent (versus −18.1 percent for the S&P 500), and the 10-year maximum drawdown was −28.9 percent (versus −50.9 percent for the S&P 500).

Equally important, there are a number of funds in this classification that rely on merger arbitrage, and that execute it in a manner that is genuinely uncorrelated with stocks and bonds. This is difficult to do, and other Lipper classifications that attempt noncorrelation do not fare as well in terms of returns, correlations, or both. Absolute Return Funds and Alternative Equity Market Neutral Funds both have high exposures to stocks, and may not diversify a portfolio as well as an Alternative Event Driven Fund. This classification is heterogeneous, so investors will have to confirm that the fund is pursuing merger arbitrage.

Alternative Event Driven Funds are suitable for a wide range of portfolios, from conservative to aggressive. Some of these event-driven strategies are more highly correlated with stocks, and are best considered as an equity complement. Others are run systematically, with small concentrations and low drawdowns, and may be used as portfolio diversifiers. The best of these funds, in our opinion, are those that consistently stick to classic merger arbitrage, which generates uncorrelated returns.

TOP TEN FUNDS

Alternative Event Driven Funds have four dominant funds that run from $1 billion to $5 billion in total net assets. The other six funds have a few hundred million in total net assets, and all funds except one had inflows in 2013. (See Tables 8.3 through 8.8.) The largest fund (MERFX) and best-performing fund (GABCX) had the greatest inflows in 2013, which will be covered in the blockbuster and spotlight section.

The second-largest fund by total net assets, the Arbitrage Fund (ARBFX), was the only fund to experience net outflows (−$278 million) in 2013. This makes sense given the fund had the weakest performance out of the top ten, up only 0.9 percent in a year when the S&P 500 was up 32.4 percent. The bottom six of the top ten funds outperformed the top four in recent years, but a few of these funds are quite new and lack brand power.

The Gabelli Enterprise Mergers & Acquisitions Fund (EMAAX), on the other hand, has brand recognition, but also high volatility. The five-year maximum drawdown was −25.5 percent and the 10-year annualized maximum drawdown was −46.7 percent—more than any other top ten fund and well above the maximum drawdown for the S&P 500 at −18.1 percent and −50.9 percent, respectively. Although EMAAX outperformed the other top ten funds, its large maximum drawdowns were not rewarded with generous returns, since it trailed the S&P 500. With high volatility,

TABLE 8.3   Top Ten Alternative Event Driven Funds as of 12/31/13: Total Assets ($ Millions)

	Symbol	Total Net Assets	Estimated Net Flows
Merger Fund	MERFX	$5,012	$448
Arbitrage Fund	ARBFX	$2,725	($278)
AQR Diversified Arbitrage Fund	ADAIX	$2,712	$163
Gabelli ABC Fund	GABCX	$1,121	$474
Touchstone Merger Arbitrage Fund	TMGAX	$691	$263
Gabelli Enterprise Mergers & Acquisitions Fund	EMAAX	$252	$29
Transamerica Arbitrage Strategy	IMUAX	$200	$76
Touchstone Arbitrage Fund	TARBX	$146	$145
Arbitrage Event-Driven Fund	AEDNX	$131	$86
Quaker Event Arbitrage Fund	QEAAX	$90	$27

Source: Lipper, a Thomson Reuters Company.

TABLE 8.4   Top Ten Alternative Event Driven Funds as of 12/31/13: Historical Returns

	One Year	Three Years Annualized	Five Years Annualized	Ten Years Annualized	Expense Ratio
Merger Fund	3.6%	3.0%	4.1%	3.5%	1.74%
Arbitrage Fund	0.9%	1.9%	3.4%	2.9%	1.99%
AQR Diversified Arbitrage Fund	1.8%	2.0%			2.37%
Gabelli ABC Fund	4.9%	4.0%	4.4%	4.5%	0.60%
Touchstone Merger Arbitrage Fund	4.7%				2.28%
Gabelli Enterprise Mergers & Acquisitions Fund	13.3%	7.1%	10.8%	4.8%	1.69%
Transamerica Arbitrage Strategy	1.4%				1.60%
Touchstone Arbitrage Fund	*Fund inception 9/30/13*				1.71%
Arbitrage Event-Driven Fund	5.7%	3.7%			1.93%
Quaker Event Arbitrage Fund	12.3%	3.9%	9.0%	6.1%	1.99%

Source: Lipper, a Thomson Reuters Company.

TABLE 8.5 Top Ten Alternative Event Driven Funds as of 12/31/13: Sharpe Ratios

	One Year	Three Years Annualized	Five Years Annualized	Ten Years Annualized
Merger Fund	0.23	0.89	1.30	0.42
Arbitrage Fund	0.09	0.66	1.11	0.25
AQR Diversified Arbitrage Fund	0.22	1.19		
Gabelli ABC Fund	0.39	1.17	1.24	0.82
Touchstone Merger Arbitrage Fund	0.34			
Gabelli Enterprise Mergers & Acquisitions Fund	0.38	1.08	0.78	0.25
Transamerica Arbitrage Strategy	0.13			
Touchstone Arbitrage Fund	*Fund inception 9/30/13*			
Arbitrage Event-Driven Fund	0.47	0.68		
Quaker Event Arbitrage Fund	0.38	0.58	1.14	0.56

Source: Lipper, a Thomson Reuters Company.

TABLE 8.6 Top Ten Alternative Event Driven Funds as of 12/31/13: Sortino Ratios

	One Year	Three Years Annualized	Five Years Annualized	Ten Years Annualized
Merger Fund	0.17	0.68	1.12	0.35
Arbitrage Fund	0.11	0.61	1.00	0.21
AQR Diversified Arbitrage Fund	0.26	1.18		
Gabelli ABC Fund	0.38	1.04	1.19	0.75
Touchstone Merger Arbitrage Fund	0.39			
Gabelli Enterprise Mergers & Acquisitions Fund	0.37	0.94	0.68	0.21
Transamerica Arbitrage Strategy	0.15			
Touchstone Arbitrage Fund	*Fund inception 9/30/13*			
Arbitrage Event-Driven Fund	0.62	0.67		
Quaker Event Arbitrage Fund	0.32	0.51	1.13	0.52

Source: Lipper, a Thomson Reuters Company.

investors are likely to opt for pure beta given the prospect of losses higher than those of the S&P 500. Despite the brand power of EMAAX, the fund's total net assets of $252 million and net flows of only $29 million in 2013 reflect the fund's volatile track record.

Quaker Event Arbitrage Fund (QEAAX) is another fund within the top ten with high volatility. The fund has a long-term record of impressive

TABLE 8.7 Top Ten Alternative Event Driven Funds as of 12/31/13: Maximum Drawdowns

	One Year	Three Years Annualized	Five Years Annualized	Ten Years Annualized
Merger Fund	−1.1%	−4.7%	−4.7%	−10.4%
Arbitrage Fund	−1.0%	−4.2%	−5.2%	−10.1%
AQR Diversified Arbitrage Fund	−0.5%	−2.0%		
Gabelli ABC Fund	−0.8%	−4.2%	−4.2%	−7.6%
Touchstone Merger Arbitrage Fund	−0.5%			
Gabelli Enterprise Mergers & Acquisitions Fund	−1.8%	−7.1%	−25.5%	−46.7%
Transamerica Arbitrage Strategy	−1.1%			
Touchstone Arbitrage Fund	Fund inception 9/30/13			
Arbitrage Event-Driven Fund	−0.6%	−5.6%		
Quaker Event Arbitrage Fund	−1.9%	−13.2%	−13.2%	−34.4%

Source: Lipper, a Thomson Reuters Company.

returns, with one-year, five-year, and 10-year annualized returns of 12.3 percent, 9.0 percent, and 6.1 percent, respectively. The one-year return of 12.3 percent is impressive, just behind the one-year return of 13.3 percent for EMAAX. However, like EMAAX, the five-year and 10-year maximum drawdowns for QEAAX were high at −13.2 percent and −34.4 percent, respectively.

On the plus side, EMAAX and QEAAX have decent Sharpe and Sortino ratios relative to the top ten funds. QEAAX's five-year annualized Sharpe and Sortino ratios of 1.14 and 1.13 are among the better measures in the top ten, with the Gabelli ABC Fund grabbing the top spot with 1.24 and 1.19. Similarly, EMAAX had the third best three-year annualized Sharpe and Sortino ratios of 1.08 and 0.94. With that said, the average maximum drawdowns often overshadow these measures, especially in comparison to the S&P 500. EMAAX's and QEAAX's expense ratios of 1.69 percent and 1.99 percent, respectively, are also greater than many of the top ten funds and near the classification average of 1.96 percent, another investor consideration.

We now compare the long-term performance of the Merger Fund (MERFX) with the Gabelli Enterprise Mergers & Acquisitions Fund (EMAAX). When investors evaluate the 10-year annualized return of MERFX with EMAAX, for example, they must consider both risk and return. EMAAX has a compound annual return of 4.8 percent over the past 10 years, a performance advantage of 130 basis points over MERFX. If what is past is prologue, investors may ask themselves if the additional

TABLE 8.8 S&P 500 Returns and Risk Data as of 12/31/13

Calendar Year Returns	
2003	28.7%
2004	10.9%
2005	4.9%
2006	15.8%
2007	5.5%
2008	−37.0%
2009	26.5%
2010	15.1%
2011	2.1%
2012	16.0%
2013	32.4%
Rolling Period Returns	
1-Year Returns	32.4%
3-Year Returns	16.2%
5-Year Returns	17.9%
10-Year Returns	7.4%
Sharpe Ratio	
1-Year Sharpe	0.97
3-Year Sharpe	1.24
5-Year Sharpe	1.04
10-Year Sharpe	0.38
Sortino Ratio	
1-Year Sortino	0.72
3-Year Sortino	1.13
5-Year Sortino	0.89
10-Year Sortino	0.31
Maximum Drawdown	
1-Year Maximum Drawdown	−2.9%
3-Year Maximum Drawdown	−16.3%
5-Year Maximum Drawdown	−18.1%
10-Year Maximum Drawdown	−50.9%

Source: Lipper, a Thomson Reuters Company.

return potential in EMAAX is worth the higher volatility, since the 10-year maximum drawdown in EMAAX is more than four times that of MERFX.

As with any high-risk, high-return strategy, there will be bursts of outperformance, such as in 2013 when EMAAX returned 13.3 percent compared to just 3.6 percent for MERFX. But once another crisis hits, advisors will have to explain to their clients why they were in such an aggressive fund, especially one that was supposed to be alternative and offer uncorrelated returns compared to the broader market indexes. For a client with high risk tolerance, however, EMAAX or QEAXX would be reasonable options within the classification. As always, advisors must understand the underlying characteristics of the funds within the classification in order to have conviction in the product they choose. Otherwise, both the client and the advisor will be tempted to bail out at the first sign of trouble.

Total net assets indicate investor interest in Alternative Event Driven Funds that are more conservatively managed. For example, the AQR Diversified Arbitrage Fund (ADAIX) had $2.7 billion in total net assets and garnered $163 million in net flows in 2013. Though ADAIX has average one-year and three-year annualized returns of only 1.8 percent and 2.0 percent, its three-year annualized Sharpe and Sortino ratios were 1.19 and 1.18—the highest within the top ten funds—and its average one-year and three-year annualized maximum drawdowns were only −0.5 percent and −2.0 percent, or the smallest maximum drawdowns within the top ten funds. This suggests that advisors and investors are seeking uncorrelated strategies within this classification, and they are piling into funds that offer attractive risk-adjusted returns.

BLOCKBUSTER AND SPOTLIGHT

The classification's blockbuster, the Merger Fund (MERFX), is an example of a less volatile fund that continues to attract significant inflows. (See Table 8.9.) Launched in January 1989, the fund pioneered the merger

TABLE 8.9 Alternative Event Driven Funds as of 12/31/13: Blockbuster and Spotlight

	Blockbuster: Merger Fund	Classification Average	Spotlight: Gabelli ABC Fund
Total Net Assets 2013 ($Mil)	$5,012	$246	$1,121
Estimated Net Flows 2013 ($Mil)	$448	$28	$474
One-Year Return	3.6%	6.4%	4.9%
Three-Year Annualized Return	3.0%	4.3%	4.0%
Five-Year Annualized Return	4.1%	7.1%	4.4%
Ten-Year Annualized Return	3.5%	4.3%	4.5%
Expense Ratio	1.74%	1.96%	0.60%

Source: Lipper, a Thomson Reuters Company.

arbitrage space, and seeks absolute, noncorrelated returns in all markets. Roy D. Behren and Michael T. Shannon have managed the fund since 2007, and take advantage of available merger and acquisition opportunities by going long in the acquisition target and shorting the acquirer's stock. Behren and Shannon also invest in bankruptcy and corporate reorganization deals, or in short-term corporate bonds when deal flow is light.

At $5 billion in total net assets and with inflows of $448 million in 2013, MERFX's time-proven and steady approach has elevated the fund to the top spot by a wide margin. The returns are certainly not the best within the top ten funds, though, and in fact the fund has lagged the classification's average returns. MERFX's average five-year and 10-year annualized returns of 4.1 percent and 3.5 percent trail the classification's average five-year and 10-year annualized returns of 7.1 percent and 4.3 percent. But the Merger Fund's five-year Sharpe and Sortino ratios of 1.30 and 1.12 are among the best relative to the top ten funds. Even more attractive are MERFX's five-year and 10-year maximum drawdowns of −4.7 percent and −10.4 percent, which are well below the S&P 500's −18.0 percent and −50.9 percent. MERFX's expense ratio of 1.74 percent also falls below the classification's average of 1.96 percent. This fund's appeal lies in its steady returns and conservative profile.

The spotlight fund, the Gabelli ABC Fund (GABCX), also has attractive risk/return characteristics. The fund is managed by Mario Gabelli, Chairman, Chief Executive Officer, and Chief Investment Officer of GAMCO Investors Inc., and was launched in May 1993. GABCX seeks total returns without excessive risk of capital loss in "various market conditions." Like any alternative fund, the name of the game is to achieve attractive returns while limiting losses. In order to achieve these objectives, the fund invests in announced mergers, spin-offs, split-ups, liquidations, and reorganizations, or even value-oriented common stocks and convertible securities. And of course, the fund invests in U.S. Treasury bills in order to act upon "non-market-correlated opportunities" that arise with short notice.

GABCX outperformed MERFX over the past 10 years, though it often lags the average returns of the classification. Nevertheless, GABCX's average annualized 10-year return of 4.5 percent beats the classification average of 4.3 percent, and its three-year annualized return of 4.0 percent is not too far behind the classification's 4.3 percent. Additionally, GABCX's 10-year Sharpe and Sortino ratios of 0.82 and 0.75 far exceed the other top ten funds, and its 10-year average maximum drawdown of −7.6 percent has provided better downside protection. Finally, the fund's expense ratio of 0.6 percent is lower than that of MERFX (1.74 percent) and the classification's average (1.96 percent).

SUMMARY

Many Alternative Event Driven Funds have an attractive risk/return profile, and may be suitable as equity complements or portfolio diversifiers. Funds that pursue a classic merger arbitrage strategy have generated the most consistent and uncorrelated returns, and are ideally suited as portfolio diversifiers. Investors should expect returns in the low single digits at best, and these are subject to cyclical movements in deal flow and merger premiums. These funds can be used for portfolios ranging from conservative to aggressive, assuming the advisor is skilled in fund selection, portfolio construction, and managing client expectations.

PROBLEMS

1. What characteristics make a merger arbitrage fund such an effective portfolio diversifier?
2. Returns in this classification have outperformed cash since 2009, but may not continue to do so. Is it more important to emphasize correlations rather than returns for Alternative Event Driven Funds?
3. If deal flow dries up, merger arbitrage funds may suffer from capacity issues. How can an advisor reconcile this with the classification's role as a portfolio diversifier?

CHAPTER 9

Alternative Global Macro Funds

Synopsis

Most of these funds are unconstrained, and can invest in any asset class or geography, leading some investors to dub them "go-anywhere" funds. The classification is heterogeneous, and performance is driven by a variety of factors that change as the manager makes new bets. Depending on the factor exposures of each strategy, these funds can be used as stock complements, bond complements, or portfolio diversifiers. The flexibility of these funds adds upside potential, but it also adds an additional layer of complexity for advisors and investors. Consequently, when using these funds, advisors must carefully identify and closely monitor the factor exposures and the impact of the fund on the portfolio's asset allocation.

DEFINITION

> *Funds that, by prospectus language, invest around the world using economic theory to justify the decision-making process. The strategy is typically based on forecasts and analysis about interest rate trends, the general flow of funds, political changes, government policies, intergovernmental relations, and other broad systemic factors. These funds generally trade a wide range of markets and geographic regions, employing a broad range of trading ideas and instruments.*
>
> Definition of the Lipper classification:
> Alternative Global Macro Funds

Alternative Global Macro Funds cover a broad swath of approaches and strategies. According to Lipper, these funds make investment decisions based on economic, monetary, and political developments around the world in order to capitalize on changes in global capital flows. Trading is discretionary as top-down managers take advantage of opportunities in different asset classes across geographic regions and industry sectors. Global macro managers may take significant long or short positions based on expected changes in equity prices, interest rates, currencies, monetary policies, or macroeconomic variables such as inflation, unemployment rates, or trade balances.

This classification generally invests using liquid assets that capture market exposures to a wide range of factors such as credit risk or liquidity risk. Most managers employ fundamental and technical analysis, and may venture into commodity strategies. Commodities such as oil, gold, and silver enable managers to react to both deflationary and inflationary environments.

Among the strategies used by global macro managers, currency strategies allow for the greatest leverage and trade based on the relative strength of currencies against one another. Managers of currency strategies follow global economic and monetary policy, in addition to the interest rates of various countries. Interest rate strategies invest in sovereign global debt—such as U.S. Treasuries or European bonds—typically in derivatives markets, enabling the use of leverage, though not using as much leverage as currency strategies typically employ.

Equity indexes are used directionally and for relative value strategies. These funds usually have long positions in countries that are growing and that have interest rates that are neutral or trending downward.

While some investors believe that Alternative Global Macro Funds lack focus, this strategy can provide diversification, and managers are able to increase the leverage of these funds by using futures, swaps, and forward contracts. This classification has high potential returns and may offer downside protection, as demonstrated in 2008 when it was relatively unscathed.

Finally, investors should note that these strategies are sometimes classified as global flexible funds or global allocation funds. The lines between classifications are fuzzy around the edges, and overlapping classifications are part and parcel of the alternatives landscape.

TOTAL NET ASSETS AND NET FLOWS

Alternative Global Macro Funds is the fourth largest Lipper alternative classification, with $35.4 billion in total net assets. (See Table 9.1.) The asset growth in this classification did not really get traction until 2010, when it had $17.5 billion in net inflows. The majority of this classification's inflows depend on one or two funds. For example, of this classification's $17.5 billion in net flows in 2010, the PIMCO Unconstrained Bond Fund (PFIUX) accounted for $10.5 billion, or 60 percent of total net flows. [Note: Bill Gross resigned from PIMCO in September of 2014, triggering massive redemptions

TABLE 9.1 Alternative Global Macro Funds: Historical Overview

	Total Net Assets ($ Millions)	Estimated Net Flows ($ Millions)	Returns	IPOs	Liquidations
2004		*No data available*			
2005					
2006	$0.10				
2007	$260	$265		12	
2008	$892	$709	−16.1%	7	*None*
2009	$4,821	$3,667	16.2%	3	
2010	$22,770	$17,501	3.4%	5	
2011	$23,233	$649	−1.4%	11	
2012	$26,903	$2,310	7.1%	4	
2013	$35,398	$9,366	2.2%	9	

Source: Lipper, a Thomson Reuters Company.

in PIMCO funds, including PFIUX.] Also in 2010, the Eaton Vance Global Macro Absolute Return Fund (EIGMX) accounted for 38 percent of estimated total net flows. So these two funds accounted for 98 percent of net flows in the classification that year, cementing their blockbuster status.

As a group, Alternative Global Macro Funds had returns of −16 percent in 2008, though this did not deter inflows in 2009. This classification had $3.7 billion of inflows, which could be mostly attributed to the PIMCO Unconstrained Bond Fund (PFIUX). PFIUX, which launched in June 2008, captured $2.8 billion of inflows during 2009, or three-fourths of the entire classification's inflows. The year 2010 was a breakout year for the classification, with inflows of $17.5 billion, with PFIUX and EIGMX leading the charge.

The year 2013 was the second largest year for net flows at $9.4 billion. As in 2010, PFIUX is largely responsible for the growth in assets, with $8.7 billion of inflows in 2013. To put this in perspective, the Legg Mason BW Absolute Return Opportunities Fund (LROIX) had inflows of $708 million, a mere 8 percent of what PFIUX garnered. The Alternative Global Macro Funds classification is large compared to other Lipper classifications, and it is highly concentrated, with one fund having largely determined its growth and success.

As a technical side note, it is worth pointing out what happens to the classification when funds have outflows during any given year. When this occurs, net flows will total more than 100 percent for the funds that are successfully gathering assets: Their inflows must more than offset the outflows. In the Alternative Global Macro Classification, EIGMX had outflows of $706 million in 2013, though this was more than offset by inflows elsewhere.

This dynamic is not behind the success of PFIUX and EIGMX, which is confirmed by comparing the net flows to the net assets for these funds. As always, investors should examine both net flows and total net assets to fully assess the dominance of a blockbuster.

Finally, turning to fund openings and closures, Alternative Global Macro Funds have had a healthy number of initial public offerings (IPOs) since 2007, though the universe of funds remains limited. There are only 16 funds, as measured by primary share class, which eliminates double-counting of funds (though all share classes are included in assets and net flows). This classification is relatively young, since only seven funds have three-year track records, which we discuss in the next section.

RISK AND RETURN

Most funds in this classification were launched within the past few years, and have not experienced a bear market. Out of the seven funds that have three-year track records, only five had positive three-year returns.

In 2013 seven out of 12 funds had negative returns despite the 32.4 percent rise in the Standard & Poor's (S&P) 500 index. Alternative Global Macro Funds' average five-year return was 6.2 percent, with Sharpe and Sortino ratios of 1.03 and 0.99. (See Table 9.2.) By contrast, the S&P 500 returned 17.9 percent and had Sharp and Sortino ratios of 1.04 and 0.89 over the same time frame.

This classification had lower relative returns over the past five years, which is typical for alternatives during a bull market. Nevertheless, the Sharpe ratio for this classification is virtually identical to that of the S&P 500 and its Sortino ratio is superior. Finally, the five-year maximum drawdown was only −12.4 percent versus −18.1 percent for the S&P 500.

TABLE 9.2 Alternative Global Macro Funds: Average Returns and Risk Ratios as of 12/31/13

	Average Return	Average Sharpe Ratio	Average Sortino Ratio	Average Maximum Drawdown
One-Year	2.2%	−0.01	−0.02	−6.28%
Annualized Three-Year	3.2%	0.59	0.55	−6.85%
Annualized Five-Year	6.2%	1.03	0.99	−12.42%
Annualized 10-Year	*No data available*			

Source: Lipper, a Thomson Reuters Company.

Alternative Global Macro Funds have generated moderately attractive returns, but it is hard to draw any firm conclusions when the five-year data occurred during a bull market (and there are no 10-year data).

FACTOR EXPOSURES

This classification is driven by a wide mix of factors, ranging from general stock and bond market exposure to more esoteric factors such as currency derivatives and short positions in optionality (i.e., buying covered puts). Since these funds are heterogeneous, advisors should evaluate bottom-up factor exposures. These exposures evolve over time since global macro managers are always changing their bets, so the factor exposures and return correlations are by no means fixed.

For example, the PIMCO Unconstrained Bond Fund (PFIUX) is driven mainly by bond market factors such as duration risk and credit risk, as well as the macroeconomic bets made by PIMCO. The Eaton Vance Global Macro Absolute Return Fund (EIGMX) is also run like a nontraditional bond fund. These funds are both relatively low-risk, and are best used as a bond complement.

At the other end of the spectrum is KCM Macro Trends Fund (KCMTX), which is primarily an equity fund. KCMTX had one-, three-, and five-year returns of 32.2 percent, 7.7 percent, and 9.7 percent. These returns compare to 32.4 percent, 16.2 percent, and 17.9 percent for the S&P 500 for the same time periods. KCMTX fits in the Alternative Global Macro Funds classification since it is globally allocated and plays "overarching trends, market biases, and future expectations regarding specific countries, regions, industries, and companies." The fund can also change its equity weighting from 0 to 100 percent. (That certainly qualifies as global macro.) Since the fund executes this strategy entirely by using stocks, it should be used as an equity complement, and any diversification benefits would be incidental.

In between these two extremes is the MFS Global Alternative Strategy Fund (DVRIX), which makes bets via both currencies and tactical trades on stocks and bonds. DVRIX has outperformed its peers over the past five years, with annualized returns of 8.5 percent versus 6.2 percent for the classification. This fund has strong Sharpe and Sortino ratios, and it derives its returns from a variety of sources that change over time. This makes the fund an ideal portfolio diversifier, assuming that MFS continues to execute well.

It is telling that seven out of 12 funds in this classification lost money in 2013, a banner year for equities. Global macro portfolio managers may have had similar outlooks for the economy and capital markets. At the start of 2013 few investors expected stocks to rally, and most managers in this space ranged from cautiously positive to passionately pessimistic. It is true that the 32 percent rally in stocks surprised most observers, but it is also true that Alternative Global Macro Funds do not seem to attract wild-eyed optimists. (This may tell us more about market sentiment than the classification, but it is worth noting.)

ASSET ALLOCATION AND FUND SELECTION

Funds in this classification can be used in any of the three basic roles for alternatives: stock complement, bond complement, or portfolio diversifier, depending on the investment process of each fund.

Perhaps the most challenging aspect of investing in Alternative Global Macro Funds is ongoing due diligence. It is relatively easy to evaluate historical performance, but this offers few clues about future performance for unconstrained portfolio managers who are making tactical and strategic bets on the global economy. A few funds are run with constraints on asset class weightings or net long/short exposures, and these funds are likely to have smaller drawdowns and tighter correlations with the underlying benchmark.

But for many of these funds, the past is not prologue, and the investor must continually reevaluate the risk/return profile of the fund. This makes it especially complicated for advisors to perform portfolio analysis, since these funds make it difficult to determine the exact asset allocation at any given point in time. This lack of transparency makes it hard to know if the fund fits the advisor's outlook for the markets, or if it still fits the client's risk profile.

One solution for this challenge is to rely on an internal fund management research team for ongoing due diligence. This group usually provides risk control analytics that show how the fund fits in an overall portfolio. These internal research teams may also provide prepackaged model portfolios that include liquid alternatives. Another solution is to simply maintain a small position size in these funds, so that a change in the underlying asset allocation will not distort the portfolio's overall risk profile.

These issues show the side effects of a "go-anywhere" fund: If it can truly go anywhere, it makes oversight much more complex.

Most Alternative Global Macro Funds can be categorized fairly cleanly into either equity complements, bond complements, or portfolio diversifiers. Once an advisor makes this decision, the next step is to decide the position size. An unconstrained fund is more complex to manage, and requires more advisor bandwidth for proper oversight. Alternatively, if the fund has clear factor exposures, the advisor may be comfortable giving the fund a standard allocation, and can offset the factor risk elsewhere in the portfolio.

The most difficult issue remains when the Alternative Global Macro Fund changes the size, nature, and direction of its bets. This could wreak havoc with correlation analytics and static asset allocation models, so the position size of this type of fund should be limited (depending on the client's goals, the firm's resources, and the advisor's outlook). In sum, these funds require extra effort to identify and monitor factor exposures and proper usage in client portfolios.

TOP TEN FUNDS

As prefaced in the section on total net assets and estimated net flows, the PIMCO Unconstrained Bond Fund (PFIUX) dominates the Alternative Global Macro Funds classification with $26.8 billion in total net assets, or 76 percent of the classification's total net assets as of 2013. (See Tables 9.3 through 9.8.) Eaton Vance grabs the next two slots with the Eaton Vance Global Macro Absolute Return Fund (EIGMX) and the Eaton Vance Global Macro Absolute Return Advantage Fund (EGRIX) with $5.5 billion and $1.1 billion in assets, respectively. EIGMX has lost assets since 2011, and outflows were $761 million in 2013, almost as much as the $801 million in the fourth largest fund, the Legg Mason BW Absolute Return Opportunities Fund (LROIX). While eight out of the 10 top funds had inflows in 2013, most were minimal—the real growth came from PFIUX.

TABLE 9.3 Top Ten Alternative Global Macro Funds as of 12/31/13: Total Assets ($ Millions)

	Symbol	Total Net Assets	Estimated Net Flows
PIMCO Unconstrained Bond Fund	PFIUX	$26,832	$8,690
Eaton Vance Global Macro Absolute Return Fund	EIGMX	$5,499	($761)
Eaton Vance Global Macro Absolute Return Advantage Fund	EGRIX	$1,090	$300
Legg Mason BW Absolute Return Opportunities Fund	LROIX	$801	$708
William Blair Macro Allocation Fund	WMCIX	$384	$312
MFS Global Alternative Strategy Fund	DVRIX	$270	$145
Altegris Macro Strategy Fund	MCRIX	$198	($124)
Transamerica Global Macro	US8939627126	$166	$74
KCM Macro Trends Fund	KCMTX	$80	$6
Orinda SkyView Macro Opportunities Fund	OMOAX	$38	$14

Source: Lipper, a Thomson Reuters Company.

TABLE 9.4 Top Ten Alternative Global Macro Funds as of 12/31/13: Historical Returns

	One Year	Three Years Annualized	Five Years Annualized	Ten Years Annualized	Expense Ratio
PIMCO Unconstrained Bond Fund	−2.2%	2.4%	5.1%		0.9%
Eaton Vance Global Macro Absolute Return Fund	−0.2%	1.1%	3.8%		1.0%
Eaton Vance Global Macro Absolute Return Advantage Fund	−0.8%	1.5%			1.7%
Legg Mason BW Absolute Return Opportunities Fund	1.3%		*No data available*		0.9%
William Blair Macro Allocation Fund	13.4%				1.4%
MFS Global Alternative Strategy Fund	8.0%	6.8%	8.5%		1.2%
Altegris Macro Strategy Fund	−7.4%				2.1%
Transamerica Global Macro	−5.0%	−2.4%	0.9%		1.5%
KCM Macro Trends Fund	32.2%	7.7%	9.7%		1.8%
Orinda SkyView Macro Opportunities Fund	0.9%				3.7%

Source: Lipper, a Thomson Reuters Company.

Half of the top ten funds had negative one-year returns, which is highly suspect for Alternative Global Macro Funds, especially given the bullish market environment. EIGMX and EGRIX, the second and third largest funds, lost 0.2 percent and 0.8 percent, respectively, and reaped three-year annualized returns of only 1.1 percent and 1.5 percent versus S&P 500's annualized three-year return of 16.2 percent. These funds had negative one-year Sharpe and Sortino ratios, and had the worst three-year Sharpe and Sortino ratios, which were 0.4 and 0.3. On the plus side, this pair of funds had three-year maximum drawdowns that were respectable versus peers and the market: EIGMX at −3.3 percent and EGRIX at −6.2 percent.

The two best performers out of the top ten funds were the William Blair Macro Allocation Fund (WMCIX) and the KCM Macro Trends Fund (KCMTX) with one-year returns of 13.4 percent and 32.2 percent, respectively. (WMCIX was launched in November 2011, hence the short

TABLE 9.5 Top Ten Alternative Global Macro Funds as of 12/31/13: Sharpe Ratios

	One Year	Three Years Annualized	Five Years Annualized	Ten Years Annualized
PIMCO Unconstrained Bond Fund	−0.13	0.92	1.70	
Eaton Vance Global Macro Absolute Return Fund	−0.02	0.44	1.60	
Eaton Vance Global Macro Absolute Return Advantage Fund	−0.04	0.33		
Legg Mason BW Absolute Return Opportunities Fund	0.03			*No data available*
William Blair Macro Allocation Fund	0.20			
MFS Global Alternative Strategy Fund	0.19	1.15	0.80	
Altegris Macro Strategy Fund	−0.32			
Transamerica Global Macro	−0.13	−0.63	−0.01	
KCM Macro Trends Fund	0.30	0.48	0.55	
Orinda SkyView Macro Opportunities Fund	0.02			

Source: Lipper, a Thomson Reuters Company.

track record.) KCMTX had strong three-year and five-year annualized returns of 7.7 percent and 9.7 percent, respectively, though its one-year return mirrors the S&P 500, suggesting a high equity beta. With greater returns comes greater risk, and this is captured in the fund's five-year annualized Sharpe and Sortino ratios, which are the second worst among the top ten funds at 0.55 and 0.52. KCMTX's five-year maximum drawdown was −22.3 percent, underperforming the S&P 500's five-year maximum drawdown of −18.1 percent. Although the fund matched the S&P 500's returns in 2013, over the long term KCMTX lagged equities and had high volatility.

BLOCKBUSTER AND SPOTLIGHT

The PIMCO Unconstrained Bond Fund (PFIUX) is a true blockbuster, driving the net flows and assets for the entire Alternative Global Macro Funds classification since its inception in June 2008. This fund is an "absolute return-oriented bond strategy," and the portfolio manager was Bill Gross, the cofounder of Pacific Investment Management Company (PIMCO).

TABLE 9.6 Top Ten Alternative Global Macro Funds as of 12/31/13: Sortino Ratios

	One Year	Three Years Annualized	Five Years Annualized	Ten Years Annualized
PIMCO Unconstrained Bond Fund	−0.11	0.91	1.72	
Eaton Vance Global Macro Absolute Return Fund	−0.02	0.40	1.53	
Eaton Vance Global Macro Absolute Return Advantage Fund	−0.03	0.30		
Legg Mason BW Absolute Return Opportunities Fund	0.02			*No data available*
William Blair Macro Allocation Fund	0.19			
MFS Global Alternative Strategy Fund	0.13	1.05	0.70	
Altegris Macro Strategy Fund	−0.30			
Transamerica Global Macro	−0.13	−0.63	−0.01	
KCM Macro Trends Fund	0.23	0.42	0.52	
Orinda SkyView Macro Opportunities Fund	0.02			

Source: Lipper, a Thomson Reuters Company.

Note: Bill Gross resigned from PIMCO in September 2014. The quantitative analysis of historical returns remains valid. But the departure of Gross means that future returns will depend on the process and judgment of the new portfolio managers, led by Dan Ivacysn, the new Group CIO of PIMCO. Ivacysn is the highly regarded co-manager of PIMCO Income (PIMIX), a fund with a solid track record. Ivacysn's co-managers on the fund are Saumil Parikh and Mohsen Fahmi. It remains to be seen, of course, if the skills of the new team are a good fit for the PIMCO Unconstrained Bond Fund.

The mandate of the fund defines its objectives broadly, and do not tie it to a specific benchmark. PFIUX invests across multiple sectors and geographies and has a duration range from negative three years to positive eight years. The fund seeks to provide the benefits of a core bond fund with greater alpha potential while limiting downside risk. PFIUX invests up to 40 percent of its assets in high-yield bonds, up to 50 percent in emerging markets bonds, and up to 35 percent in foreign currencies, and carries no maximum on non-U.S.-dollar-denominated securities.

In 2013, PFIUX made some bad bets on bonds and lost −2.2 percent, slightly below the Barclays iShares Core U.S. Aggregate Bond ETF's

TABLE 9.7 Top Ten Alternative Global Macro Funds as of 12/31/13: Maximum Drawdowns

	One Year	Three Years Annualized	Five Years Annualized	Ten Years Annualized
PIMCO Unconstrained Bond Fund	−3.8%	−3.8%	−3.8%	
Eaton Vance Global Macro Absolute Return Fund	−3.3%	−3.3%	−3.3%	
Eaton Vance Global Macro Absolute Return Advantage Fund	−6.2%	−6.2%		
Legg Mason BW Absolute Return Opportunities Fund	−7.8%			*No data available*
William Blair Macro Allocation Fund	−7.0%			
MFS Global Alternative Strategy Fund	−5.7%	−5.7%	−18.2%	
Altegris Macro Strategy Fund	−8.5%			
Transamerica Global Macro	−10.3%	−16.1%	−18.7%	
KCM Macro Trends Fund	−7.1%	−22.3%	−22.3%	
Orinda SkyView Macro Opportunities Fund	−5.5%			

Source: Lipper, a Thomson Reuters Company.

−2 percent, and 440 basis points below the classification's returns of 2.2 percent. Nevertheless, PFIUX had inflows of $8.7 billion in 2013, highlighting PIMCO's brand power. The fund's five-year annualized return of 5.1 percent lags the classification average of 6.2 percent, but the fund has the highest five-year annualized Sharpe and Sortino ratios out of the top ten funds, both at 1.7. This compares to the five-year Sharpe and Sortino ratios of the Barclays iShares Core U.S. Aggregate Bond ETF (AGG) of 1.49 and 1.41. PFIUX also has the lowest five-year maximum drawdown in the top ten at −3.8 percent, slightly above the −3.7 percent for the AGG. This low maximum drawdown is not surprising, since a bond-oriented fund will usually have lower volatility. The fund has decent returns with solid risk measures, and its expense ratio of 0.90 percent is even lower than that of the spotlight fund, DVRIX.

The superior risk/return characteristics of the MFS Global Alternative Strategy Fund (DVRIX) warranted a spotlight for this classification. Launched in December 2007, the fund seeks total returns through individual securities, top-down market allocation, and active currency management. The fund's portfolio managers, Joseph C. Flaherty Jr. (lead) and Natalie I.

TABLE 9.8   S&P 500 Returns and Risk Data as of 12/31/13

Calendar Year Returns	
2003	28.7%
2004	10.9%
2005	4.9%
2006	15.8%
2007	5.5%
2008	−37.0%
2009	26.5%
2010	15.1%
2011	2.1%
2012	16.0%
2013	32.4%
Rolling Period Returns	
1-Year Returns	32.4%
3-Year Returns	16.2%
5-Year Returns	17.9%
10-Year Returns	7.4%
Sharpe Ratio	
1-Year Sharpe	0.97
3-Year Sharpe	1.24
5-Year Sharpe	1.04
10-Year Sharpe	0.38
Sortino Ratio	
1-Year Sortino	0.72
3-Year Sortino	1.13
5-Year Sortino	0.89
10-Year Sortino	0.31
Maximum Drawdown	
1-Year Maximum Drawdown	−2.9%
3-Year Maximum Drawdown	−16.3%
5-Year Maximum Drawdown	−18.1%
10-Year Maximum Drawdown	−50.9%

Source: Lipper, a Thomson Reuters Company.

Shapiro, oversee the team responsible for security selection, while UBS's Curt Custard, Jonathan Davies, and Andreas Koester oversee the team managing market exposure. The portfolio management team has essentially made both currency and asset class bets. In 2013, the fund had inflows of $145 million, bringing net assets to $270 million. Though small, it is still the sixth-largest fund within the Alternative Global Macro Funds classification.

TABLE 9.9 Alternative Global Macro Funds as of 12/31/13: Blockbuster and Spotlight

	Blockbuster: PIMCO Unconstrained Bond Fund	Classification Average	Spotlight: MFS Global Alternative Strategy Fund
Total Net Assets 2013 ($Mil)	$26,832	$694	$270
Estimated Net Flows 2013 ($Mil)	$8,690	$184	$145
One-Year Return	−2.2%	2.2%	8.0%
Three-Year Annualized Return	2.4%	3.2%	6.8%
Five-Year Annualized Return	5.1%	6.2%	8.5%
Ten-Year Annualized Return		*No data available*	
Expense Ratio	0.9%	1.7%	1.15%

Source: Lipper, a Thomson Reuters Company.

DVRIX has outperformed the classification average over the past five years, with a five-year annualized return of 8.5 percent versus the classification's 6.2 percent. The fund's one-year return of 8.0 percent significantly outpaced the classification's one-year return of 2.2 percent during a weak year for the strategy. Aside from the KCM Macro Trends Fund (KCMTX)—which has high beta and volatility—DVRIX reaped the best returns out of the top ten funds over one-year, three-year, and five-year periods.

From a risk standpoint, the fund's three-year annualized Sharpe and Sortino ratios of 1.15 and 1.05 beat the other funds within the top ten. DVRIX's five-year maximum drawdown was −18.1 percent, matching the S&P 500, but its three-year maximum drawdown of −5.7 percent was superior to the S&P 500's −16.3 percent. Though the beta is high, the fund has a robust track record of risk and return. As an added benefit, the fund's expense ratio of 1.15 percent is 55 basis points less than the classification average.

SUMMARY

Given the wide range of strategies and factor exposures in this classification, advisors should evaluate each fund on its own merits. The go-anywhere approach is most appropriate for sophisticated advisors and aggressive investors, especially since most of these funds have limited track records. Alternative Global Macro Funds need a high level of ongoing due diligence, so advisors need additional tools to help them research and monitor these funds.

PROBLEMS

1. Why do investors call global macro strategies "go-anywhere" funds?
2. The factor exposures for these funds vary widely, and they evolve over time. What challenges does this create for ongoing due diligence?
3. A global macro manager may make bets that are contrary to the advisor's outlook. When would this make sense?
4. Some global macro funds have no constraints on asset allocation. How does this affect portfolio construction?

CHAPTER 10

Alternative Long/Short Equity Funds

Synopsis

Alternative Long/Short Equity Funds are a popular gateway product for investors who are new to alternatives, and the classification has broadened beyond equities to include other asset classes. These funds are more homogeneous than most Lipper alternative classifications, which allows for more detailed and rigorous factor analysis and more direct comparisons of fund manager performance. The homogeneity of these funds enables them to be used nearly universally as an equity complement, and each fund offers various degrees of market exposure and factor tilts. Since there are more than 160 funds in the classification, investors have no reason to limit themselves to the classification's blockbuster, the MainStay Marketfield Fund. To help winnow these choices, this chapter has additional content about the fund selection process.

DEFINITION

Funds that employ portfolio strategies combining long holdings of equities with short sales of equity, equity options, or equity index options. The funds may be either net long or net short, depending on the portfolio manager's view of the market.

Definition of the Lipper classification:
Alternative Long/Short Equity Funds

The Alternative Long/Short Equity Funds classification originally focused on stocks, but has expanded to include bonds, commodities, and occasionally currencies. This strategy has a high correlation to equities—an attractive feature in bull markets when other alternative strategies tend to underperform. Since this strategy has a high correlation to stocks, it is best used as an equity complement. Concerns about interest rates have also attracted investors to long/short fixed income strategies, which entails active management of both credit and duration risk.

The rapid growth of Alternative Long/Short Equity Funds is based partly on the familiarity of the strategy, which provides investors with something of a gateway product into the alternatives space. The classification is vulnerable to depreciation in the underlying assets, given its short equity exposures, and investors may lose interest in these funds if returns seem inferior to pure equity strategies (especially in a bull market). Nevertheless, the classification has attracted healthy growth in assets over the past several years.

TOTAL NET ASSETS AND NET FLOWS

Alternative Long/Short Equity Funds is the second largest classification by total net assets within the Lipper alternatives classifications, totaling $44 billion, or 14 percent of all liquid alt assets. (See Table 10.1.) About half of these assets were amassed in 2013, when net flows were almost $19.9 billion—more than the total net assets of six other Lipper alternative classifications. In the years leading up to 2013, the classification grew at a swift pace, with a modest dip in 2008. Assets fell from almost $9.1 billion in 2007 to less than $8.0 billion in 2008, when the average returns for the classification were −29.5 percent. This return is better than the −37.0 percent drop in the Standard & Poor's (S&P) 500, but the decline still surprised many investors who thought "long/short" meant that these funds had a neutral exposure to equity markets.

TABLE 10.1 Alternative Long/Short Equity Funds: Historical Overview

	Total Net Assets ($ Millions)	Estimated Net Flows ($ Millions)	Returns	IPOs	Liquidations
2004	$3,283	$896	7.6%	1	
2005	$5,142	$1,634	5.3%	6	
2006	$7,881	$2,325	8.1%	6	2
2007	$9,060	$847	5.0%	18	4
2008	$7,954	$1,048	−29.5%	17	4
2009	$11,062	$2,404	19.7%	14	10
2010	$13,660	$2,656	5.5%	19	10
2011	$15,354	$1,661	−2.7%	16	11
2012	$20,025	$4,649	4.7%	17	10
2013	$44,016	$19,869	15.9%	22	7

Source: Lipper, a Thomson Reuters Company.

This strategy's returns loosely shadow those of the S&P 500, showing that these funds have a pronounced long equity bias. The allocation to stocks potentially boosts returns over long time horizons, though it challenges investors to deconstruct returns in order to separate the alpha from the beta.

The high equity exposure has fueled healthy long-term returns for Alternative Long/Short Equity Funds: Ten-year annualized returns for the classification are 4.8 percent, with much higher returns for shorter time periods. These funds lost –29.5 percent in 2008, almost as much as the S&P 500 (–37.0 percent). The classification rebounded to 19.7 percent returns in 2009, so these funds do catch a big chunk of market upswings. This is not guaranteed, however, since the classification fell –2.7 percent in 2011 when the S&P 500 rose 2.1 percent. Alternative Long/Short Equity Funds resemble a subdued form of equity exposure, with higher tracking error due to the high active share of long/short strategies. (Advisors could use this analytical perspective for long/short fixed income strategies as well, now that the classification has expanded beyond equities.)

The appeal of this classification appears almost immune to investment performance: Asset growth continues to be strong whether or not these funds outperformed during the prior year, or even when the funds lost money. Perhaps the strategy attracts investors who seek the prospect of equity upside during upturns and a hedge during downturns, even though these funds have generally not been able to deliver on this promise.

This classification certainly does not lack variety: The Alternative Long/Short Equity Funds classification boasts 161 primary share classes— a generous assortment of products for advisors to sort and filter. The high level of initial public offerings (IPOs) reflects the strategy's popularity, and it has also had a steady stream of liquidations. Liquidations often accompany cyclical surges of IPO activity, especially in a space with hundreds of funds—far more than most Lipper alternative classifications.

RISK AND RETURN

Alternative Long/Short Equity Funds' high correlation to the equity market has enabled the strategy to achieve solid 10-year and five-year returns of 4.8 percent and 8.8 percent, respectively. (See Table 10.2.) The 10-year maximum drawdown of –35.0 percent includes the crash of 2008, and was better than the S&P 500's maximum drawdown of –50.9 percent. Meanwhile, the classification's five-year maximum drawdown of –16.3 percent was modestly better than the S&P 500's –18.1 percent.

What does this mean? This classification's returns, although healthy, trail those of the S&P 500, which would be acceptable if it were not for

TABLE 10.2 Alternative Long/Short Equity Funds: Average Returns and Risk Ratios as of 12/31/13

	Average Return	Average Sharpe Ratio	Average Sortino Ratio	Average Maximum Drawdown
One-Year	15.9%	0.27	0.27	−4.0%
Annualized Three-Year	6.4%	0.56	0.50	−13.4%
Annualized Five-Year	8.8%	0.64	0.60	−16.3%
Annualized 10-Year	4.8%	0.22	0.20	−35.1%

Source: Lipper, a Thomson Reuters Company.

the propensity for maximum drawdowns that nearly match equity indexes. For example, Alternative Long/Short Equity Funds had annualized three-year and five-year returns of 6.4 percent and 8.8 percent compared to the S&P's 16.2 percent and 17.9 percent. But the three-year maximum drawdown of −13.4 percent is only 200 basis points below the S&P's annualized three-year maximum drawdown.

This implies that investors were better off in large-capitalization stocks, which offered twice the returns and modest additional risk. The S&P 500's Sharpe and Sortino ratios outshined those of Alternative Long/Short Equity Funds by a wide margin: The S&P's five-year annualized Sharpe and Sortino ratios were 1.04 and 0.89, versus the classification's 0.64 and 0.60.

For those interested in deeper analysis, Andrew Clark suggests an analysis of downside deviation ratios. Investors could also consider the use of conditional value at risk (CVaR) to help evaluate the trade-off between returns and maximum drawdowns.

FACTOR EXPOSURES

Andrew Clark of Lipper has done extensive work on the factor exposures that drive Alternative Long/Short Equity Funds. Clark published the results of his studies in a series of articles in *Lipper Insight* beginning on January 11, 2014 (http://lipperinsight.thomsonreuters.com/2014/01/using-risk-factors-understand-longshort-equity-mutual-fund-returns-part-1/).

Clark tested 45 primary share class funds that had a five-year track record. He considered their exposure to standard Fama-French factors (market beta, market capitalization, and price-to-book ratio), as well as tilts toward low volatility and high dividend yield.

In this study Clark found that these standard risk factors could explain:

- More than 50 percent of returns for 36 of the 45 funds
- Eighty to 85 percent of returns for 10 of the 45 funds

Which risk factors?

- Forty-three funds had a positive tilt to high dividend yield.
- Twelve funds had a positive tilt to small-cap stocks.

Regarding alpha, Clark found:

- Thirty funds had positive alpha.
- Two funds had positive alpha that was statistically significant.

So despite the many stylistic variations used to execute strategies among Alternative Long/Short Equity Funds, standard risk factors can largely explain returns.

This sounds like a recipe for replication in an exchange-traded fund (ETF). Clark highlights, however, that volatility plays a nonlinear role in almost all Alternative Long/Short Equity Funds, making passive replication problematic. It remains the responsibility of the portfolio manager to balance the volatility factor with the other factors that drive returns.

Here we list in alphabetical order six funds highlighted elsewhere in this chapter. We show the R-squared value for each fund, which indicates the percentage variation in returns that was explained by the risk factors previously outlined: market beta, market capitalization, price-to-book ratio, dividend tilt, and volatility tilt. These R-squared values show how much these factor exposures drive returns for each fund.

Fund	R-Squared
Highland Long/Short Equity Fund	0.66
Hussman Strategic Growth Fund	0.66
MainStay Marketfield Fund	0.69
Robeco Boston Partners Long/Short Research Fund	0.63
Schooner Fund	0.81
Wasatch Long/Short Fund	0.78

The Schooner Fund and the Wasach Long/Short Fund have the highest R-squared values, at 0.81 and 0.78, respectively. This means that risk factors explain 81 percent of the performance of the Schooner Fund and 78 percent of the Wasatch Long/Short Fund's performance. These two funds had identical Sharpe ratios for the five years ending 12/31/13, at 0.88. For Schooner and Wasach the five-year returns (and maximum drawdowns) were:

- Schooner 10.4 percent (−15.2 percent)
- Wasatch 13.4 percent (−13.0 percent)

Thus, these two funds were broadly similar in their risk/return profiles. We cannot draw firm conclusions about these similarities, however, since we would have to know exactly what the factor exposures were for each fund and how these evolved over time. As Clark noted, the changes in factor exposures—and especially in volatility—can have a large impact on returns.

The other funds in this sample have lower R-squared values, ranging from 0.63 to 0.69. The returns of these four funds have varied widely over the past five years, and it would require considerable analysis to fully deconstruct and explain historical returns.

ASSET ALLOCATION AND FUND SELECTION

Alternative Long/Short Equity Funds make an ideal equity complement to a portfolio. This classification is homogeneous compared to other Lipper classifications in the alternatives space, making it easier to generalize. The analysis of factor exposures shows that equity market beta remains the primary driver of returns, so investors should expect limited diversification benefits from adding these funds to a portfolio. Due to the homogeneity of this classification and the clarity of the underlying factors, the rest of this section covers fund selection.

Fund selection begins with an evaluation of historical returns, risk ratios, and maximum drawdowns. This helps identify attractive funds and raises questions that can be addressed by evaluating fund filings, marketing literature, in-house due diligence, third-party research, and direct discussion with the portfolio manager. Although this sounds burdensome, much of it involves a routine examination of the same factors repeatedly.

This brings us to the *qualitative* part of fund manager selection, some of which is beyond the scope of this book. Evaluating alternative managers is a specialized process, partly because the securities and strategies are esoteric.

There are some simple rules of thumb that due diligence teams typically look for when evaluating fund managers, and these apply to virtually any investment strategy, including this classification. The following are some of the attributes that advisors and investors should seek during the fund selection process:

- A concrete description of the fund's philosophy, process, and execution
- Experienced people and adequate firm resources
- A minimum of vague, sweeping claims (boilerplate language is a necessary evil in the fund prospectus, but the marketing material should be specific)
- Clear expectations for the strategy:
  - What it is and what it is not
  - When it works and when it does not

- Accountability when explaining investment performance
- Performance attribution in quarterly reports
- A well-defined connection showing how the fund's performance reflects the fund's process
- Candor with investors when performance is poor

The prospectus expense ratios for this classification are high at 2.6 percent. Due to temporary fee waivers, however, the *net* expense ratios for most funds are lower (in some cases, much lower). Our general philosophy about fees is that they are secondary to risk and return. Some investors see this issue differently, and believe that fees should be an investor's primary concern. This is partly because fees are the easiest risk to manage, and fees are the only factor that is known with certainty in advance.

Why not just buy an index product that replicates long/short equity returns? Based on the analysis from Lipper, it appears difficult to duplicate the performance of Alternative Long/Short Equity Funds by using a low-cost passive approach. Nevertheless, expense ratios merit analysis, and some questions the advisor should ask are:

- Is this an attractive strategy? (That is, does it improve the portfolio?)
- If so, is this fund the most cost-effective way to get access to this strategy? (Depending on the account size, there might be a more cost-effective and tax-efficient form of the strategy in a separately managed account.)
- What are the inherent costs to the investment process? (Does it require lots of expensive data? Lots of bottom-up research? High-caliber portfolio managers?)
- Does this fund offer the best return potential for the given strategy? (If the client is suitable for a traditional hedge fund, he or she might get better returns. Some asset managers, such as AQR Capital Management, now offer similar alternatives in both a limited partnership structure and a mutual fund structure.)

This process is merely a launching point for advisors, who may have different priorities, resources, and fund selection processes. These questions are meant as food for thought about fund manager due diligence and the portfolio construction process.

TOP TEN FUNDS

MainStay Marketfield Fund (MFLDX) is not only a blockbuster within Alternative Long/Short Equity Funds, but also within the entire mutual fund world. (We discuss MFLDX in detail under "Blockbuster and Spotlight," later.) The other funds in the top ten have much lower total net assets and net flows than MFLDX, which may make them appear small. But eight other funds in the top ten are billion-dollar funds, making them both highly successful and profitable funds for their parent companies. (See Tables 10.3 through 10.8.)

Only two top ten funds experienced outflows in 2013: The Hussman Strategic Growth Fund (HSGFX) had outflows of $1.8 billion and the Highland Long/Short Equity Fund (HEOZX) had outflows of $21 million. The risk/return profile of HEOZX remains attractive, and outflows of $21 million, though not ideal, are small relative to its total net assets of $1.0 billion. Conversely, HSGFX's outflows are warranted in light of the fund's underperformance and unfavorable risk measures over the past 10 years.

HSGFX has a 10-year annualized return of −0.9 percent. The fund's five-year and one-year returns of −3.5 percent and −6.6 percent are alarming in a five-year bull run, while most funds in the top ten were up at least 7 percent to 8 percent over both time periods. The Sharpe and Sortino ratios for HSGFX over each time period are also negative, unlike any other fund in the top ten—the worst being the three-year annualized Sharpe and Sortino ratios of −0.85 and −0.84. In addition, HSGFX's 10-year maximum drawdown is not the worst out of the top ten at −28.4 percent, but its three-year and five-year average maximum drawdowns of −22.9 percent and −24.6 percent are the worst on the list. This strategy's market beta necessitates greater risk, and may lead to losses more akin to those that sometimes occur in the equity market, but HSGFX's negative returns do

TABLE 10.3 Top Ten Alternative Long/Short Equity Funds as of 12/31/13: Total Assets ($ Millions)

	Symbol	Total Net Assets	Estimated Net Flows
MainStay Marketfield Fund	MFLDX	$19,341	$13,297
Diamond Hill Long-Short Fund	DIAMX	$3,013	$197
Robeco Boston Partners Long/Short Research Fund	BPIRX	$2,964	$2,201
Wasatch Long/Short Fund	FMLSX	$2,574	$647
Virtus Dynamic AlphaSector Fund	EMNAX	$2,330	$1,584
Neuberger Berman Long Short Fund	NLSIX	$1,979	$1,662
Hussman Strategic Growth Fund	HSGFX	$1,269	($1,836)
Highland Long/Short Equity Fund	HEOZX	$1,028	($21)
PIMCO EqS Long/Short Fund	PMHIX	$1,006	$604
Robeco Boston Partners Long/Short Equity Fund	BPLSX	$856	$83

Source: Lipper, a Thomson Reuters Company.

TABLE 10.4 Top Ten Alternative Long/Short Equity Funds as of 12/31/13: Historical Returns

	One Year	Three Years Annualized	Five Years Annualized	Ten Years Annualized	Expense Ratio
MainStay Marketfield Fund	16.9%	11.2%	15.6%		2.7%
Diamond Hill Long-Short Fund	22.9%	11.1%	10.1%	7.7%	1.9%
Robeco Boston Partners Long/Short Research Fund	17.8%	11.3%			2.8%
Wasatch Long/Short Fund	19.0%	9.6%	13.4%	6.8%	1.5%
Virtus Dynamic AlphaSector Fund	36.0%	8.7%	6.8%	2.3%	3.1%
Neuberger Berman Long Short Fund	14.5%				1.8%
Hussman Strategic Growth Fund	−6.6%	−6.0%	−3.5%	−0.9%	1.1%
Highland Long/Short Equity Fund	20.7%	7.3%	9.0%		2.4%
PIMCO EqS Long/Short Fund	34.5%				1.5%
Robeco Boston Partners Long/Short Equity Fund	7.9%	8.7%	24.3%	12.7%	4.3%

Source: Lipper, a Thomson Reuters Company.

not justify such drastic maximum drawdowns. Put simply, this fund has consistently lost money in a bull market.

More promising funds include the Robeco Boston Partners Long/Short Research Fund (BPIRX) and Wasatch Long/Short Fund (FMLSX), third and fourth on the list of the top ten funds by total net assets. BPIRX had a breakout year in 2013, with $2.2 billion in net flows, thereby reaching $3.0 billion in total net assets. Although the fund is relatively new, having been launched in October 2010, it generated robust one-year and three-year returns of 17.8 percent and 11.3 percent. BPIRX also has attractive risk/return ratios, with three-year Sharpe and Sortino ratios of 1.14 and 0.95. With solid returns, high Sharpe and Sortino ratios, and a three-year maximum drawdown of −11.5 percent—below the classification average of −13.36 percent—BPIRX has fared well relative to the classification and the top ten funds, even though it has never endured a bear market.

TABLE 10.5 Top Ten Alternative Long/Short Equity Funds as of 12/31/13: Sharpe Ratios

	One Year	Three Years Annualized	Five Years Annualized	Ten Years Annualized
MainStay Marketfield Fund	0.30	1.07	1.06	
Diamond Hill Long-Short Fund	0.38	0.96	0.69	0.49
Robeco Boston Partners Long/Short Research Fund	0.40	1.14		
Wasatch Long/Short Fund	0.27	0.73	0.88	0.42
Virtus Dynamic AlphaSector Fund	0.33	0.72	0.69	0.11
Neuberger Berman Long Short Fund	0.36			
Hussman Strategic Growth Fund	−0.21	−0.85	−0.61	−0.32
Highland Long/Short Equity Fund	0.30	0.76	0.94	
PIMCO EqS Long/Short Fund	0.49			
Robeco Boston Partners Long/Short Equity Fund	0.21	1.31	1.40	0.72

Source: Lipper, a Thomson Reuters Company.

TABLE 10.6 Top Ten Alternative Long/Short Equity Funds as of 12/31/13: Sortino Ratios

	One Year	Three Years Annualized	Five Years Annualized	Ten Years Annualized
MainStay Marketfield Fund	0.34	1.04	1.11	
Diamond Hill Long-Short Fund	0.38	0.91	0.64	0.44
Robeco Boston Partners Long/Short Research Fund	0.30	0.95		
Wasatch Long/Short Fund	0.26	0.65	0.83	0.38
Virtus Dynamic AlphaSector Fund	0.27	0.73	0.69	0.11
Neuberger Berman Long Short Fund	0.30			
Hussman Strategic Growth Fund	−0.20	−0.84	−0.60	−0.30
Highland Long/Short Equity Fund	0.28	0.66	0.86	
PIMCO EqS Long/Short Fund	0.59			
Robeco Boston Partners Long/Short Equity Fund	0.22	1.29	1.34	0.66

Source: Lipper, a Thomson Reuters Company.

TABLE 10.7 Top Ten Alternative Long/Short Equity Funds as of 12/31/13: Maximum Drawdowns

	One Year	Three Years Annualized	Five Years Annualized	Ten Years Annualized
MainStay Marketfield Fund	−2.7%	−9.4%	−15.5%	
Diamond Hill Long-Short Fund	−2.9%	−12.3%	−21.7%	−40.6%
Robeco Boston Partners Long/Short Research Fund	−2.4%	−11.5%		
Wasatch Long/Short Fund	−3.6%	−13.0%	−13.0%	−29.3%
Virtus Dynamic AlphaSector Fund	−6.7%	−13.1%	−14.0%	−21.6%
Neuberger Berman Long Short Fund	−3.2%			
Hussman Strategic Growth Fund	−6.9%	−22.9%	−24.6%	−28.4%
Highland Long/Short Equity Fund	−3.4%	−8.3%	−8.3%	
PIMCO EqS Long/Short Fund	−4.0%			
Robeco Boston Partners Long/Short Equity Fund	−3.7%	−6.9%	−21.7%	−39.3%

Source: Lipper, a Thomson Reuters Company.

FMLSX, on the other hand, experienced the 2008 financial crisis since it was launched in August 2003. The fund's 10-year and five-year annualized returns are 6.8 percent and 13.4 percent. These returns do not beat the other funds within the top ten, but they are competitive. Furthermore, the fund had the third best five-year annualized Sharpe and Sortino ratios of 0.88 and 0.83, behind the blockbuster, MFLDX, and HEOZX (which on net had worse returns). The fund's five-year annualized maximum drawdown was also among the lowest within the top ten at −13.0 percent. The fund has achieved solid returns and risk measures throughout a full market cycle, which are characteristics advisors should seek, even if the fund does not hit the ball out of the park in every time frame.

The top ten funds within the Alternative Long/Short Equity Funds classification had relatively similar returns, though the funds' maximum drawdowns greatly differed. This dispersion suggests a mix of alpha and beta, and highlights the need for bottom-up research from advisors when picking funds: Looking at returns is insufficient, since investors tend to chase performance and panic when performance falters.

BLOCKBUSTER AND SPOTLIGHT

The MainStay Marketfield Fund (MFLDX) was launched in July 2007, and targets low-volatility absolute returns in excess of the risk-free rate by going

TABLE 10.8 S&P 500 Returns and Risk
Data as of 12/31/13

Calendar Year Returns

2003	28.7%
2004	10.9%
2005	4.9%
2006	15.8%
2007	5.5%
2008	−37.0%
2009	26.5%
2010	15.1%
2011	2.1%
2012	16.0%
2013	32.4%

Rolling Period Returns

1-Year Returns	32.4%
3-Year Returns	16.2%
5-Year Returns	17.9%
10-Year Returns	7.4%

Sharpe Ratio

1-Year Sharpe	0.97
3-Year Sharpe	1.24
5-Year Sharpe	1.04
10-Year Sharpe	0.38

Sortino Ratio

1-Year Sortino	0.72
3-Year Sortino	1.13
5-Year Sortino	0.89
10-Year Sortino	0.31

Maximum Drawdown

1-Year Maximum Drawdown	−2.9%
3-Year Maximum Drawdown	−16.3%
5-Year Maximum Drawdown	−18.1%
10-Year Maximum Drawdown	−50.9%

Source: Lipper, a Thomson Reuters Company.

long and short in equity securities, fixed income instruments, commodities, futures, options, and even ETFs. Although the fund was acquired by Main-Stay in October 2012, the current advisor remains the fund's subadvisor: the President and Chief Investment Officer of Oscar Gruss & Son, Michael C. Aronstein. Aronstein and his management team have a top-down approach, and also hold some small-cap positions, which has become more difficult as the fund has grown. Consequently, management has shifted allocations heavily toward ETFs and large-cap stocks, and performance through the first half of 2014 has been weak.

With total net assets of $19.3 billion, MFLDX tops rival funds in the classification by a wide margin. (See Table 10.9.) In fact, the fund accounts for 44 percent of the total net assets in Alternative Long/Short Equity Funds. MFLDX's 2013 inflows alone were three times the size of the second largest fund within the classification. The fund's rapid growth has caused some challenges as the fund adapts to a larger asset base. With that said, MFLDX has five-year and three-year annualized returns of 15.6 percent and 11.2 percent, well above the classification average of 4.8 percent and 8.8 percent. The fund's five-year annualized Sharpe and Sortino ratios of 1.06 and 1.11 were second best among the top ten funds, and its average maximum drawdowns are on the lower end as well: Its three-year and five-year annualized maximum drawdowns are −9.4 percent and −15.5 percent, respectively, which are modestly superior to the S&P 500's −16.3 percent and −18.1 percent. On the whole, MFLDX has achieved attractive returns relative to the classification, while limiting maximum drawdowns to a reasonable level. It will cost the investor, however, with a prospectus expense ratio of 2.7 percent compared to the classification's 2.6 percent average. [Note: MFLDX has

TABLE 10.9 Alternative Long/Short Equity Funds as of 12/31/13: Blockbuster and Spotlight

	Blockbuster: MainStay Marketfield Fund	Classification Average	Spotlight: Schooner Fund
Total Net Assets 2013 ($Mil)	$19,341	$176	$228
Estimated Net Flows 2013 ($Mil)	$13,297	$73	$144
One-Year Return	16.9%	15.9%	17.0%
Three-Year Annualized Return	11.2%	6.4%	6.6%
Five-Year Annualized Return	15.6%	8.8%	10.4%
Ten-Year Annualized Return		4.8%	
Expense Ratio	2.7%	2.6%	1.80%

Source: Lipper, a Thomson Reuters Company.

struggled in 2014, with returns of −9.0% through September 30, 2014. This shows the volatile and unpredictable performance of long/short funds that have a broad mandate.]

A potentially cheaper alternative is the Schooner Fund (SCNAX), which has a prospectus net expense ratio of 1.8 percent. The authors chose SCNAX as the spotlight for the Alternative Long/Short Equity Funds classification due to its unique approach to investing. Schooner Investment Group was founded in 2008 and launched SCNAX in August 2008. The fund's portfolio managers include Gregory R. Levinson, Chief Executive Officer and Chief Investment Officer of the Advisor, and the Managing Director of Trading of the Advisor, Anthony B. Fusco.

SCNAX invests in equities, convertible securities warrants, and rights and single-issuer equity call option securities of U.S. large-cap companies (over $5 billion). The managers write covered calls and use put options in order to reduce the fund's overall volatility, or to hedge the fund's equity exposure. (Buying puts can be an expensive form of insurance, depending on market conditions and the fund manager's execution.) The fund also invests in debt securities, particularly convertible debt securities, to generate income and capital appreciation.

Although SCNAX's total net assets are only $228 million (still above the classification average of $176 million), the fund is growing, having garnered net flows of $144 million in 2013. SCNAX has performed above average relative to the Alternative Long/Short Equity Funds classification: The fund's one-year and five-year annualized returns are 17.0 percent and 10.4 percent versus the classification's 15.9 percent and 8.8 percent. The five-year annualized Sharpe and Sortino ratios of 0.88 and 0.84 also stack up well against the top ten funds by total net assets, which average 0.72 and 0.70; additionally, its five-year annualized maximum drawdown of −15.2 percent is below the top ten funds' average five-year maximum drawdown of −17.0 percent.

SUMMARY

Alternative Long/Short Equity Funds make an ideal equity complement for portfolios, since the funds are driven primarily by equity beta. The wide variety of funds in this classification offers an unusually broad selection: There are 161 funds here, and nine have more than $1 billion in assets. This presents an opportunity for advisors to add value for clients through rigorous due diligence, thoughtful usage of the fund for specific client goals, and the construction of fully diversified and cost-effective portfolios.

PROBLEMS

1. What are the key factors that drive risk and return for Alternative Long/ Short Equity Funds?
2. MainStay Marketfield dominates this classification. Does this reflect the fund's performance, marketing prowess, or both?
3. This classification offers a deep selection of funds with similar attributes. Assuming an advisor has screened funds based on risk and return, what are some questions the advisor should ask the fund manager? How does your process for fund selection differ from the process outlined in this chapter?
4. There are different ways to access long/short equity strategies. What makes a client suitable for each solution?

CHAPTER 11

Alternative Managed Futures Funds

Synopsis

Alternative Managed Futures Funds offer noncorrelated returns that help diversify portfolios, and this makes these funds unusual among liquid alternatives, which usually have high exposure to equities and other traditional risk factors. This classification also stands out for being relatively homogeneous, since the funds are driven by many of the same trend-following algorithms. Poor returns in recent years have convinced some investors that managed futures funds are merely a bear market hedge. This is misleading, however, since these funds can offer valuable diversification benefits, and the blockbuster success of AQR Capital shows the rewards of consistently strong performance. High fees remain a challenge for this classification, and can make these funds an expensive tool for diversification.

DEFINITION

Funds that invest primarily in a basket of futures contracts with the aim of reduced volatility and positive returns in any market environment. Investment strategies are based on proprietary trading strategies that include the ability to go long and/or short.

Definition of the Lipper classification:
Alternative Managed Futures Funds

Volatile returns have made managed futures a controversial strategy. The classification's rock-star outperformance in 2008 and the subsequent underperformance have created confusion about its role in a portfolio: Is it a bear market hedge or an uncorrelated strategy? As we discuss in this chapter, the authors believe that managed futures is an uncorrelated strategy that provides long-term diversification.

Lipper defines Alternative Managed Futures Funds in terms of their usage of algorithms to manage volatility, mainly by trading index exposures. These funds include algorithmic volatility management and trend-following strategies, and they have an embedded call-like option that enables the fund to trend upward with the market, albeit not as much as the underlying index.

Alternative Managed Futures Funds include strategies that actively trade long or short, futures and forward contracts, physical commodities, financial assets, and exchange rates. In this manner, funds in this classification attempt to capture absolute returns through systematic, rules-based algorithms. Most funds employ commodity trading advisors (CTAs), who are professional money managers specializing in futures markets. As the name suggests, the roots of CTAs were in commodities, though most managed futures funds have expanded to include nearly all asset classes. While a CTA's expertise is invaluable, the high fee structure is a stiff headwind for performance, especially when the market experiences low volatility.

The capital markets environment of 2009 through 2012 has not been particularly hospitable to the approach used by these strategies. Risk-on/risk-off environments are not conducive to systematic, trend-following strategies since the market has been unpredictable, and many trades get stopped out before they become profitable. A layering of fees also impedes results, and has prevented many funds from breaking even. Alternative Managed Futures Funds can still improve risk-adjusted returns over the long term by creating higher lows in a diversified portfolio, thereby boosting compound annual average returns.

TOTAL NET ASSETS AND NET FLOWS

Alternative Managed Futures Funds is the smallest classification within the Lipper universe for liquid alts. The first three years of flows are solely reflective of the Guggenheim Managed Futures Strategy Fund (RYMFX), the trailblazer of the classification. (See Table 11.1.)

The entrance of new funds did not gain momentum until 2010, and readers should bear in mind that launching a fund takes a significant amount of time. The process in this classification most likely commenced after 2008, when managed futures vastly outperformed the equity market. Inflows peaked in 2011 at $4.5 billion after a burst of initial public offerings (IPOs), and the classification had $10.7 billion in assets in 2013 after a strong year for net flows, which reached $1.8 billion.

TABLE 11.1 Alternative Managed Futures Funds: Historical Overview

	Total Net Assets ($ Millions)	Estimated Net Flows ($ Millions)	Returns	IPOs	Liquidations
2004					
2005	*No data available*				
2006					
2007	$244	$231		1	
2008	$1,252	$963	8.3%		
2009	$2,330	$1,155	−4.5%	1	
2010	$4,091	$1,775	−0.5%	6	
2011	$8,251	$4,593	−5.0%	11	
2012	$8,468	$657	−4.8%	9	
2013	$10,691	$1,845	0.4%	5	2

Source: Lipper, a Thomson Reuters Company.

RISK AND RETURN

In 2008 managed futures performed exceptionally well in the hedge fund space, attracting great attention thereafter. Only one fund—RYMFX—was available in an Investment Company Act of 1940 ('40 Act) wrapper to capitalize on this strategy, and it gained 8.3 percent in a year when the Standard & Poor's (S&P) 500 index fell 37.0 percent. Managed futures underperformed in the years that ensued, partly due to a bull market, and the poor returns disappointed investors after such a promising year in 2008.

Alternative Managed Futures Funds earned an average annualized return of −3.2 percent over the three-year period ending in 2013. (See Table 11.2.) This is the most appropriate time frame for analysis since most

TABLE 11.2 Alternative Managed Futures Funds: Average Returns and Risk Ratios as of 12/31/13

	Average Return	Average Sharpe Ratio	Average Sortino Ratio	Average Maximum Drawdown
One-Year	0.41%	−0.002	−0.002	−9.1%
Annualized Three-Year	−3.17%	−0.43	−0.42	−19.4%
Annualized Five-Year	−4.82%	−0.56	−0.55	−29.2%
Annualized 10-Year		*No data available*		

Source: Lipper, a Thomson Reuters Company.

of these funds are new: Other than RYMFX, three years is the longest track record advisors can expect.

Due to negative returns, this classification's annualized three-year Sharpe and Sortino ratios are −0.43 and −0.42. These measures lag stocks by a wide margin, given the S&P 500's three-year Sharpe ratio of 1.24 and three-year Sortino ratio of 1.13. But what is even more distressing is the classification's three-year annualized maximum drawdown of −19.4 percent compared to the S&P's −16.3 percent. The funds not only underperformed, but were more volatile, to boot.

The classification managed to finish in positive territory in 2013, up 0.41 percent, with a number of strong showings among the top ten funds. But the classification still produced negative Sharpe and Sortino ratios that year (both −0.002). The classification's one-year maximum drawdown was also poor, at −9.05 percent compared to the S&P 500's −2.9 percent.

The positive performance of many managed futures funds in 2013 coincided with a strong year for equities. Not only does this contradict the notion that this classification is solely a bear market hedge, but it also proved as a rewarding year for patient investors who genuinely sought long-term diversification.

FACTOR EXPOSURES

Research by Andrew Clark of Lipper shows that managed futures funds have minimal beta exposures, making the strategy unique among alternative classifications tracked by Lipper:

> After "cleaning" our data, i.e., reducing any spurious or random correlations, we see that all but managed-futures funds are heavily affected by beta. This makes sense because managed-futures funds tend to have some or a significant exposure to commodities.
>
> *Source:* http://lipperinsight.thomsonreuters.com/
> 2013/11/constructing-funds-of-alternatives-funds/

This confirms that these funds have an uncorrelated risk/return profile. This lack of correlation frustrated many investors after 2008, a banner year for managed futures that created great expectations. These funds tend to perform well in trending markets, though typically not during the inflection points between bull and bear markets.

When will managed futures face a favorable climate? These environments are difficult, if not impossible, to predict. Indeed, if this level of market timing were possible, investors would have no need for diversification, since tactical moves would suffice for risk management.

Investors need to have doggedly realistic expectations to successfully use Alternative Managed Futures Funds. This strategy is truly uncorrelated, which means it will often be "out of sync and out of favor." If an investor does not understand this aspect of the strategy and its inherently unpredictable nature, the advisor should avoid this classification.

ASSET ALLOCATION AND FUND SELECTION

Alternative Managed Futures Funds offer the ideal form of portfolio diversification in the form of uncorrelated returns. It is critical that both advisors and clients begin the asset allocation process with this in mind, and with all of the patience it implies.

This is a homogeneous group of funds, so fund selection is fairly straightforward compared to other Lipper alternative classifications. Since the best use of these funds in asset allocation is diversification, fund selection should be based on uncorrelated long-term returns. The caveats in this classification include short track records and high fees for many funds.

Assuming that the advisor can find a fund that consistently delivers uncorrelated returns, the strategy would merit a significant allocation as a long-term holding in both aggressive and conservative portfolios. In fact, the strategy might prove especially useful in aggressive portfolios with high equity weightings, and that are in greatest need of diversification.

TOP TEN FUNDS

The funds within the Alternative Managed Futures Funds classification are hardly mature: Nine out of the top ten funds by total net assets remain under $1 billion, and four funds lost assets in 2013. (See Tables 11.3 through 11.8.) The Natixis ASG Managed Futures Strategy Fund (ASFYX), the second largest in the classification, had only $838 million in total net assets in 2013, which is relatively small for a leading fund in a Lipper alternative classification. Moreover, ASFYX had $15 million of outflows in 2013. The other eight funds have assets below the $500 million mark, and if not experiencing outflows, have had insignificant inflows. These are signs of disappointed and confused investors who have lost patience with a strategy that they most likely do not fully understand.

TABLE 11.3 Top Ten Alternative Managed Futures Funds as of 12/31/13: Total Assets ($ Millions)

	Symbol	Total Net Assets	Estimated Net Flows
AQR Managed Futures Strategy Fund	AQMIX	$5,886	$2,852
Natixis ASG Managed Futures Strategy Fund	ASFYX	$838	($15)
Transamerica Managed Futures Strategy	US8935092994	$498	$132
361 Managed Futures Strategy Fund	AMFZX	$490	$365
Equinox MutualHedge Futures Strategy Fund	MHFAX	$422	($376)
Altegris Managed Futures Strategy Fund	MFTIX	$396	($520)
LoCorr Managed Futures Strategy Fund	LFMAX	$373	$4
Guggenheim Managed Futures Strategy Fund	RYMFX	$305	($562)
Altegris Futures Evolution Strategy Fund	EVOAX	$295	$15
Aspen Managed Futures Strategy	MFBPX	$180	$55

Source: Lipper, a Thomson Reuters Company.

The year 2013 proved more successful for the strategy, as only three of the top ten funds had negative returns. ASFYX outperformed its peers within the top ten, gaining 12.8 percent in 2013; the fund returned 0.3 percent over the three-year annualized period. The fund's one-year Sharpe ratio (0.14) and Sortino ratio (0.13) and three-year annualized Sharpe and Sortino ratios of 0.03 fare well among its peers, though its three-year annualized maximum drawdown of –18.81 percent exceeds the S&P 500's –16.3 percent.

Conversely, the Altegris Managed Futures Strategy Fund (MFTIX) continued to struggle in 2013, losing –3.6 percent. MFTIX has a three-year annualized return of –4.6 percent and a maximum drawdown of –18.6 percent during that same period; its three-year annualized Sharpe and Sortino ratios are –0.49 and –0.47.

We now come to the issue of fees. Though backed by a premiere brand—Altegris Advisors LLC—this fund shows that management fees can be a major headwind for many funds within the classification. MFTIX enlists several subadvisors, and no matter their skill, the layering of fees inherent to a multimanager structure eats away at returns. This particular fund's expense ratio of 1.89 percent is below the classification average of

TABLE 11.4 Top Ten Alternative Managed Futures Funds as of 12/31/13: Historical Returns

	One Year	Three Years Annualized	Five Years Annualized	Ten Years Annualized	Expense Ratio
AQR Managed Futures Strategy Fund	9.4%	1.8%			1.40%
Natixis ASG Managed Futures Strategy Fund	12.8%	0.3%			1.48%
Transamerica Managed Futures Strategy	9.4%	1.8%			1.42%
361 Managed Futures Strategy Fund	3.0%		*No data*		2.15%
Equinox MutualHedge Futures Strategy Fund	−3.2%	−1.8%	*available*		2.31%
Altegris Managed Futures Strategy Fund	−3.6%	−4.6%			1.89%
LoCorr Managed Futures Strategy Fund	−5.5%				2.62%
Guggenheim Managed Futures Strategy Fund	4.3%	−4.9%	−4.6%		1.61%
Altegris Futures Evolution Strategy Fund	0.7%				1.94%
Aspen Managed Futures Strategy	6.3%				1.81%

Source: Lipper, a Thomson Reuters Company.

2.16 percent, but expense ratios remain high for this classification, and act as a drag on returns.

BLOCKBUSTER AND SPOTLIGHT

The AQR Managed Futures Strategy Fund (AQMIX) disrupted the Alternative Managed Futures Funds classification, accumulating assets at a brisk pace since its inception in January 2010. AQMIX is a blockbuster by any measure, and the fund accounts for 55 percent of the total net assets in the classification. The fund had inflows of $2.9 billion in 2013—more than triple the assets in the second largest fund. (See Table 11.9.)

TABLE 11.5 Top Ten Alternative Managed Futures Funds as of 12/31/13: Sharpe Ratios

	One Year	Three Years Annualized	Five Years Annualized	Ten Years Annualized
AQR Managed Futures Strategy Fund	0.16	0.19		
Natixis ASG Managed Futures Strategy Fund	0.14	0.03		
Transamerica Managed Futures Strategy	0.16	0.19		
361 Managed Futures Strategy Fund	0.09			
Equinox MutualHedge Futures Strategy Fund	−0.06	−0.21		*No data available*
Altegris Managed Futures Strategy Fund	−0.06	−0.49		
LoCorr Managed Futures Strategy Fund	−0.07			
Guggenheim Managed Futures Strategy Fund	0.08	−0.68	−0.53	
Altegris Futures Evolution Strategy Fund	0.01			
Aspen Managed Futures Strategy	0.12			

Source: Lipper, a Thomson Reuters Company.

AQR Capital Management launched the fund, and its managers include Managing and Founding Principal Clifford S. Asness, PhD; Founding Principal John M. Liew, PhD; Principal Brian K. Hurst; Principal Yao Hua Ooi; and Ari Levine. The fund's quantitative approach dates back to the roots of AQR's founders in quantitative research at Goldman Sachs.

AQMIX assumes long and short positions in more than 100 liquid futures and forward contracts across four asset classes: global equities, fixed income, currencies, and commodities. Trades are informed by trend-following signals, and position sizes are adjusted based on an instrument's risk and the probability of a trend continuing.

The Guggenheim Managed Futures Strategy Fund (RYMFX) also employs quantitatively driven, trend-following strategies that take global long and short positions in equities, fixed income, commodities, and currencies. Though the fund's investment objective is to "achieve absolute returns," actual performance has fallen short.

TABLE 11.6 Top Ten Alternative Managed Futures Funds as of 12/31/13: Sortino Ratios

	One Year	Three Years Annualized	Five Years Annualized	Ten Years Annualized
AQR Managed Futures Strategy Fund	0.15	0.18		
Natixis ASG Managed Futures Strategy Fund	0.13	0.03		
Transamerica Managed Futures Strategy	0.15	0.18		
361 Managed Futures Strategy Fund	0.12			*No data available*
Equinox MutualHedge Futures Strategy Fund	−0.06	−0.21		
Altegris Managed Futures Strategy Fund	−0.06	−0.47		
LoCorr Managed Futures Strategy Fund	−0.07			
Guggenheim Managed Futures Strategy Fund	0.07	−0.65	−0.52	
Altegris Futures Evolution Strategy Fund	0.01			
Aspen Managed Futures Strategy	0.11			

Source: Lipper, a Thomson Reuters Company.

RYMFX pioneered the classification—the reason for its designation as the spotlight—and did not see rivals enter the space until two years after its inception in March 2007. The fund's investment advisor, Security Investors, LLC, operates under Guggenheim Investments, and its portfolio managers include Senior Vice President Michael P. Byrum, CFA; Senior Managing Director Jayson Flowers; Portfolio Manager Ryan A. Harder, CFA; and Global Chief Executive Officer B. Scott Minerd.

AQMIX has provided intense competition for RYMFX. When analyzing the flows of each fund in the classification, a shift of flows from RYMFX into AQMIX becomes evident. RYMFX had the field to itself from 2007 through 2009, when net flows reached $1.1 billion. Net flows for RYMFX fell sharply in 2010 when AQMIX entered the space, and the weak performance of RYMFX eventually led to outflows in 2012: RYMFX had outflows of $1.3 billion in 2012 while AQMIX had inflows of $1.0 billion. In 2013, RYMFX had outflows of $562 million compared to AQMIX's inflows of

TABLE 11.7 Top Ten Alternative Managed Futures Funds as of 12/31/13: Maximum Drawdowns

	One Year	Three Years Annualized	Five Years Annualized	Ten Years Annualized
AQR Managed Futures Strategy Fund	−7.1%	−9.9%		
Natixis ASG Managed Futures Strategy Fund	−9.3%	−18.8%		
Transamerica Managed Futures Strategy	−7.1%	−10.1%		
361 Managed Futures Strategy Fund	−2.9%		*No data available*	
Equinox MutualHedge Futures Strategy Fund	−11.0%	−15.7%		
Altegris Managed Futures Strategy Fund	−11.2%	−18.6%		
LoCorr Managed Futures Strategy Fund	−14.1%			
Guggenheim Managed Futures Strategy Fund	−8.8%	−23.3%	−28.4%	
Altegris Futures Evolution Strategy Fund	−13.6%			
Aspen Managed Futures Strategy	−3.5%			

Source: Lipper, a Thomson Reuters Company.

$2.9 billion. Thus, the launch of AQMIX seems to have directly affected RYMFX.

Investment performance helps explain the flows out of RYMFX and the flows into AQMIX. RYMFX's one-year and three-year annualized returns of 4.3 percent and −4.9 percent trail AQMIX's 9.4 percent and 1.8 percent. AQMIX's three-year annualized Sharpe and Sortino ratios of 0.19 and 0.18 lead the top ten funds, compared to RYMFX's −0.68 and −0.65, which lag the top ten funds. Similarly, AQMIX has the best three-year annualized maximum drawdown of −9.9 percent out of the top ten funds, whereas RYMFX has the worst at −23.2 percent. Poor returns and high maximum drawdowns are a recipe for assets to migrate elsewhere, and AQMIX offers some of the classification's best returns and lowest maximum drawdowns. In addition, AQMIX's expense ratio of 1.4 percent is lower than RYMFX's 1.61 percent, a welcome advantage in a classification plagued with high fees.

TABLE 11.8 S&P 500 Returns and Risk
Data as of 12/31/13

Calendar Year Returns	
2003	28.7%
2004	10.9%
2005	4.9%
2006	15.8%
2007	5.5%
2008	−37.0%
2009	26.5%
2010	15.1%
2011	2.1%
2012	16.0%
2013	32.4%
Rolling Period Returns	
1-Year Returns	32.4%
3-Year Returns	16.2%
5-Year Returns	17.9%
10-Year Returns	7.4%
Sharpe Ratio	
1-Year Sharpe	0.97
3-Year Sharpe	1.24
5-Year Sharpe	1.04
10-Year Sharpe	0.38
Sortino Ratio	
1-Year Sortino	0.72
3-Year Sortino	1.13
5-Year Sortino	0.89
10-Year Sortino	0.31
Maximum Drawdown	
1-Year Maximum Drawdown	−2.9%
3-Year Maximum Drawdown	−16.3%
5-Year Maximum Drawdown	−18.1%
10-Year Maximum Drawdown	−50.9%

Source: Lipper, a Thomson Reuters Company.

TABLE 11.9 Alternative Managed Futures Funds as of 12/31/13: Blockbuster and Spotlight

	Blockbuster: AQR Managed Futures Strategy Fund	Classification Average	Spotlight: Guggenheim Managed Futures Strategy Fund
Total Net Assets 2013 ($Mil)	$5,886	$126	$305
Estimated Net Flows 2013 ($Mil)	$2,852	$21	($562)
One-Year Return	9.4%	0.41%	4.3%
Three-Year Annualized Return	1.8%	−3.17%	−4.9%
Five-Year Annualized Return		−4.82%	−4.6%
Ten-Year Annualized Return		No data available	
Expense Ratio	1.40%	2.16%	1.61%

Source: Lipper, a Thomson Reuters Company.

SUMMARY

Alternative Managed Futures Funds serve as ideal portfolio diversifiers for patient investors. They are especially useful for clients who do not qualify for managed futures in a hedge fund format (though alternative mutual funds often lag the performance of their hedge fund peers). The entrance of AQR Capital into the space in 2010 has been a profile of success in liquid alternatives: a blockbuster with a strong brand and robust performance. Investors should be mindful of fees in this classification, so that they do not overpay for diversification.

PROBLEMS

1. What is the difference between a portfolio hedge and a portfolio diversifier?
2. What is the proper way to evaluate fees when choosing products that offer diversification benefits? Does it depend on the client's goals and time frame?
3. The strong performance of managed futures in 2008 created great expectations. Investors became impatient with returns in subsequent years, though results improved in 2013. What lessons does this provide about alternatives going forward?
4. What can investors learn from the success of AQR Capital Management in managed futures? Does this suggest that investors should consider an active approach to managed futures? Or do high fees argue for passive exposure to the strategy?

CHAPTER 12

Alternative Multi-Strategy Funds

Synopsis

Alternative Multi-Strategy Funds give investors access to multiple strategies in a single fund. This one-stop shopping has been a popular way to access alternatives, and these funds can be effective portfolio diversifiers. The downside of this approach is layering of fees, short track records, and reduced transparency. In light of these challenges, investors who need diversification and reduced volatility can always consider holding more cash.

DEFINITION

> *Funds that, by prospectus language, seek total returns through the management of several different hedge-like strategies. These funds are typically quantitatively driven to measure the existing relationship between instruments and in some cases to identify positions in which the risk-adjusted spread between these instruments represents an opportunity for the investment manager.*
>
> Definition of the Lipper classification:
> Alternative Multi-Strategy Funds

Alternative Multi-Strategy Funds allocate assets to a wide variety of alternative strategies simultaneously, either directly or by using a fund of funds (FOF) approach. For example, these funds can use subadvisors to invest in multiple strategies, such as long/short equity, equity market neutral, global macro, and so on. This structure can provide access to traditional hedge funds, albeit with reduced transparency. Although Alternative Multi-Strategy Funds often generate low returns, this classification offers diversification benefits due to its relatively low correlation with traditional asset classes.

The classification's appeal rests in its offering of a bundled approach, providing a diverse set of strategies to complement the stock and bond holdings in a portfolio. This packaged approach appeals to many advisors,

TABLE 12.1   Alternative Multi-Strategy Funds: Historical Overview

	Total Net Assets ($ Millions)	Estimated Net Flows ($ Millions)	Returns	IPOs	Liquidations
2004	$3			1	
2005	$228	$13		1	
2006	$734	$369	6.3%	2	
2007	$1,454	$605	5.5%	3	
2008	$1,155	$148	−21.3%	1	
2009	$1,495	$460	11.7%	5	
2010	$2,455	$850	7.5%	4	
2011	$5,319	$2,886	−1.7%	5	
2012	$8,739	$3,147	4.4%	9	
2013	$15,658	$5,727	4.9%	9	1

Source: Lipper, a Thomson Reuters Company.

though it reduces transparency and makes it difficult to monitor risks and evaluate performance since the underlying positions are in funds that may be allocated to various managers.

TOTAL NET ASSETS AND NET FLOWS

Alternative Multi-Strategy Funds is a young and small classification, comprising 5 percent of the assets within the Lipper alternative classifications. The classification's total net assets, now almost $15.7 billion, have grown steadily over the past 10 years. (See Table 12.1.) Alternative Multi-Strategy Funds did not exceed $1 billion in assets until 2007. In fact, the classification did not come into its own until 2011, when it exceeded $5 billion in total net assets. Although 2013 saw a burst of interest with inflows of $5.7 billion, the classification has not experienced the boom/bust cycles that are typical of other classifications within the liquid alternatives space.

The classification's net flows have grown uniformly—though slowing in 2008—and this steady climb likely reflects the relatively stable returns of these funds. A number of initial public offerings (IPOs) have been launched since the 2008 crash, and there has been only one liquidation.

RISK AND RETURN

Most funds within the Alternative Multi-Strategy Funds classification have three-year track records, and only one fund within the top ten has a five-year

TABLE 12.2 Alternative Multi-Strategy Funds: Average Returns and Risk Ratios as of 12/31/13

	Average Return	Average Sharpe Ratio	Average Sortino Ratio	Average Maximum Drawdown
One-Year	4.9%	0.14	0.13	−3.8%
Annualized Three-Year	3.2%	0.46	0.41	−8.2%
Annualized Five-Year	5.8%	0.61	0.56	−12.0%
Annualized 10-Year	*No data available*			

Source: Lipper, a Thomson Reuters Company.

track record. Due to the rally in stocks from 2009 to 2013, funds in this classification performed better when they had a higher equity exposure. Sometimes this bet is clearly evident, and sometimes it is not. Since this classification has not experienced a full market cycle, any analysis of equity beta is provisional.

Alternative Multi-Strategy Funds provide modest upside potential with reduced volatility. These characteristics are also evident in Alternative Market Neutral Funds and Alternative Long/Short Equity Funds. (Alternative Multi-Strategy Funds had healthier returns than Alternative Equity Market Neutral Funds, with similar average drawdowns.) All three of these Lipper alternative classifications offer equity exposure with defensive elements, and potentially better returns than cash. Alternative Multi-Strategy Funds could be considered a more aggressive form of market-neutral strategies, and a more conservative form of long/short strategies.

The returns of Alternative Multi-Strategy Funds over one year and three years are 4.9 percent and 3.2 percent, respectively, with maximum drawdowns of −3.8 percent and −8.2 percent. (Most funds in the classification date back only three years.) The historical returns of this classification capture a fraction of the equity market's upside over the same time horizons, and the classification's three-year annualized Sharpe and Sortino ratios of 0.46 and 0.41 are about one-third the level of the Standard & Poor's (S&P) 500 index. (See Table 12.2.)

This classification is clearly defensive, and advisors must manage client expectations accordingly. Investors will not capture the upside of equities, but they may be spared the worst of the downside. These funds may be appropriate when advisors are especially concerned about risk, because of either market conditions or a client's situation. Advisors should keep in mind that this classification is new, and most funds remain untested by a bear market.

FACTOR EXPOSURES

The oldest and largest fund in the group is the Natixis ASG Global Alternatives Fund (GAFYX), which has broad exposures to hedge fund strategies. Likewise for the fund spotlight, the IQ Hedge Multi-Strategy Tracker ETF (QAI). Deconstructing the performance of these funds proves challenging since the classification has a broad range of underlying exposures, and the lack of extensive track records makes it difficult to analyze returns.

The true test of these funds will come during the next market downturn, when their underlying exposures to market factors of all types will be revealed. Until then, investors should not assume that these funds would act defensively during a market crash, which often exposes a lack of liquidity in investments that had previously traded freely. Sometimes a crisis shows that there is "a big trade and a little door," leading to fire-sale prices as funds liquidate assets to meet redemptions at a time when market prices are already declining.

In the meantime, investors should pay careful attention to the underlying holdings and strategies in the funds, provided by the fund fact sheets and regulatory filings (especially the fund prospectus and the statement of additional information). If the advisor does not have time to analyze these filings, he or she should have access to third-party research that offers analysis and updates.

ASSET ALLOCATION AND FUND SELECTION

These funds have the potential to make simple portfolio diversifiers due to the wide range of strategies, though the lack of transparency and the added layer of fees are genuine concerns. One option is to get exposure through a passive vehicle, such as an exchange-traded fund (ETF). This addresses both fees and transparency, since the factor exposures are clearer. An ETF will not have as much potential for outperformance, but it should be considered where suitable, such as in smaller accounts.

It is possible that the portfolio is better off holding additional cash, which always has perfect liquidity during a crisis, of course. In addition, cash holdings provide the opportunity for treasure hunting during bear markets, an option that is not available if the client's funds are fully invested.

Most of these funds have outperformed cash, even after fees, but that is a rather low performance hurdle over the past five years during a bull market. If a portfolio had been invested in 75 percent cash and 25 percent equities, the risk/return profile would have also been superior to cash, and would have had lower historical volatility than stocks. This is hardly a groundbreaking insight, but it is worth mentioning given the challenges of finding investments that diversify and reduce volatility.

TOP TEN FUNDS

Funds with strong brand names hold the most assets within the Alternative Multi-Strategy Funds classification, in which many funds have track records of three years or less. The Natixis ASG Global Alternatives Fund (GAFYX) had total net assets of $2.4 billion in 2013, and this was unusually small for the market leader in an alternatives classification. (We cover GAFYZ in greater detail in the Blockbuster and Spotlight section of this chapter.) (See Tables 12.3 through 12.8.)

The second largest fund, AQR Multi-Strategy Alternative Fund (ASAIX), had gathered $1.5 billion in net assets, after inflows of $645 million in 2013. The success of this fund reflects AQR Capital Management's clout in alternatives, since ASAIX was launched only in July 2011.

Potential investors should note, however, that ASAIX is no more accessible to the average investor than a hedge fund is: With a $5 million minimum investment, AQR has effectively eliminated the average retail investor from

TABLE 12.3 Top Ten Alternative Multi-Strategy Funds as of 12/31/13: Total Assets ($ Millions)

	Symbol	Total Net Assets	Estimated Net Flows
Natixis ASG Global Alternatives Fund	GAFYX	$2,429	$1,039
AQR Multi-Strategy Alternative Fund	ASAIX	$1,529	$645
Principal Global Multi-Strategy Fund	PSMIX	$1,264	$701
Blackstone Alternative Multi-Manager Fund	BXMMX	$1,122	$1,058
Arden Alternative Strategies Fund	ARDNX	$1,075	$262
Russell Multi-Strategy Alternative Fund	RMSSX	$949	$153
John Hancock Alternative Asset Allocation Fund	JAAAX	$885	$481
Columbia Active Portfolios Multi-Manager Alternative Strategies Fund	CPASX	$752	$169
Neuberger Berman Absolute Return Multi-Manager Strategies Fund	NABIX	$745	$209
IQ Hedge Multi-Strategy Tracker ETF	QAI	$629	$290

Source: Lipper, a Thomson Reuters Company.

TABLE 12.4 Top Ten Alternative Multi-Strategy Funds as of 12/31/13: Historical Returns

	One Year	Three Years Annualized	Five Years Annualized	Ten Years Annualized	Expense Ratio
Natixis ASG Global Alternatives Fund	16.1%	5.3%	6.4%	*No data available*	6.4%
AQR Multi-Strategy Alternative Fund	4.5%				3.6%
Principal Global Multi-Strategy Fund	5.5%				2.3%
Blackstone Alternative Multi-Manager Fund	*Fund inception August 6, 2013*				3.3%
Arden Alternative Strategies Fund	6.6%				3.4%
Russell Multi-Strategy Alternative Fund	3.0%				2.1%
John Hancock Alternative Asset Allocation Fund	4.0%	3.4%			1.7%
Columbia Active Portfolios Multi-Manager Alternative Strategies Fund	9.0%				1.7%
Neuberger Berman Absolute Return Multi-Manager Strategies Fund	9.9%				2.3%
IQ Hedge Multi-Strategy Tracker ETF	5.2%	3.1%			0.9%

Source: Lipper, a Thomson Reuters Company.

this fund. In fact, most hedge funds are more accessible than this product, and this is a case where an Investment Company Act of 1940 ('40 Act) structure does not democratize access to an investment strategy.

The John Hancock Alternative Asset Allocation Fund (JAAAX) is one of the few funds within the top ten with three years of returns. JAAAX's total net assets are below $1 billion, though the fund had inflows of $481 million in 2013, more than the inflows of half of the funds within the top ten. The fund's three-year Sharpe and Sortino ratios were 0.52 and 0.43,

TABLE 12.5 Top Ten Alternative Multi-Strategy Funds as of 12/31/13: Sharpe Ratios

	One Year	Three Years Annualized	Five Years Annualized	Ten Years Annualized
Natixis ASG Global Alternatives Fund	0.31	0.63	0.81	*No data available*
AQR Multi-Strategy Alternative Fund	0.14			
Principal Global Multi-Strategy Fund	0.24			
Blackstone Alternative Multi-Manager Fund	*Fund inception August 6, 2013*			
Arden Alternative Strategies Fund	0.27			
Russell Multi-Strategy Alternative Fund	0.13			
John Hancock Alternative Asset Allocation Fund	0.14	0.52		
Columbia Active Portfolios Multi-Manager Alternative Strategies Fund	0.25			
Neuberger Berman Absolute Return Multi-Manager Strategies Fund	0.47			
IQ Hedge Multi-Strategy Tracker ETF	0.14	0.66		

Source: Lipper, a Thomson Reuters Company.

slightly below those of GAFYX, but JAAAX had a three-year maximum drawdown of −9.1 percent, which is roughly 300 basis points better than GAFYX.

Two funds within the top ten had attractive risk/return profiles: Arden Alternative Strategies Fund (ARDNX) and the Neuberger Berman Absolute Return Multi-Manager Strategies Fund (CPASX). ARDNX and CPASX returned 6.6 percent and 9.9 percent, respectively, in 2013, with superior one-year Sharpe ratios of 0.27 and 0.47. These funds also had low maximum drawdowns of −2.8 percent for ARDNX and −1.2 percent for CPASX. Neither fund has weathered a bear market, so their success is untested by crisis.

The most attractive risk measures for this classification are the low drawdowns and low correlations to stocks and bonds. Alternative Multi-Strategy

TABLE 12.6 Top Ten Alternative Multi-Strategy Funds as of 12/31/13: Sortino Ratios

	One Year	Three Years Annualized	Five Years Annualized	Ten Years Annualized
Natixis ASG Global Alternatives Fund	0.3	0.55	0.74	*No data available*
AQR Multi-Strategy Alternative Fund	0.13			
Principal Global Multi-Strategy Fund	0.21			
Blackstone Alternative Multi-Manager Fund	*Fund inception August 6, 2013*			
Arden Alternative Strategies Fund	0.26			
Russell Multi-Strategy Alternative Fund	0.13			
John Hancock Alternative Asset Allocation Fund	0.12	0.43		
Columbia Active Portfolios Multi-Manager Alternative Strategies Fund	0.22			
Neuberger Berman Absolute Return Multi-Manager Strategies Fund	0.4			
IQ Hedge Multi-Strategy Tracker ETF	0.11	0.56		

Source: Lipper, a Thomson Reuters Company.

Funds can limit drawdowns and outperform cash, so the classification merits consideration.

BLOCKBUSTER AND SPOTLIGHT

Natixis ASG Global Alternatives Fund (GAFYX) was launched in September 2008, making it the oldest fund within the top ten. GAFYX accounts for 15 percent of the assets within Alternative Multi-Strategy Funds, and is still growing rapidly with inflows of more than $1 billion in 2013. (See Table 12.9.) The fund has five portfolio managers, two of whom are Andrew Lo, Massachusetts Institute of Technology professor and

TABLE 12.7 Top Ten Alternative Multi-Strategy Funds as of 12/31/13: Maximum Drawdowns

	One Year	Three Years Annualized	Five Years Annualized	Ten Years Annualized
Natixis ASG Global Alternatives Fund	−4.5%	−12.1%	−12.1%	*No data available*
AQR Multi-Strategy Alternative Fund	−3.7%			
Principal Global Multi-Strategy Fund	−2.8%			
Blackstone Alternative Multi-Manager Fund	*Fund inception August 6, 2013*			
Arden Alternative Strategies Fund	−2.5%			
Russell Multi-Strategy Alternative Fund	−3.4%			
John Hancock Alternative Asset Allocation Fund	−3.2%	−9.1%		
Columbia Active Portfolios Multi-Manager Alternative Strategies Fund	−3.2%			
Neuberger Berman Absolute Return Multi-Manager Strategies Fund	−1.2%			
IQ Hedge Multi-Strategy Tracker ETF	−4.5%	−4.5%		

Source: Lipper, a Thomson Reuters Company.

Cofounder of AlphaSimplex Group, and Jeremiah Chafkin, CEO and President of AlphaSimplex Group; the fund also has a subadvisor from Reich & Tang Asset Management, LLC.

GAFYX invests across multiple hedge funds based on proprietary algorithms that analyze their risk factors and domestic and international exposures relative to equities, bonds, interest rates, commodities, and currencies. Accordingly, the fund assumes long and short positions in 25 to 30 exchange-traded futures and forward contracts that represent the "broad market exposures of the hedge fund industry," while maintaining "volatility at or below a targeted level to limit the magnitude of potential loss." (Source: Natixis web site.) By doing so, the fund aims to achieve absolute returns and capital appreciation with limited volatility. In a sense, this fund is

TABLE 12.8 S&P 500 Returns and Risk
Data as of 12/31/13

Calendar Year Returns	
2003	28.7%
2004	10.9%
2005	4.9%
2006	15.8%
2007	5.5%
2008	−37.0%
2009	26.5%
2010	15.1%
2011	2.1%
2012	16.0%
2013	32.4%
Rolling Period Returns	
1-Year Returns	32.4%
3-Year Returns	16.2%
5-Year Returns	17.9%
10-Year Returns	7.4%
Sharpe Ratio	
1-Year Sharpe	0.97
3-Year Sharpe	1.24
5-Year Sharpe	1.04
10-Year Sharpe	0.38
Sortino Ratio	
1-Year Sortino	0.72
3-Year Sortino	1.13
5-Year Sortino	0.89
10-Year Sortino	0.31
Maximum Drawdown	
1-Year Maximum Drawdown	−2.9%
3-Year Maximum Drawdown	−16.3%
5-Year Maximum Drawdown	−18.1%
10-Year Maximum Drawdown	−50.9%

Source: Lipper, a Thomson Reuters Company.

TABLE 12.9 Alternative Multi-Strategy Funds as of 12/31/13: Blockbuster and Spotlight

	Blockbuster: Natixis ASG Global Alternatives Fund	Classification Average	Spotlight: IQ Hedge Multi-Strategy Tracker ETF
Total Net Assets 2013 ($Mil)	$2,429	$126	$629
Estimated Net Flows 2013 ($Mil)	$1,039	$45	$290
One-Year Return	16.1%	4.9%	5.2%
Three-Year Annualized Return	5.3%	3.2%	3.1%
Five-Year Annualized Return	6.4%	5.8%	
Ten-Year Annualized Return	*No data available*		
Expense Ratio	1.36%	2.35%	0.94%

Source: Lipper, a Thomson Reuters Company.

delivering exposure to hedge funds as an asset class, within the limitations of a '40 Act structure. Generally speaking, restrictions on leverage and illiquid securities tend to limit returns for mutual funds that imitate hedge funds.

This fund has outperformed its respective classification over the past five years: GAFYX's three-year return of 5.3 percent beat the classification by 210 basis points, and its one-year return of 16.1 percent greatly exceeded the classification's one-year return of 4.9 percent. The fund's one-year Sharpe and Sortino ratios were both 0.3, which surpassed the other funds within the top ten. GAFYX had annualized three-year Sharpe and Sortino ratios of 0.63 and 0.55. These were in the middle of the pack, though there are not enough funds to make a statistically robust comparison. GAFYX had one-year and three-year maximum drawdowns of −4.5 percent and −12.1 percent, worse than the other top ten funds, but the fund has delivered solid returns over the past five years. The fund has an expense ratio of 1.36 percent—about 100 basis points below the classification average. Overall, GAFYX appears to have done a solid job of delivering hedge fund beta in a mutual fund wrapper.

The authors chose the IQ Hedge Multi-Strategy Tracker ETF (QAI) as the spotlight in the Alternative Multi-Strategy Funds classification due to the fund's risk/return characteristics, and as a means to highlight its structure as an ETF tracker, a product that is becoming more relevant within the liquid alts space.

Similar to GAFYX, QAI is one of the few funds within its classification to have a track record that extends five years, with an inception date of March 2009. The fund "seeks to track, before fees and expenses, the performance of the IQ Hedge Multi-Strategy Index." The index tries to replicate the "risk-adjusted return characteristics of hedge funds using multiple hedge fund investment styles." According to the fund's fact sheet, these styles include long/short equity, global macro, market neutral, event driven, fixed income arbitrage, and emerging markets styles. By doing so, QAI targets the performance of hedge funds in the aggregate, with low correlation to the equity market. Since the fund tracks an index, there is minimal active management.

QAI barely made the top ten rankings with total net assets of $629 million; in 2013, the fund had healthy inflows of $290 million. The fund's one-year return of 5.2 percent beat the classification average of 4.9 percent, and its three-year annualized return of 3.1 percent just missed the classification average of 3.2 percent. (QAI trailed the blockbuster, GAFYX, during both periods.) Although the returns do not necessarily stand out, the fund's three-year annualized Sharpe and Sortino ratios of 0.66 and 0.56 are superior to those of the other two funds in the top ten that also have three-year track records, including GAFYX. The three-year maximum drawdown for QAI was an attractive −4.5 percent, well below its peers in the top ten. The one-year maximum drawdown for QAI was also −4.5 percent, and was a bit below average. In true ETF fashion, the QAI has a low expense ratio of 0.94 percent, lower than its rivals in the classification (nearly all of which are mutual funds).

SUMMARY

Alternative Multi-Strategy Funds offer the diversification benefits of alternatives in a mutual fund wrapper, and may serve as a portfolio completion tool for clients who own stocks and bonds and are unfamiliar with alternatives. The defensive nature of these funds is their main attraction, and they are a low-risk way for an investor to improve the risk/return profile of the overall portfolio. Given their historical returns and risk profiles, the blockbuster and spotlight funds are not a bad place to begin the fund selection process.

PROBLEMS

1. What is the ideal role for these products?
2. What is the downside of this structure?
3. If a portfolio needs diversification, is the client better off with a passive product in this category?
4. Cash also diversifies and reduces volatility. How should an advisor consider cash in portfolio construction? How should the choices be presented to clients?
5. What expectations should clients have for these funds?

CHAPTER 13

Dedicated Short Bias Funds

Synopsis

Dedicated Short Bias Funds are the most heterogeneous of all Lipper alternative classifications. The funds have inverse exposure to a wide array of securities from across the globe and across the asset class spectrum. This diversity generates an enormous dispersion of returns, and makes these funds ideal for hedging and tactical bets. These products are extremely risky, however, and misuse has led to ongoing regulatory scrutiny.

DEFINITION

Funds that employ portfolio strategies consistently creating a "net short" exposure to the market. This classification also includes short-only funds, i.e., funds pursuing short sales of stock or stock index options.

Definition of the Lipper classification:
Dedicated Short Bias Funds

Dedicated Short Bias Funds aim to capture the inverse or negative multiple of an index's return. Seventy-four percent of the 166 funds in this classification are packaged in an exchange-traded fund (ETF) wrapper. These funds track underlying indexes composed of stocks, bonds, commodities, and equity sectors. Consequently, these products are usually used by professional traders and investors for tactical bets, or to hedge long exposures within portfolios. The majority of these funds are highly leveraged, and this leads to a wide dispersion of returns; in any given time period, this classification typically has the broadest range of returns of any Lipper alternative classification.

Depreciation has been a gale-force headwind for asset growth over the past five years, amid a bull market for equities. Nonetheless, this classification has garnered tens of billions of dollars' worth of assets during that same time period.

TOTAL NET ASSETS AND NET FLOWS

Dedicated Short Bias Funds make up the second smallest classification with total net assets of $15.1 billion in 2013, or 5 percent of assets in all 11 Lipper alternative classifications. (See Table 13.1.) This classification grew relatively slowly through 2007, and experienced outflows of $1.5 billion in 2008. The crash of 2008 was a banner year for returns, as the classification reaped returns of 35.5 percent compared to the loss by the Standard & Poor's (S&P) 500 index of 37.0 percent, leading to staggering inflows of $19.9 billion in 2009. These inflows are huge by any measure, larger than both the total net assets in five other Lipper alternative classifications, *and* the assets in Dedicated Short Bias Funds during any year since the classification's inception.

How can this be? The bull market from 2009 through 2013 led to an influx of assets into Dedicated Short Bias Funds, reflecting bearish bets during a bull market. But the funds have experienced steady depreciation: From 2009 to 2013, the classification returned −30.1 percent on average, while total net assets have not grown significantly. The strategy had inflows of $43.4 billion during those five years, but market depreciation has offset nearly all of the inflows.

Dedicated Short Bias Funds are still relevant in terms of investor usage—the classification has seen significant activity comparatively in terms of initial public offerings (IPOs) and liquidations. The strategy continues to be popular with traders, most of whom do not hold the funds for very long.

The high number of liquidations reflects the low level of assets held in the typical Dedicated Short Bias Fund. The table in the Blockbuster and Spotlight section shows that the average fund in this classification has $94 million

TABLE 13.1   Dedicated Short Bias Funds: Historical Overview

	Total Net Assets ($ Millions)	Estimated Net Flows ($ Millions)	Returns	IPOs	Liquidations
2004	$1,462	$530	−15.3%	6	
2005	$2,135	$746	−3.6%	3	
2006	$3,232	$1,917	−13.1%	17	
2007	$8,664	$5,925	−8.5%	33	3
2008	$9,581	($1,564)	35.5%	16	4
2009	$14,073	$19,942	−50.6%	14	1
2010	$13,016	$5,632	−34.2%	26	8
2011	$14,684	$5,174	−11.7%	17	3
2012	$15,500	$5,500	−23.5%	7	18
2013	$15,136	$7,150	−30.6%	6	6

Source: Lipper, a Thomson Reuters Company.

in assets. Stripping out the leading fund, however, brings the average fund size down to $55 million. This level of assets is at the edge of economic viability for a mutual fund, given the overhead costs. These tend to be niche funds, and they also require a more complex and expensive investment management process to oversee the short-selling process.

Covering all of these costs on a small asset base may explain why this classification has an average expense ratio of 1.42 percent. The small asset base and high fees may suppress demand and encourage liquidations. This dynamic creates a bit of a catch-22, since the economics of niche funds are a continual challenge in an industry that rewards economies of scale so generously.

Within this classification, 74 percent of these funds are exchange-traded products such as ETFs and exchange-traded notes (ETNs), which hold 57 percent of the assets. The blockbuster fund in the classification is a mutual fund, and with $6 billion in assets it skews the median fund size. As for fees, exchange-traded products typically have lower expense ratios, with an average of 0.99 percent. Conversely, mutual funds within this classification charge 1.76 percent, bringing the overall expense ratio up to 1.42 percent.

RISK AND RETURN

Dedicated Short Bias Funds have the widest dispersion of returns among all Lipper alternative classifications, as evidenced in the Top Ten Funds section. Overall, the classification has underperformed dramatically, yielding average annualized five-year and one-year returns of −34.2 percent and −30.6 percent, respectively. (See Table 13.2.) The average maximum drawdowns over these same periods were −90.5 percent and −39.5 percent.

Unsurprisingly, the Sharpe and Sortino ratios were mostly negative. The average one-year Sortino ratio is 0.13 and the one-year Sharpe ratio is −0.11, while the annualized five-year Sharpe and Sortino ratios are −0.74

TABLE 13.2 Dedicated Short Bias Funds: Average Returns and Risk Ratios as of 12/31/13

	Average Return	Average Sharpe Ratio	Average Sortino Ratio	Average Maximum Drawdown
One-Year	−30.6%	−0.11	0.13	−39.5%
Annualized Three-Year	−25.1%	−0.58	−0.61	−71.7%
Annualized Five-Year	−34.2%	−0.74	−0.77	−90.5%
Annualized 10-Year	−16.4%	−0.33	−0.36	−89.0%

Source: Lipper, a Thomson Reuters Company.

and −0.77. These funds have the worst risk measures of all the Lipper alternative classifications.

Negative returns and extreme maximum drawdowns are unattractive at first blush, but must be seen in context. During the past five years, these funds have been on the wrong side of a one-way bet as the equity market produced impressive returns. This classification—like other liquid alternatives—typically underperforms in a bull market, and high leverage magnifies adverse returns.

FACTOR EXPOSURES

Unlike other alternative classifications, generalities would be misleading, and top-down screening can only separate these funds into the asset classes they cover and the degree of leverage they offer. There is not much more to add to this analysis, though the complete range of factor exposures for these funds is evident in the Top Ten Funds section.

ASSET ALLOCATION AND FUND SELECTION

Before we consider asset allocation, we must assess the proper benchmark for this classification. As one might expect, many of the funds in this classification use the Lipper Dedicated Short Bias Funds Index. The challenge with this approach, of course, is that these funds use varying degrees of leverage, and they may short different underlying securities, ranging from biotechnology stocks to precious metals. This diversity of exposures means that no benchmark can accurately reflect the wide range of securities in this classification. Since these funds have radically different factor exposures, there is little screening to be done up front, and the full responsibility for fund selection lies in the hands of the investor, the advisor, or the creator of the model portfolio.

As for fees, it is worth noting that the expenses for Dedicated Short Bias Funds include both management fees and investment expenses. These investment expenses are interest and dividends that the fund manager must pay to the counterparty. (When a fund sells borrowed securities, it owes the dividends to the owner.) These fees can be considerable: According to the prospectus of one fund, these expenses averaged 3.2 percent for the five years ending in 2013.

With those caveats in mind, there are many proper roles for these funds in client portfolios, such as:

- *Tactical bets*: Nearly all of these funds are meant for short-term trading, since the erosion of capital can be extremely rapid.

- *Hedging*: These funds can help hedge against ordinary risks and tail risks. Advisors may also hold these funds to hedge client-specific risks, such as legacy positions in stocks with large capital gains, or incentive stock options that have not yet vested.
- *Diversification*: It is possible to use these funds to seek uncorrelated returns in a fully diversified portfolio. This usage is debatable, however, since it is hard to make the case for the strategic use of a depreciating asset.

Given the riskiness of these funds, regulators give these holdings extra scrutiny during audits of advisors, and some wirehouse firms have banned them from their platforms. This regulatory scrutiny follows widespread misuse of these products, and triggered a $9 million settlement with four banks in May 2012, followed by a $1 million settlement with one securities firm in January 2014. In fact, regulators have censured advisors not for fraud, but for *ignorance* of how these products work.

- In 2011 the Financial Industry Regulatory Authority (FINRA) barred a registered representative from the industry because of inappropriate recommendations regarding nontraditional ETFs for two clients. The advisor's misconduct was because he did not understand the purpose of the ETFs or their risks (*Source*: FINRA Letter of Acceptance, Waiver and Consent No. 2009020930301, November 3, 2011).
- In 2012 FINRA barred a branch manager with 25 years of experience for poor supervision of leveraged and inverse ETFs, and for lax oversight of unsolicited trades (*Source*: FINRA Letter of Acceptance, Waiver and Consent No. 2010021688101, March 14, 2012).

So advisors must be careful in their use of these funds not only for investment reasons, but also for compliance and suitability purposes.

TOP TEN FUNDS

The assets held within the top ten funds in the Dedicated Short Bias Funds classification are much smaller than other alternative classifications. Only three funds have total net assets over $1 billion. (See Tables 13.3 through 13.8.) Despite the small asset base of these products, every top ten fund had positive inflows in 2013, with the exception of the VelocityShares Daily Inverse VIX Short-Term ETN (XIV). Ironically, XIV is the only fund that had a positive one-year return (105.3 percent). The fund offers daily inverse exposure to the performance of the S&P 500 VIX Short-Term Futures Index, or the first- and second-month VIX futures contracts traded on the Chicago

TABLE 13.3 Top Ten Dedicated Short Bias Funds as of 12/31/13: Total Assets ($ Millions)

	Symbol	Total Net Assets	Estimated Net Flows
PIMCO StocksPLUS AR Short Strategy Fund	PSTIX	$5,999	$2,873
ProShares Short S&P500	SH	$1,403	$86
ProShares UltraShort S&P500	SDS	$1,368	$891
Direxion Daily Small Cap Bear 3x Shares	TZA	$560	$804
ProShares Short Russell2000	RWM	$478	$189
ProShares UltraPro Short S&P500	SPXU	$413	$436
VelocityShares Daily Inverse VIX Short-Term ETN	XIV	$407	($287)
Direxion Daily Financial Bear 3x Shares	FAZ	$407	$409
ProShares UltraShort QQQ	QID	$359	$262
ProShares Short Dow30	DOG	$262	$75

Source: Lipper, a Thomson Reuters Company.

TABLE 13.4 Top Ten Dedicated Short Bias Funds as of 12/31/13: Historical Returns

	One Year	Three Years Annualized	Five Years Annualized	Ten Years Annualized	Expense Ratio
PIMCO StocksPLUS AR Short Strategy Fund	−24.6%	−12.6%	−12.0%	−2.1%	0.64%
ProShares Short S&P500	−25.8%	−16.8%	−18.9%		0.90%
ProShares UltraShort S&P500	−45.2%	−32.2%	−36.3%		0.90%
Direxion Daily Small Cap Bear 3x Shares	−68.6%	−55.1%	−64.0%		1.01%
ProShares Short Russell2000	−30.6%	−19.4%	−23.7%		0.95%
ProShares UltraPro Short S&P500	−60.1%	−46.3%			0.93%
VelocityShares Daily Inverse VIX Short-Term ETN	105.3%	42.0%			1.35%
Direxion Daily Financial Bear 3x Shares	−64.4%	−51.5%	−68.6%		1.02%
ProShares UltraShort QQQ	−49.4%	−36.4%	−44.5%		0.95%
ProShares Short Dow30	−24.2%	−16.2%	−17.6%		0.95%

Source: Lipper, a Thomson Reuters Company.

TABLE 13.5 Top Ten Dedicated Short Bias Funds as of 12/31/13: Sharpe Ratios

	One Year	Three Years Annualized	Five Years Annualized	Ten Years Annualized
PIMCO StocksPLUS AR Short Strategy Fund	−0.39	−0.88	−0.72	−0.21
ProShares Short S&P500	−0.40	−1.21	−1.16	
ProShares UltraShort S&P500	−0.40	−1.28	−1.25	
Direxion Daily Small Cap Bear 3x Shares	−0.41	−1.37	−1.47	
ProShares Short Russell2000	−0.39	−1.09	−1.17	
ProShares UltraPro Short S&P500	0.05	−0.38		
VelocityShares Daily Inverse VIX Short-Term ETN	0.18	0.53		
Direxion Daily Financial Bear 3x Shares	−0.39	−1.28	−1.37	
ProShares UltraShort QQQ	0.07	−0.27	−0.45	
ProShares Short Dow30	−0.38	−1.26	−1.19	

Source: Lipper, a Thomson Reuters Company.

TABLE 13.6 Top Ten Dedicated Short Bias Funds as of 12/31/13: Sortino Ratios

	One Year	Three Years Annualized	Five Years Annualized	Ten Years Annualized
PIMCO StocksPLUS AR Short Strategy Fund	−0.37	−0.97	−0.80	−0.25
ProShares Short S&P500	−0.36	−1.29	−1.23	
ProShares UltraShort S&P500	−0.36	−1.34	−1.30	
Direxion Daily Small Cap Bear 3x Shares	−0.37	−1.39	−1.46	
ProShares Short Russell2000	−0.36	−1.16	−1.21	
ProShares UltraPro Short S&P500	0.19	−0.42		
VelocityShares Daily Inverse VIX Short-Term ETN	0.15	0.44		
Direxion Daily Financial Bear 3x Shares	−0.35	−1.30	−1.37	
ProShares UltraShort QQQ	0.40	−0.31	−0.5	
ProShares Short Dow30	−0.36	−1.31	−1.25	

Source: Lipper, a Thomson Reuters Company.

TABLE 13.7 Top Ten Dedicated Short Bias Funds as of 12/31/13: Maximum Drawdowns

	One Year	Three Years Annualized	Five Years Annualized	Ten Years Annualized
PIMCO StocksPLUS AR Short Strategy Fund;	−24.6%	−37.7%	−58.6%	−58.6%
ProShares Short S&P500	−25.8%	−45.5%	−72.2%	
ProShares UltraShort S&P500	−45.2%	−71.2%	−93.2%	
Direxion Daily Small Cap Bear 3x Shares	−68.6%	−91.7%	−99.7%	
ProShares Short Russell2000	−30.6%	−52.2%	−80.6%	
ProShares UltraPro Short S&P500	−57.2%	−90.9%		
VelocityShares Daily Inverse VIX Short-Term ETN	−23.0%	−72.8%		
Direxion Daily Financial Bear 3x Shares	−64.4%	−91.9%	−99.9%	
ProShares UltraShort QQQ	−47.0%	−86.9%	−97.8%	
ProShares Short Dow30	−24.2%	−41.9%	−70.1%	

Source: Lipper, a Thomson Reuters Company.

Board Options Exchange; thus, the fund benefits when the near month VIX futures contracts are in contango. XIV is an exchange-traded note (ETN) backed by Credit Suisse, and advisors should always be mindful of potential credit risk and counterparty risk of the issuer.

XIV's three-year return of 42 percent outperforms not only the other funds within the top ten, but also every other fund within the classification as a whole. Additionally, its annualized three-year Sharpe and Sortino ratios are 0.53 and 0.44, which are bright spots among Dedicated Short Bias Funds. This ETN's annualized three-year maximum drawdown was −72.81 percent, and this highlights the fund's volatility in spite of its impressive returns.

Another fund that performed exceptionally well in 2013 was the Direxion Daily Gold Miners Bear 3x Shares (DUST), up 181 percent, making it the top performer in the classification for the year. The fund seeks 300 percent of the inverse of the performance of the Market Vectors Gold Miners ETF; in other words, should its prospective index fall 15 percent, DUST would theoretically gain 45 percent.

The key word, however, is *theoretically*, since these funds use derivatives and are designed to track the underlying index over one day. Holding these funds longer than one day will generate returns that are not two or three times the underlying index. The longer the period of time, the greater the deviation will be from a strict two or three times replication. The mathematical reasons involve compounding, volatility drag, and path dependency,

TABLE 13.8 S&P 500 Returns and Risk Data as of 12/31/13

Calendar Year Returns	
2003	28.7%
2004	10.9%
2005	4.9%
2006	15.8%
2007	5.5%
2008	−37.0%
2009	26.5%
2010	15.1%
2011	2.1%
2012	16.0%
2013	32.4%
Rolling Period Returns	
1-Year Returns	32.4%
3-Year Returns	16.2%
5-Year Returns	17.9%
10-Year Returns	7.4%
Sharpe Ratio	
1-Year Sharpe	0.97
3-Year Sharpe	1.24
5-Year Sharpe	1.04
10-Year Sharpe	0.38
Sortino Ratio	
1-Year Sortino	0.72
3-Year Sortino	1.13
5-Year Sortino	0.89
10-Year Sortino	0.31
Maximum Drawdown	
1-Year Maximum Drawdown	−2.9%
3-Year Maximum Drawdown	−16.3%
5-Year Maximum Drawdown	−18.1%
10-Year Maximum Drawdown	−50.9%

Source: Lipper, a Thomson Reuters Company.

but the key point is that this is not tracking error per se. These products are designed to track an index for one day, and they are reset daily. They are not designed to capture returns for longer holding periods that compound the deviation between the returns of the fund and the underlying index.

This long-term behavior of returns confirms that these funds are designed for short holding periods. Taxation is another reason for brief holding periods, since these funds are taxed at a short-term capital gains rate. So there is no point in holding on to one of these funds in order to qualify for long-term capital gains treatment.

Most important, investors should note that these are highly leveraged products that can lose vast amounts of money. For example, the Direxion Daily Financial Bear 3x Shares (FAZ) fund—included within the top ten funds for the classification—returned −68.6 percent and −64.0 percent over one-year and annualized five-year periods. This fund is similar to DUST in that it seeks 300 percent of the inverse of the daily performance, though it is benchmarked against the Russell 1000 Financial Services Index. FAZ's annualized five-year Sharpe and Sortino ratios were both −1.37, among the worst of the top ten funds, and the five-year annualized maximum drawdown was −99.9 percent. That is not a typographical error: This fund lost 99.9 percent of its value during the worst drawdown period between 2009 and 2013. Nevertheless, hope springs eternal, and the estimated net flows in 2013 were $409 million. That is $2 million more than FAZ's net assets that year of $407 million. So investors continue to refill the asset pool that market depreciation is draining away.

Likewise, the ProShares UltraShort S&P 500 (SDS) attracted massive inflows of $891 million in 2013, despite a loss of 45.2 percent. SDS has had weak long-term performance, too, with five-year annualized returns of −36.3 percent and a five-year Sortino ratio of −1.3. SDS's five-year annualized maximum drawdown is an alarming −93.2 percent. Since the fund seeks a return that is two times the inverse of the daily performance of the S&P 500, these severe losses are to be expected. In fact, one could argue the fund did better than expected in 2013: While the S&P 500 returned 32.4 percent, SDS should have lost 97.2 percent, but it fell less than half that figure. (This difference might be explained by volatility drag and compounding.)

Dedicated Short Bias Funds are volatile, as the top ten funds demonstrate. Investors can earn huge returns, or suffer greatly. In 2013, 35 funds (out of the classification's 166) lost more than half of their value. Advisors and investors must have conviction about a bearish bet on a particular equity sector, commodity, stock, or other investment in order to use these types of funds; the investor's risk profile must also comport with the highly leveraged nature of these products.

BLOCKBUSTER AND SPOTLIGHT

PIMCO launched the PIMCO StocksPLUS AR Short Strategy Fund (PSTIX) in July 2003. (See Table 13.9.) Bill Gross was portfolio manager of the fund through September 2014, when he resigned from PIMCO. The fund is now

TABLE 13.9 Dedicated Short Bias Funds as of 12/31/13: Blockbuster

	Blockbuster: PIMCO StocksPLUS AR Short Strategy Fund	Classification Average	Spotlight: None
Total Net Assets 2013 ($Mil)	$5,999	$94	*Not applicable*
Estimated Net Flows 2013 ($Mil)	$2,873	$43	
One-Year Return	−24.6%	−30.6%	
Three-Year Annualized Return	−12.6%	−25.1%	
Five-Year Annualized Return	−12.0%	−34.2%	
Ten-Year Annualized Return	−2.1%	−16.4%	
Expense Ratio	0.64%	1.42%	

Source: Lipper, a Thomson Reuters Company.

co-managed by Saumil Parikh and Mohsen Fahmi. The fund uses derivatives to short positions in the S&P 500, a common and efficient way to short stocks. The unusual part of the process is how the fund manages the cash left over after collateral is posted for the derivatives. The fund attempts to enhance returns by actively managing this cash in a bond portfolio with an absolute return orientation. Essentially, PSTIX seeks better returns than the inverse of the S&P 500 on a daily basis.

PSTIX's total assets are a hair shy of $6 billion, dominating a classification where the average fund has assets of $94 million (excluding PSTIX, the average is $55 million). In 2013, the fund's inflows totaled $2.9 billion, more than the $1.4 billion in net assets of the second largest fund, ProShares Short S&P500 (SH). Note that despite the negative one-year return for PSTIX, it had inflows of almost $3 billion in 2013.

This fund's blockbuster status makes sense given the fund's risk/return characteristics compared to the classification as a whole, and compared to other funds within the top ten. PSTIX's average one-year and annualized five-year returns of −24.6 percent and −12.0 percent outperformed the other top ten funds (except for XIV), and the classification average of −30.6 percent and −34.2 percent during the same time periods.

The Sharpe and Sortino ratios for PSTIX also beat most of the other top ten funds: Its one-year Sharpe and Sortino ratios are −0.39 and −0.37, and its five-year Sharpe and Sortino ratios are 0.72 and 0.80 (second best). PSTIX's one-year and five-year maximum drawdowns of −24.55 percent and −58.60 percent pale in comparison to the significant drawdowns of its peers. Finally, the fund's low expense ratio of 0.64 percent compares quite favorably to the classification average of 1.42 percent.

There is no spotlight fund for Dedicated Short Bias Funds. These products are used primarily as short-term hedges or directional bets, and the range of choices spans virtually all asset classes. Thus, no single fund serves as an accurate representative of the classification.

SUMMARY

Dedicated Short Bias Funds have the potential for rapid and substantial gains or losses, and should be used prudently. These funds are designed to be short-term holdings, and they require careful research, thoughtful risk management, and continual oversight. If these conditions are met, funds in this classification can be useful tools for tactical bets and tail risk hedging as part of a fully diversified portfolio.

PROBLEMS

1. These funds are unusually risky. How can they be used in portfolios for investors with different risk tolerances?
2. Returns in this classification vary widely, and investors need to track them closely. How does this affect the weighting of positions and the risk management tools that advisors use?
3. These funds are designed for daily tracking of an index. When the funds are held for longer periods, what makes performance vary from the benchmark?

CHAPTER 14

Lipper Alternative Classifications Summary

Synopsis

This chapter summarizes our research on Lipper's 11 alternative classifications. We evaluate the roles that these funds can serve in portfolios and how well the funds have functioned in these roles. We also discuss the relative size and historical popularity of each classification, the impact of blockbuster funds, and the degree to which funds in each classification are either homogeneous or heterogeneous.

LIPPER ALTERNATIVE CLASSIFICATION ROLES

Table 14.1 summarizes the five roles that alternative funds can play in an investment portfolio. (In addition, all funds have the potential for alpha, or outperformance versus their benchmark.) Some alternative funds can serve more than one role, depending on the specific exchange-traded fund (ETF) or mutual fund, and the other holdings in an investor's portfolio.

For example, Alternative Equity Market Neutral Funds can increase risk if the fund has high equity beta, and if the portfolio already has a high exposure to stocks. Another fund in the same classification could decrease risk if the fund has low beta and diversifies the portfolio. The roles described in Table 14.1 offer guidelines for usage, and are a necessary simplification of complex underlying factor exposures.

The historical asset growth of alternative funds reflects investor demand for the benefits that alternative funds can offer. These benefits are often described in the marketing of alternatives, and have contributed to the rising popularity of these products. We discuss in this chapter how well each classification has historically fulfilled its potential role in a portfolio, and the implications for usage of these funds by investors and advisors.

TABLE 14.1 The Roles of Each Alternative Classification in a Portfolio

Classification	Equity Complement	Fixed Income Complement	Portfolio Diversifier	Tactical Hedge	Directional Bet
Absolute Return Funds			x		
Alternative Active Extension Funds	x				
Alternative Credit Focus Funds		x			
Alternative Currency Strategies Funds				x	x
Alternative Equity Market Neutral Funds	x	x	x		
Alternative Event Driven Funds	x		x		
Alternative Global Macro Funds	x	x	x		
Alternative Long/Short Equity Funds	x				
Alternative Managed Futures Funds			x		
Alternative Multi-Strategy Funds	x	x	x		
Dedicated Short Bias Funds				x	x

ABSOLUTE RETURN FUNDS

Absolute Return Funds attracted significant demand after the financial crisis, growing to become the third largest Lipper classification with total net assets of $39.6 billion. A wide variety of strategies spanning all asset classes are employed to achieve positive returns in excess of cash or a risk-free benchmark. Yet many of these strategies are unproven and have not experienced a bear market, and most funds that did exist during the crash of 2008 lost money, when the classification returned −16.3 percent on average. This classification has high equity beta, and has not lived up to its absolute return mandate relative to both positive returns and downside protection.

These funds are used primarily as portfolio diversifiers, and require considerable active management by the asset manager due to the use of short selling and a broad range of asset classes. The variety of approaches used throughout this classification necessitates bottom-up research to uncover funds that have limited correlation to stocks and bonds, since this is the root of long-term diversification. Returns for this strategy have been modest due to its absolute return mandate, and fund screening should focus on low systematic risk and low tail risk to enhance a portfolio's risk/return profile.

This classification has expanded rapidly, garnering total net flows of $14 billion in 2013. As investors seek new tools for portfolio diversification, this classification has bright prospects for continued growth.

ALTERNATIVE ACTIVE EXTENSION FUNDS

This classification is less alternative than its peer groups: Alternative Active Extension Funds are best suited as equity complements, or as substitutes for U.S. equity exposure (i.e., large-cap stocks). Given this classification's high volatility and historical correlations to stocks, these funds best serve as an equity complement to help diversify a large-cap portion of a portfolio.

Alternative Active Extension Funds is a homogeneous classification, and assets are highly concentrated in one fund. This classification is the second smallest among the 11 Lipper alternative classifications, with total net assets of $11.1 billion. These funds hold long and short positions in equities, and the most popular allocation is a 130/30 structure, whereby a portfolio manager has a net long position of 100 percent (hence the nickname "beta one strategies"). Generally speaking, portfolio managers in this classification seek a long-only exposure with limited short selling, anchored in the objective of outperforming an index. This approach can generate alpha, and while the leverage potentially enhances returns, it also amplifies risk.

This classification has a high correlation to the Standard & Poor's (S&P) 500 index, and many funds emulate the large-cap benchmark; the divergence typically lies in the strategy's short positions. The 10 largest funds by total net assets within the classification have historically earned a narrow range of returns, with greater maximum drawdowns than the S&P 500 due to the use of leverage and consequent higher beta. The historical volatility of these funds has contributed to lower Sharpe and Sortino ratios relative to the S&P 500, and this strategy often underperforms the index.

ALTERNATIVE CREDIT FOCUS FUNDS

This classification has become the largest Lipper alternative classification with total net assets of $83.3 billion. Income strategies are especially important to baby boomers in retirement—a huge pool of assets. Alternative Credit Focus Funds have attracted high demand as investors seek higher yields during an extended period of low interest rates. Investors also seek active management of interest rate risk, especially as rates transition from near-zero levels as conventional wisdom expects.

The goals of these strategies range from conservative to aggressive, with some funds focusing on capital preservation and others seeking total returns. Regardless of the risk profile, portfolio managers in this classification often use relative value strategies in fixed income vehicles such as investment grade corporate bonds, mortgage-backed securities, bank loans, emerging market debt, and Treasuries. This classification has a high correlation to fixed income markets, though its low correlation to long-only bond funds helps these funds limit losses. Investors should keep in mind, however, that these funds have been stress-tested by rising rates for only short periods of time.

Alternative Credit Focus Funds serve as a bond complement, and help diversify the fixed income allocation of a portfolio. This classification is likely to continue to grow and dominate in the liquid alternative universe as rates climb over the next few years, and as investors seek enhanced income, inflation protection, capital preservation, and active management of interest rate risk.

ALTERNATIVE CURRENCY STRATEGIES FUNDS

Alternative Currency Strategies Funds have total net assets of only $12.8 billion, since this is a specialized strategy that makes specific bets on the direction of a currency relative to the U.S. dollar. These funds have historically had low returns and high volatility, as their exposure to currencies provides more beta than alpha.

Buy-and-hold strategies are not usually appropriate for Alternative Currency Strategies Funds, and the value added to portfolios lies in the advisor's ability to pick the right fund at the right time. These funds are not strategic diversifiers, but better serve as tactical hedges and targeted bets.

Alternative Currency Strategies Funds enable advisors to act on thematic plays based on macroeconomics, political risks, technical trends, and so forth. These funds are useful as a hedge against the fall of the U.S. dollar, which we saw in 2004 when they outperformed. Advisors can use these products as a satellite holding to reduce risk in a core position with undesirable currency risk. More specifically, investors can use these funds to hedge the currency exposure of foreign stock and bond positions, and to generate alpha or preserve purchasing power in the country in which an investor is domiciled.

Nevertheless, this strategy does not generate significant risk-adjusted returns. This classification is uncorrelated to most holdings in a portfolio, but Alternative Currency Strategies Funds are not effective as long-term passive holdings, nor have they served as effective portfolio diversifiers due to their historically low returns and high volatility. These funds are best used as a hedge and for speculative trading.

ALTERNATIVE EQUITY MARKET NEUTRAL FUNDS

Alternative Equity Market Neutral Funds make up a sizable classification with total net assets of $26 billion. This strategy has a low risk/low return profile as it aims to neutralize beta by assuming long and short positions in equities of the same sector, industry, country, style, and market capitalization. These funds also have exposures to credit spreads, optionality, and market capitalization, so a bottom-up approach is necessary in fund selection, as some funds are more aggressive than others. Advisors must take note of the factor exposures that drive each fund, and should manage client expectations appropriately given the strategy's low volatility and high correlation to cash. While these funds lag equities in bull markets, they have promising potential to limit losses during bear markets: In 2008, the classification lost only −2.4 percent versus the S&P 500's decline of −37 percent.

This strategy serves many roles, depending on a fund's factor exposures and the advisor's investment approach. Funds with exposures to equities serve as equity complements, and funds with exposures to bonds as bond complements. Alternative Equity Market Neutral Funds can also act as effective portfolio diversifiers for investors with long-term goals and appropriate expectations.

ALTERNATIVE EVENT DRIVEN FUNDS

Alternative Event Driven Funds require exceptional skill and robust processes by asset managers, and this may explain why this classification accounts for a mere 4.3 percent of all Lipper alternative classifications with total net assets of $13.3 billion. This strategy exploits pricing inefficiencies caused by corporate events, such as mergers and acquisitions, bankruptcies, spin-offs, and corporate reorganization deals. Thus, these funds offer exposure to equity or credit arbitrage, thereby serving as a portfolio diversifier due to their low correlation with stocks and bonds (if run systematically).

Funds that practice classic merger arbitrage are often uncorrelated; by contrast, other funds have more beta and are best suited as equity complements. Overall performance for this classification has been healthy, with a high correlation to equities but lower drawdowns during bear markets. Potential risks include this classification's sensitivity to merger spreads and the cyclicality of deal flow, and advisors should set return expectations in the low single digits.

ALTERNATIVE GLOBAL MACRO FUNDS

Alternative Global Macro Funds often undertake an unconstrained approach, with exposures across asset classes and across the globe. Some funds focus on stocks and bonds, whereas others add exposures to currency derivatives, short positions in optionality, and other exotic bets. Since managers make tactical and strategic bets on the global economy, these funds are often criticized as go-anywhere funds. But this flexibility adds upside potential, and Alternative Global Macro Funds have attracted huge flows in a short period of time. The classification came into existence in 2006, yet assets spiked in 2010, and grew to $35.4 billion in 2013.

Given this classification's heterogeneous nature, these funds can serve as an equity complement, bond complement, or portfolio diversifier depending on the manager's investment style. Alternative Global Macro Funds are complex and unconstrained, and require more due diligence than the average Lipper alternative classification to identify and monitor factor exposures and proper usage within client portfolios. These funds have a short track record with a wide range of returns, so we cannot yet draw firm conclusions about the success or failure of this classification.

ALTERNATIVE LONG/SHORT EQUITY FUNDS

Alternative Long/Short Equity Funds make up the second largest classification ($44 billion total net assets) out of the 11 Lipper alternative classifications, and with good reason: This classification is easy to understand, making it an ideal gateway product for investors who are new to alternatives. This strategy typically focuses on equities, but has grown to include bonds, commodities, and even currencies. In particular, long/short fixed income strategies have attracted investors who are concerned about rising rates, since these funds provide active management of credit and duration risk.

This classification is homogeneous and highly correlated with equities, and it best serves as an equity complement. Historical returns have been mixed and volatility has been high, so fund selection is critical. With more than 160 funds, advisors have a broad spectrum from which to choose, which requires rigorous factor analysis and fund manager due diligence. Advisors must evaluate a fund's varying degrees of market exposures and factor tilts, and match these to client goals in order to build a cost-effective and fully diversified portfolio.

ALTERNATIVE MANAGED FUTURES FUNDS

Alternative Managed Futures Funds is the smallest classification with total net assets of $10.7 billion. These funds use algorithmic volatility management and trend-following strategies that go long or short in derivatives, commodities, financial assets, and exchange rates. Most funds employ commodity trading advisors who specialize in the futures markets. The use of these subadvisors often acts as a headwind for performance, though, due to the high fee structure.

Though managed futures achieved attractive returns during the 2008 financial crisis, the strategy underperformed during the ensuing bull market. (Please note that the majority of funds were launched after 2008, and remain untested by a market crash.) Nevertheless, the authors believe these funds act as an uncorrelated strategy that provides long-term diversification, not a bear market hedge as some have come to believe, given the strategy's poor returns over the past few years. Like most alternative strategies, managed futures lag in bull markets, and advisors must manage client expectations accordingly. Alternative Managed Futures Funds are effective as portfolio diversifiers, but advisors must be cognizant of high fees so that they do not overpay for diversification.

ALTERNATIVE MULTI-STRATEGY FUNDS

Alternative Multi-Strategy Funds provide one-stop shopping, covering multiple strategies in one fund. This bundled approach has helped the classification garner a healthy $15.7 billion in assets, which continue to grow at a steady pace. These funds allocate assets to a wide variety of strategies either directly or by using a fund of funds approach, which provides access to traditional hedge funds, albeit with reduced transparency.

This classification offers diversification benefits due to its low correlation with traditional asset classes, thereby acting as a complement to both stock and bond holdings in a portfolio. The funds have short track records, and the broad range of underlying exposures proves challenging when analyzing returns. Advisors must carefully evaluate the underlying holdings and strategies of each fund, and keep both fees and transparency in mind (an ETF can help address these concerns).

Alternative Multi-Strategy Funds serve as portfolio diversifiers, and provide a low-risk way for advisors to enhance the risk/return profiles of client portfolios. At best, investors should expect these funds to outperform cash, and in some cases holding more cash may be a better alternative for advisors and clients in search of diversification and reduced volatility.

DEDICATED SHORT BIAS FUNDS

Dedicated Short Bias Funds account for almost 5 percent of all Lipper alternative classifications, with total net assets of $15.1 billion in 2013. This is a niche strategy that seeks to capture the inverse or negative multiple of an index's return, composed of stocks, bonds, commodities, and equity sectors. These products are typically packaged in an ETF wrapper, and are used by professional traders or investors for tactical bets or to hedge long exposures within portfolios.

This classification is highly leveraged and has the widest dispersion of returns of all Lipper alternative classifications. Moreover, due to these funds' varying factor exposures, fund selection rests completely on the advisor or investor. There is no way to systematically screen funds since no single benchmark accurately reflects the wide range of securities covered in this classification. Advisors should also note that fees for Dedicated Short Bias Funds include both management fees and investment expenses that are unique to short strategies (such as interest and dividends that the fund manager must pay to the counterparty). This classification endures ongoing regulatory scrutiny due to the strategy's inherent high risk, and advisors must be careful of the suitability and compliance nuances that accompany these funds.

Dedicated Short Bias Funds are best used as tactical bets over short time horizons due to the potential for a rapid erosion of capital. They can also be used as hedges against tail risks or client-specific risks, such incentive stock options that have not yet vested. Additionally, these funds have the potential to serve as a portfolio diversifier, as a means to achieve uncorrelated returns in a fully diversified portfolio, though the potential for large, sudden losses undercuts the viability of this role.

CHAPTER **15**

Portfolio Construction

Synopsis

This chapter offers a practical look at asset allocation and the potential roles of liquid alternatives. We focus heavily on how portfolio construction has evolved in the shadow of the financial crisis, toward solutions that are more tactical, customized, transparent, and cost-effective. A combination of exchange-traded funds (ETFs) and liquid alternatives helps address these needs, and the authors describe the Micro-Endowment Model as a tool that may help the portfolio construction process. The chapter closes with a dozen questions that may help advisors as they evaluate the role of liquid alts in their own practices.

HOLISTIC AND GOALS-BASED

Traditional portfolio construction begins with an evaluation of risk tolerance, and classifies clients as aggressive, moderate, conservative, or somewhere in between with regard to risk. This is part of the client's suitability assessment, and has its roots in regulatory and compliance requirements. This process should not be limited, however, to labeling people and putting each of their accounts into a so-called risk bucket.

Consequently, many advisors now focus on a goals-based approach, and emphasize how to meet more holistic goals such as lifetime income or multigenerational wealth. These goals require a comprehensive approach, and include an assessment of a client's income, assets, liabilities, trust and estate needs, and a host of other issues. So while risk tolerance is a good place to start, it is by no means complete.

MACRO ENVIRONMENT

Advisors also have to consider the macroeconomic environment so they can adapt as market conditions change. Figure 15.1 shows strategic and tactical tilts being combined with the suitability assessment to create a customized portfolio. Some advisors rely on home office and third-party research for top-down guidance, and some advisors make these decisions themselves. Either way, customization of portfolios requires an artful blending of inputs to meet the client's needs given the current macroeconomic outlook.

Investors have been deeply impacted by the crash of 2008, followed by the New Normal, the New Neutral, or however one might describe today's economy and the outlook for capital markets. Perhaps the biggest impact has been on retirement income solutions, since retirees are challenged by low real interest rates, bursts of market volatility, higher costs of living, and rising longevity for baby boomers. This confluence of factors has led investors on a global scavenger hunt for enhanced income, exploring frontier markets and the far corners of the asset class spectrum. Many retirement income solutions now include assets such as dividend stocks, emerging market bonds, high-yield bonds, real estate investment trusts (REITs), master limited partnerships (MLPs), and so forth. Investors may also underweight government bonds in their portfolio, due to concerns about low real returns and the threat of rising rates. The danger is that as investors reach for yield, they are

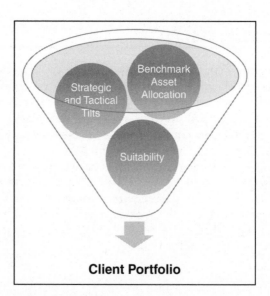

FIGURE 15.1 The Initial Ingredients of the Asset Allocation Process

stretching their risk tolerance beyond reasonable limits, and may find that these income portfolios do not offer diversification or liquidity during the next market crisis.

CORRELATIONS CONVERGE

One of the most valuable lessons of 2008 has to do with how different asset classes trade during a crisis. The financial crisis sparked a rise in the 30-day historical correlations of the 10 industry sectors in the Standard & Poor's (S&P) 500 to the index as a whole, which exceeded 90 percent during some periods in 2011. During this period of high correlation, markets have experienced a risk-on/risk-off pattern of trading. This high level of correlations has abated in the past couple of years, falling to even just below 70 percent during some periods in 2013 and mid-2014 at the time this book was being written.

The high correlations after the crisis have partly been due to central banks printing money. This coordination of global monetary policy has dominated the outlook for the real economy and for financial assets, and has been a primary driver of an extended bull market. Alternative strategies have fallen out of favor since diversification is no longer a top investor priority. As the authors like to say, "Bull markets cause amnesia" as investors forget about the benefits of diversification. (The same could be said for bear markets, which make investors forget about the benefits of taking risks.)

High correlations may not last, however, since a market environment with lower correlations is more historically normal. Low correlations allow differences in returns to stand out, as capital markets allocate scarce resources: Investments flow into productive assets and out of less productive assets. This movement of capital is inevitable in a globally linked economy, though this is easy to forget after an extended period of government intervention.

As market conditions shift, investor preferences will also shift, and diversification will again become a top priority. Investors still seek the flexibility to make tactical and strategic changes in asset allocation (especially after the financial crisis), and the desire for both diversification and liquidity helps explain the appeal of liquid alternatives.

EVOLUTION OF INVESTMENT MANAGEMENT AFTER THE CRASH

The crash of 2008, the convergence of correlations, and other macroeconomic events have caused profound changes in the investment process. Figure 15.2 attempts to summarize these high-level changes in portfolio management.

FIGURE 15.2 Trends in Portfolio Design
Source: Right Blend Investing, LLC.

First on the list is a shift from investment benchmarks to client goals. This is one of the most important changes for asset allocation and portfolio design, and it reflects a deep-seated and long-lasting response to the tech crash of 2000, the lost decade for equities, and the financial crash of 2008. Investors have lost faith in "buy-and-hold forever," which can seem like a portfolio on autopilot. Investors can get low-cost diversification via a target-date fund or through the guidance offered by discount brokers and online tools.

This has led to demand for greater flexibility in portfolio design. Investors increasingly seek strategic and tactical advice that customizes the portfolio for their individual circumstances and for the current market environment. Investors want simple solutions that are tailored to their needs, rather than complex solutions that are impressive but may be rigidly applied, or that have underlying strategies that are illiquid or have "a big trade and a little door" during a crisis.

This does not mean that the asset allocation process needs to be on hair-trigger alert, or that short-term performance should dominate fund selection. A long-term approach is essential for investment strategies that are inherently illiquid, such as private equity that rewards buy-and-hold investors with an illiquidity premium (excess returns that reflect the low liquidity of the underlying asset). A long-term approach is also necessary for most alternative strategies, such as managed futures, since these strategies may be out of sync with the market for long periods of time. Finally, a long-term approach is invariably required for most types of alpha generation, since investment styles go in and out of fashion in unpredictable ways. Some strategies need a full market cycle to demonstrate their value, and should not be used as sources of liquidity or as sources of cash when tactical changes are made to the portfolio.

As a side note, this assumes that some assets should be used as preferred sources of liquidity during the rebalancing of portfolios. Some portfolio managers believe that changes in asset allocation should be made evenly across all asset classes and all holdings during any rebalancing of portfolios. As a practical matter, many advisors use exchange-traded funds (ETFs) and passive funds as buffers for liquidity needs and tactical changes in the portfolio. There is room for disagreement on how to rebalance portfolios that combine liquid and illiquid holdings.

The key change in the wealth management process is that clients increasingly demand active management of the asset mix to reflect their goals and their time frames. Clients also expect more frequent adjustments based on the market outlook, so they are looking for an investment process that has evolved to be more flexible and customized.

Another response to the crash listed in Figure 15.2 has been a changing perspective from "low-cost" to "cost-effective." Best practices in portfolio construction now blend active and passive solutions throughout the portfolio, and focus on low costs for market beta and premium fees for niche strategies. This results in an overall portfolio that is cost-effective for the client and that allows a reasonable fee for an advisor.

We recognize that some investors focus exclusively on low-cost diversification via passive products and passive investment management. This puts the entire burden for asset allocation and security selection on these individuals, who may not have the time, resources, interest, or expertise to manage their own money. Liquid alternatives are especially complex and demanding, and intermediaries such as investment advisors and other professional investors own the vast majority of these products. Consequently, this book focuses on how those intermediaries manage portfolios.

Moving toward the middle of Figure 15.2, we note that style boxes were once considered the cornerstone of portfolio diversification. Investment styles such as large-cap versus small-cap and growth versus value are still part of the puzzle, but these style boxes play a smaller role in portfolio diversification. A global perspective is now considered essential, too, and so are nontraditional sources of diversification such as alternatives and real assets. This approach to portfolio management casts a wide net in the search for uncorrelated assets, and especially for securities that will remain uncorrelated during a market crisis. This search has given many advisors new respect for cash as an asset class, since cash has a virtually perfect track record for noncorrelation during a crisis.

The evolution of risk is next on the list, since investors now focus less on volatility and more on the permanent losses of capital or purchasing power. (This does not include upside volatility—few investors are alarmed when the portfolio suddenly rises in value, of course.)

This redefinition of risk came to the fore in 2008, when retirees and near retirees suffered losses of 25 percent or more in many balanced portfolios. These losses early in retirement have a disproportionate impact on the ability of the portfolio to generate lifetime income, and clients effectively suffer a permanent loss in purchasing power if they withdraw assets during a bear market. The importance of downside risk explains why the analysis in this book focuses so heavily on maximum drawdowns.

Another change in thinking has occurred because of the frequency of sudden large losses. The outlier events during the past decade have made investors less comfortable with reversion to the mean, and in portfolio optimization that blindly relies on historical returns. When mean reversion comes up, some advisors ask: "What mean will prices revert to? And when will they revert?" Investors have become familiar with black swans, tail risk, and changing correlations, and this undermines their faith in risk management approaches that are purely quantitative.

The final point in Figure 15.2 examines a change in thinking about a sustainable withdrawal rate for a retirement portfolio that generates lifetime income. An old rule of thumb among advisors was that a 4 percent withdrawal rate was a prudent sustainable rate for a diversified portfolio of stocks and bonds. As interest rates collapsed, however, the assumptions behind the 4 percent rule came under stress. Current thinking now uses a wider range of income-producing products, such as MLPs and REITs, and there has been a surge of interest in dividend growth investing. Advisors are also discussing how investors can adapt by adjusting their spending to market conditions, such as inflation and the timing of bear markets. The key concern among investors and advisors is that they seek more active, flexible approaches to retirement income, and fewer rigid rules.

CORE/SATELLITE INVESTING

A core/satellite approach is simple to execute and easy to explain to clients, and offers an excellent way to distinguish low-cost beta from high-cost alpha. Figure 15.3 shows a core/satellite approach that has passive strategies in the core and active strategies in the satellite. Passive strategies include mutual funds and ETFs, and perhaps even some forms of smart beta (e.g., stock indexes that use equal weights instead of weightings based on market capitalization). Passive products can be used for beta exposure to stocks, bonds, real assets, and certain alternative assets, and they reduce costs while increasing liquidity and transparency.

The core/satellite approach described in Figure 15.3 allocates the satellite to active strategies, and this allocation could include anything from actively managed mutual funds to holdings in a single stock or bond. The satellite approach works well with hedge funds and private equity, too, and with any expensive or illiquid strategy that does not form the core of the portfolio. The separation of alpha and beta not only lowers costs, but it can also allow advisors to customize portfolios more easily for individual clients, using the satellite of the portfolio for client-specific needs (such as socially responsible investment choices or legacy holdings with large accumulations of capital gains). This core/satellite approach could also allow advisors to use ETFs in the satellite. This would facilitate tactical changes in asset allocation, and allow advisors to be more responsive to market conditions. The simplicity of the core/satellite approach has made

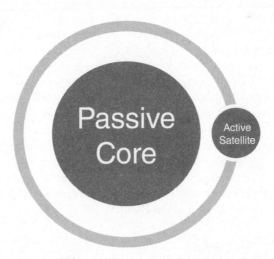

FIGURE 15.3 A Simple Core/Satellite Approach

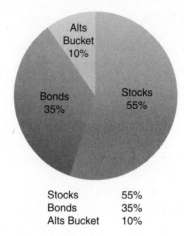

Stocks	55%
Bonds	35%
Alts Bucket	10%

FIGURE 15.4   The Bucket
Approach to Alts

it increasingly popular among advisors, and the authors believe that the
benefits of this approach make it an ideal fit for the trends in portfolio
design described earlier in Figure 15.2.

Just as the core/satellite approach may be the simplest way to blend
alpha and beta, the bucket approach may be the simplest way to add alts to
a portfolio. As shown in Figure 15.4, the advisor or investor picks a single
product to diversify the stock/bond allocations in the portfolio. If the portfolio started with a 60/40 mix of stocks and bonds, the advisor could add
a 10 percent allocation to alternatives and reduce the other asset classes by
5 percent each. The bucket approach might even put the entire alternatives
allocation in a single fund.

For many situations, this approach is fine. A larger allocation may not
be suitable for the client, and the advisor may not have the time or resources
to do extensive due diligence. The bucket approach offers one-stop shopping
for alts, and many products are designed for precisely this role as a portfolio
diversifier.

The downside of this approach is high fees and low transparency. A
fund-of-funds approach involves a layering of fees, and details about the
underlying exposures and positions may not be available on a timely basis.
This is the trade-off for simplicity and convenience, and it is up to the advisor
to decide what makes sense for the client.

MICRO-ENDOWMENT MODEL

An approach that addresses the need for both low costs and complete diversification is shown in Table 15.1. The Micro-Endowment Model combines

TABLE 15.1 The Micro-Endowment Model: Asset Allocation Framework

Asset Class	Allocation	Role in Portfolio and Type of Fund
Equity		
	20% to 30%	Equity Beta: Passive Fund
	5% to 15%	Equity Complement: Liquid Alts
	5% to 15%	Diversifier: Liquid Alts
Fixed Income		
	10% to 20%	Fixed Income Beta: Passive Fund
	5% to 10%	Fixed Income Complement: Liquid Alts
	5% to 10%	Diversifier: Liquid Alts
Real Assets		
	0% to 15%	Beta Exposures: ETFs
Alternative		
	0% to 10%	Tactical Hedge: ETF/Liquid Alts
	0% to 10%	Directional Bet: ETF/Liquid Alts
	5% to 20%	Diversifier: Liquid Alts
Cash	0% to 10%	Liquidity
	100%	

elements of core/satellite investing with targeted exposures to liquid alternatives. This offers the benefits of liquidity and transparency, along with low costs for the client. Research by Right Blend Investing, LLC, in 2012 showed that portfolios with a 13 percent allocation to real assets and a 10 percent allocation to liquid alternatives could achieve a weighted average expense ratio of 25 to 35 basis points. This analysis assumed that passive funds were 77 percent of the portfolio, and fees have edged lower since that time.

In addition to passive funds, the Micro-Endowment Model incorporates liquid alternatives in many different roles, ranging from equity complement to tactical hedge. In equities, the portfolio allocates 30 percent of assets to a passive fund in order to capture equity beta with low costs and high liquidity, transparency, and tax efficiency. The portfolio also allocates 5 to 15 percent of assets to liquid alternatives that serve other roles such as equity complements or portfolio diversifiers.

In this example, the lion's share of equity and fixed income assets is allocated to passive funds in order to keep costs down. But all of these numbers are general illustrations, and subject to change depending on the baseline asset allocation, tactical tilts, client suitability, and availability of funds with an attractive risk/return profile. These are by no means fixed allocations, and the advisor is free to change the allocations based on his or her opinion about what is best for the client.

The Micro-Endowment process assumes that the people building the portfolio have properly identified the underlying factor exposures of each fund, and have identified its proper role as an equity complement, fixed income complement, and so on. Chapters 3 through 13 offer a detailed description of each Lipper classification, and show how each fund fulfills each role.

The Limits of the Micro-Endowment Model

There are natural limits to applying any model that relies on theoretical approaches used by pensions, endowments, and foundations. These institutions have an investment process that is usually quantitatively rigorous and applied in a disciplined manner over time horizons measured in decades.

This approach may be ideal for institutions, but it is impractical for individuals. Every client relationship must eventually address a wide variety of random life events that involve money. This includes death, divorce, new jobs, retirement, medical issues, sale of the family business, and so on. Adapting to these events is part of what makes investment advice an art, and not a science. We believe that the Micro-Endowment Model can be a useful tool, but we leave the application in the hands of the advisor.

Quest for Alpha

Throughout this book we have focused on factor analysis as a key method to distinguish funds. This assumes that correlations to major asset classes and certain factor exposures are the primary drivers of investment performance. We then defined the roles of liquid alternatives in terms of these factor exposures.

Like any strategy, liquid alternatives may also generate alpha. We define alpha as the potential outperformance compared to a benchmark or factor exposure, or some other form of market beta. Disentangling alpha from beta is difficult enough, which is why much of the analysis in this book attempts to deconstruct investment performance into factor exposures. An analysis of alpha requires an even more extensive due diligence process than the one we have undertaken, beginning with quantitative screening and finishing with qualitative evaluations. We hope that the asset allocation process outlined in this chapter is a step forward in the quest for alpha, and for using liquid alts to help clients achieve their goals.

SUMMARY

It is essential for advisors to have a cohesive framework for portfolio design and asset allocation before they consider using liquid alternatives. The portfolio construction process and the needs of individual clients will determine the proper usage of liquid alternatives in each of their different roles as portfolio diversifiers, equity complements, and so forth. It is critical to have an investment process in place so that advisors can successfully incorporate liquid alts into client portfolios. The approach can be simple or complex, and we close the chapter with questions that may help advisors develop a process or enhance an existing process that fits the needs of their clients, their firm, and their practice.

QUESTIONS

1. The investment process begins with client goals and a suitability assessment. How do you assess client goals in financial planning and portfolio construction? Do you emphasize standardized models or customization to each client's needs?
2. Standardization of the asset allocation process is efficient, but may lack flexibility for individual clients. Customization is attractive to clients, but it is less scalable, and makes it hard for an advisor to build and manage a large book of business. How do you balance these competing forces in your practice?
3. Market conditions often drive client preferences in asset allocation and portfolio design, and short-term volatility requires a response from advisors. How do you distinguish between long-term and short-term trends in your asset allocation process and in your communications with clients?
4. Long-term trends in markets require changes in asset allocation, and may eventually affect portfolio design. How do you adjust to secular trends in your asset allocation process? How do you adapt your portfolio design?
5. Asset allocation and portfolio design can be simple or complex, depending on the client, the advisor, and the firm. How does each of these factors affect the complexity or simplicity of your investment process?
6. Financial planning is the initial input in portfolio design. How do you add value as an advisor during the planning process? How does planning impact the ongoing client relationship in your practice?
7. What role do you have in the investment process? Are you more comfortable as an asset gatherer or as an investment manager? What are the pros and cons of each role for an advisor?
8. How does financial planning affect the portfolio construction process at your firm? Does client suitability directly determine a client's asset allocation, or do you have a role in this process as an advisor?

9. Client communications often refer to the asset allocation process. Do you also link communications with the financial planning needs of individual clients?

10. Does your firm offer an integrated approach that connects financial planning to portfolio construction and to client reporting and communication?

11. Do you believe that liquid alternatives have a role to play in client portfolios? How will the inclusion of these products affect your practice and your value proposition as an advisor?

12. Liquid alts are complex products that are rapidly evolving. Does your firm offer educational material about their usage in portfolios?

CHAPTER 16

Volatility Management

Synopsis

Most approaches to portfolio construction manage volatility by offering a mix of stocks and bonds, and by using portfolio optimization based on the concept of an efficient frontier. The addition of uncorrelated liquid alternative strategies to the asset mix adds another source of diversification. Volatility management can be challenging to explain to clients, so we offer two illustrations of volatility drag that show how volatility can erode long-term returns.

We assume that most advisors are familiar with the efficient frontiers and portfolio management techniques based on mean variance optimization. This aspect of modern portfolio theory is well established, and is an excellent foundation for volatility management.

Adding alternatives to the portfolio has additional benefits, but only to the degree that the strategy is actually uncorrelated to the rest of the portfolio. Chapters 3 through 13 identify the different factor exposures of liquid alts funds, and most of them have high correlations to traditional sources of beta. Alternative Managed Futures Funds are one exception, since many of these funds are genuinely uncorrelated with stocks and bonds.

Unfortunately, investors often have trouble accepting the full implications of what it means to be out of sync with the market. Uncorrelated funds will lag during bull markets, and this can be difficult to explain to clients after a long period of high equity returns. This is why we like to say that bull markets cause amnesia about the benefits of diversification, and they discourage investors from holding uncorrelated strategies such as liquid alts. This client behavior makes it tempting for advisors to build portfolios that rely exclusively on traditional sources of beta for returns, and that rely on optimization for risk management.

Adding uncorrelated alternative strategies to the mix, however, can expand the efficient frontier in ways that are not possible when an investor relies solely on traditional asset classes.

With this introduction aside, we now launch into two illustrations that show why volatility management is so important, and we focus on how volatility drag hurts the long-term returns for a portfolio.

HOW VOLATILITY DRAG REDUCES COMPOUND RETURNS

Volatility drag describes the impact of volatility on compound annual returns. This deterioration of returns is difficult to detect in the short run, since the noise of market volatility masks the signal from volatility drag. Consequently, financial literature often encourages investors to ignore volatility in the short run and to focus on long-term returns. This is generally true, but it masks the damage done by gyrations in the returns of a portfolio.

For example, the capital asset pricing model (CAPM) links investment returns with volatility, and assumes that greater volatility produces higher expected returns. Hence, CAPM assumes that the volatility of returns rewards investors with a risk premium over the risk-free rate. This risk premium implies that, over the long run, stocks will outperform bonds, bonds will outperform cash, and high-beta stocks will outperform the equity market as a whole. The implications of the CAPM are sometimes misunderstood, however, since some investors presume that volatility *itself* rewards long-term investors and bolsters portfolio performance.

In order to illustrate the effect of volatility on compound returns, we include two charts: one showing returns for a fixed initial investment of $10,000 (Figure 16.1) and one showing returns when the client takes distributions from the portfolio (Figure 16.2). The time frame in both portfolios is 30 years, and year zero may occur at any point in someone's life. We show three levels of volatility that a portfolio may experience over these 30 years:

- *No volatility*: Returns are steady at 7 percent from year 1 through year 30.
- *Moderate volatility*: Returns alternate from 17 percent in year 1 to −3 percent in year 2. This two-year cycle repeats through year 30.
- *High volatility*: Returns alternate from 25 percent in year 1 to −11 percent in year 2. This two-year cycle repeats through year 30.

All three levels of volatility—high, moderate, and no volatility—have an average annual return of 7 percent, as shown in Table 16.1. Figure 16.1

TABLE 16.1 Growth of $10,000 Assuming 7 Percent Returns and Different Levels of Volatility

	Growth of $10,000	After 4% Distribution	
High Volatility	7.0%	7.0%	Average Annual Return
	5.5%	1.4%	Compound Annual Growth Rate
	$49,488	$15,243	Portfolio after 30 Years
	395%	52%	Cumulative 30-Year Returns
Moderate Volatility	7.0%	7.0%	Average Annual Return
	6.5%	2.5%	Compound Annual Growth Rate
	$66,737	$21,058	Value of $10,000 after 30 Years
	567%	106%	Cumulative 30-Year Returns
No Volatility	7.0%	7.0%	Average Annual Return
	7.0%	3.0%	Compound Annual Growth Rate
	$76,123	$24,273	Value of $10,000 after 30 Years
	661%	143%	Cumulative 30-Year Returns

shows returns for a fixed investment, and Figure 16.2 shows returns during the distribution phase, when 4 percent of the year-end balance is distributed as income to the client. The 4 percent rule assumes that a balanced portfolio can sustain annual distributions of 4 percent each year, so we thought this would be a good place to start.

The portfolios in these two illustrations grow at different rates, and the differences in performance among these three examples shows up in the compound annual growth rate (CAGR) of each portfolio. For math geeks, the CAGR is also called the geometric mean, while the average annual return is the arithmetic mean.

In Figure 16.1, the portfolio with no volatility grows in a steady curve, earning 7 percent annually. As a result, the portfolio's initial 10,000 reaches $76,123 in year 30. Figure 16.2 shows the distribution phase, and the same portfolio earns 3 percent annually since 4 percent is distributed. This portfolio reaches $24,273 in year 30.

Adding volatility to the picture changes the outcomes. The portfolio with moderate volatility follows a sawtooth pattern of returns, rallying in one year and dropping subsequently in a cyclical pattern. The portfolio advances 17 percent during each rally, and retreats 3 percent during each downturn, still achieving a 7 percent average annual return but only a 6.5 percent CAGR. This portfolio will be worth $66,737 in year 30, or 14 percent less than the portfolio with no volatility. In Figure 16.2, the portfolio has a 4 percent distribution and it grows to $21,058 in year 30, or 15 percent less than the portfolio with no volatility.

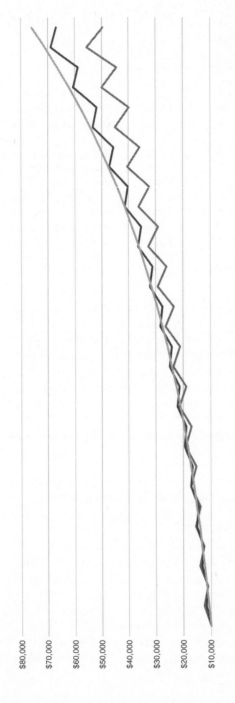

FIGURE 16.1 Growth of $10,000 Assuming 7 Percent Returns and Different Levels of Volatility

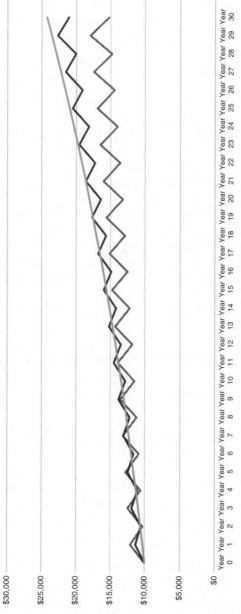

FIGURE 16.2 Growth of $10,000 Net of a 4 Percent Distribution Rate

The portfolio with high volatility undergoes a boom/bust cycle of 25 percent returns and 11 percent declines, represented by its jagged peaks and valleys in the chart. While the average annual return is still 7 percent, the CAGR is only 5.5 percent, and the portfolio will grow to only $49,488 in year 30, or 54 percent less than the portfolio with no volatility. In Figure 16.2, the portfolio in distribution ends up with $15,243 in year 30, or 60 percent less than the portfolio with no volatility.

Table 16.1 summarizes the results of each portfolio's returns over 30 years. The portfolio with no volatility delivers a cumulative 30-year return of 661 percent and a compound annual growth rate, or geometric mean, of 7 percent. Having steady returns means that the portfolio experiences no volatility drag. In Figure 16.2, the portfolio with no volatility and a 4 percent distribution rate also avoids volatility drag, achieving a cumulative 30-year return of 143 percent and a CAGR of 3 percent, since 4 percent is withdrawn each year.

Conversely, the portfolio with moderate volatility achieves a cumulative return of 567 percent and a CAGR of 6.5 percent, while the portfolio with high volatility fares even worse, with a cumulative 30-year return of 395 percent and a CAGR of 5.5 percent. When in distribution, the portfolios with moderate volatility and high volatility deliver cumulative 30-year returns of 106 percent and 52 percent, respectively, and CAGRs of 2.5 percent and 1.4 percent (the latter is less than half the CAGR of the portfolio with no volatility).

Readers should note that the levels of volatility in these examples are well within historical norms, and far worse scenarios could materialize. Additionally, the example assumes that the return sequences start with a rally, which makes the charts look slightly better in the first few years. (Though it may be counterintuitive, the long-term results are identical regardless of whether the example begins with a positive year or a negative year.)

Volatility erodes returns even though it is not easy to see. This is especially true in the early years, when the year-to-year fluctuations in value mean that the portfolios with moderate and high volatility are sometimes worth more than the portfolio with no volatility. In this sense, noisy returns obscure the signal of volatility drag. The impact of volatility drag is relentless, however, and shows conclusively that higher levels of volatility gradually and progressively erode portfolio returns over time.

Volatility, in and of itself, is *not* advantageous. But it is not necessarily disadvantageous, either, if managed appropriately by constructing diversified portfolios. This is where liquid alts come in, since some of these strategies provide uncorrelated returns that help reduce volatility and enhance long-term returns.

TALKING POINTS FOR CLIENTS

While liquid alternatives are a potential solution for volatility drag, advisors must be able to explain this concept to clients: They must democratize access to liquid alts through education of their clients. Access to alternative strategies has already been democratized, since the products are now available in Investment Company Act of 1940 ('40 Act) wrappers. But in order to fully take advantage of this access, investors need education about these products to capitalize on the benefits they offer to portfolio construction.

As one example, if a product has negative correlation to equities, an advisor must identify how it can be used as an effective vehicle to hedge equity market risk. Likewise, an advisor must explain how a product with low correlation reduces volatility, which over a long investment horizon will mitigate the erosion of returns from volatility drag.

Most important, an advisor must use concepts like volatility management to put liquid alternatives in context. Investors are tempted to avoid liquid alternative products during a bull market since uncorrelated strategies tend to underperform. Advisors can help manage client expectations by explaining the long-term benefits of volatility management. Volatility drag is a tricky concept to explain, but managing volatility through sophisticated portfolio construction techniques is one example of how advisors can validate their role and the fees they earn.

BEHAVIORAL DISCIPLINE

Moreover, advisors also add value when democratizing the education of concepts such as volatility drag and the role of liquid alternatives in portfolios. One of the benefits of alternatives is that these products can temper the harmful behavioral effects of volatility. Volatility often causes clients to panic, and impedes an advisor's ability to execute a disciplined plan. For example, clients who panic may bail out of a strategy and withdraw funds during a market trough. Uncorrelated strategies in a portfolio may prevent clients from bailing out at the bottom.

Another benefit of alternatives strategies is higher lows via volatility management. This is especially important when clients have unexpected liquidity needs. Long-term horizons are simple and attractive in theory, but life is full of surprises, and this includes liquidity events such as death, illness, marriage, divorce, and so forth. The combination of unpredictable life events and a fickle market highlights the importance of liquidity and volatility management, so that portfolios are better prepared for unforeseen financial needs.

One of the biggest opportunities in '40 Act alternatives is volatility management for retirees, given the large asset base of baby boomers and their need for income in a low-yield environment. Retirees who seek lifetime income need fully diversified portfolios and volatility management, and they may benefit from new products and strategies.

One reason is that retirement portfolios are especially vulnerable to a bear market in early retirement, since it greatly increases the odds that the client will eventually run out of money. Once assets are withdrawn, the portfolio cannot benefit from a market rebound. (Monte Carlo simulations can reveal this risk, which is also called the "sequence of returns" problem.) The need for lifetime income is an enormous challenge, and allows advisors to add value by offering more robust portfolio construction.

SUMMARY

Volatility management is one way that advisors can add real value during the portfolio construction and fund selection process. When using uncorrelated strategies, advisors must also commit to client education, since concepts like volatility drag are not easy to grasp. Advisors who combine effective usage of liquid alts with effective education are creating better portfolios for clients, a superior value proposition for themselves, and a healthier wealth management franchise.

CHAPTER 17

Suitability and Fees

Synopsis

Discussions about liquid alternatives can sometimes overlook suitability, or get sidetracked by a preoccupation with fees. Granted, alternative mutual funds usually do have high expense ratios compared to traditional mutual funds. The key question is: Are they worth it? If advisors do their homework, they can find funds with a risk/return profile that justifies a premium fee, especially in the context of the portfolio's overall costs and goals.

This chapter also discusses the value proposition of investment advisors. Fee compression is spreading throughout the wealth management industry, sometimes with good reason, and sometimes not. Advisors have a key role to play in the investment process when they take time to understand the client's goals and connect these goals with the appropriate set of investment solutions. This process can be enhanced by considering sophisticated products such as liquid alts, and this is one way that advisors can serve clients better.

SUITABILITY AND RESULTS

Advisors who have long-term client relationships are already familiar with the importance of suitability. Suitability screening is often done defensively, in order to prevent compliance problems, and focuses mainly on risk tolerance. Forward-looking advisors who use a goals-based approach to financial planning may see suitability in a more positive light, as a means to help clients reach their objectives, and keep them engaged with their financial success over time. Successful advisors may use suitability discussions to deepen their relationship with clients by getting to know them better, and perhaps even expanding their book of business through client referrals.

Suitability plays a less visible role as advisors shift gears from financial planning to portfolio construction. But it is critical to properly assess client needs and to match these needs with the right portfolio. A proper assessment and reassessment may even help generate better investment results. After all, a client who understands the portfolio is less likely to panic when performance is poor. A related issue is client communications, since an advisor who educates a client about new strategies now has a more sophisticated client who is ready for a broader spectrum of investments. Sometimes the best investment opportunities lie in complex strategies run by sophisticated managers, and client communication and education open the door to these opportunities.

This perspective on suitability highlights the value of a healthy advisory relationship. A do-it-yourself approach is great for Home Depot, where the products are usually simple and the risks of failure are low. In this case, it makes sense to emphasize low prices. But a DIY approach to investing can be catastrophic, so it is a mistake to assume that the cheapest portfolio is the best portfolio. In some cases, a sophisticated approach with complex products can add value, especially when the advisor takes the time and effort to thoroughly understand the client's needs, concerns, and objectives.

INTERVIEWS

In order to gain a deeper understanding of the issues involved, we consulted individuals within the mutual fund industry. Here are two perspectives.

Kathy Nalywajko, CTFA

Kathy Nalywajko, CTFA, is an investment advisor and a principal of Legg Mason Investment Counsel. In the following interview Nalywajko discusses her perspective on suitability, and how advisors can use it to help clients reach their investment goals *and* get better investment performance. She also discusses the value added that advisors offer, and how fees fit into the advisory relationship. In some ways, a healthy advisor/client relationship is like a healthy doctor/patient relationship: It is a joint effort, and clients who collaborate with you enjoy the full benefits of a successful relationship.

How do you make the case for investment advice?

That question has some hidden assumptions: Why is investing something people automatically think they *should* do themselves? I don't assume I can fix my own car, and I may not choose to clean my own house. Maybe I lack the skills, and maybe it is not an optimal use of my time. There are issues of convenience, knowledge, and emotion. If we were robots, there would be a lot less to write about. How we react to things is important—you can't discount emotions in the investment process.

How do you discuss fees in the context of your value proposition as an advisor?

Advice delivery is not primarily about fees. Why should it be? The world has so many investors and so many clients, and there are different ways to meet different needs.

For example, what if you said that you wanted to date "the best person in the world." What does *that* mean? How would you define the experience and the relationship you're seeking? There are plenty of choices for people when it comes to personal relationships, and there are plenty of choices when it comes to investment advice. So we have to frame questions about advisory relationships in a constructive, meaningful way.

I understand that fees eat at returns, but so does doing nothing. It is usually benign neglect that costs you. It's a combination of benign neglect, bad decisions, and emotional decisions. Perhaps clients are overly conservative and sitting on cash, and they just ride the market in the worst possible way: getting in at the top and getting out at the bottom.

The industry does not operate in vacuum: People are unusual, unique, and emotional. As an advisor, you are trying to figure out how to serve a variety of people, and fees are not really the driver of the value proposition. Fees are part of the experience, but so are communication, risk management, behavioral finance, and emotional discipline.

We have an Investment Policy Statement for every client, with communication standards. If you call, you will get a call back within 24 hours. If you call and say it's an emergency, we'll get back to you within three hours. So a client knows what to expect. The Investment Policy Statement outlines all aspects of the client experience and client expectations. We document what we said, and revisiting is critical. Focusing on one aspect (such as fees) is totally misleading.

Some academics focus heavily on fees. What are they missing?

When many academics look at investing, they focus exclusively on fees. *But this presumes that investors can do a good job at managing their money.* In this case, the academic perspective assumes what it is trying to prove: that investors already have the willingness and ability to do the job well.

What about expense ratios for funds?

'40 Act funds report performance net of fees. The primary focus should be on the net results for the client. Does the product improve the risk/return profile of the portfolio? Does it help the client achieve his or her goals? Sometimes you get what you pay for: Some forms of active management are inherently expensive, since they require data, research, and experienced professionals.

'40 Act funds also offer access to strategies and consistent reporting, and with audited results. You have to put some premium on the liquidity, too.

Todd Hiller

Todd Hiller is Director of Market Research at Oppenheimer Funds, and has extensive experience studying investor needs, investment products, and the mutual fund industry. He notes that mutual funds and exchange-traded funds (ETFs) are not stand-alone products. Hiller also offers a perspective about how fee pressures will affect advisors and the delivery of investment advice.

How would you describe the value proposition of Oppenheimer for clients?

Oppenheimer brings unconventional wisdom to the marketplace for investors. The firm has product strengths in areas of the marketplace that are less understood. We have a forward-looking philosophy about asset management, and we go to places where people are looking to go: emerging markets, floating-rate notes, master limited partnerships (MLPs). This evolves as the market evolves.

Best of breed and open architecture solutions have affected the concept of the fund family. How do you see it?

The shift to best of breed has certainly challenged the mutual fund industry. But best of breed is a natural part of any maturing industry. Advisors are embracing best of breed, and that makes sense for them as fiduciaries: They are holding mutual funds accountable in an open architecture world. But this puts unusual pressure on fund families.

Mutual fund firms were originally all about access to different products that people would use to build diversified portfolios. (Some firms went with a specific philosophy, but these are few and far between.) So for those firms that are just providing access to products, it was inevitable that these commodity providers would get weeded out. The fund industry remains undefined in many ways. It has become a game of having something compelling to say (entertainment, for some) and it has turned product quality into a game. But outperformance comes over market cycles, and doesn't lend itself to cursory analysis.

What role will technology play?

There will be disruptive innovation from the technology industry. The Internet is naturally disruptive, and offers price discovery about funds and lots of research on funds. But the complexity can be overwhelming for investors, so I think people will use a combination of technology and people to get them the solutions they want.

Historically, we're used to treating Internet tools as distinct, and competitive with the role of an advisor. *Investor behavior shows that investors increasingly want multiple sources of advice.* Access to advice has historically been available only via a human being, but technology is changing that. As technology improves access to research and advice, it is putting pressure on advisors to take their game to the next level.

We see this as a fundamental shift. This is a result of living in the tool-based age. You can already access basic information to build a diversified portfolio from ETFs and passive funds. Automation is here, but it's really another tool in the advisor's tool bucket. It's not an either/or decision to use online tools or an advisor. Investors can use both.

What about account aggregation? Is this important to investors?

Account aggregation is important to advisors since they want to manage all of a client's money. But do investors want their advisor to have access to all of their financial information? Many investors like to break up their advice among different people. This is a change that has been caused by the Internet and the financial crash. People are nervous about sharing information and aggregating all their assets at one place. There is no shortage of options in the marketplace, which is as it should be, since people want choice. People like to shop at Wal-Mart for price and variety, and then shop at a specialty retailer for niche products and high-end services.

How will advisors have to change?

Some advisors are having difficulty adapting to this challenge. They have to recognize that perhaps they cannot get *all* of a household's assets, even if they are serving the client well. Advisors want to provide holistic advice, but this may be an outdated model in many situations. Perhaps account aggregation makes sense for high-net-worth clients who don't mind paying for convenience, and who have the assets to make it profitable for the advisor.

It works to provide holistic advice and financial planning when the client has $2 million in assets and generates $20,000 of revenue. It does not work when the client has $250,000 of assets and generates $2,000 or less in revenue.

We've had fee compression throughout the mutual fund industry. How will this affect advisors?

Fee compression and commoditization are going to affect the entire value chain for advice delivery and asset management. How will this play out for the delivery of advice? This remains an open question.

Commoditization is happening to some advisors just as it has already happened to asset managers. This is not something that is openly discussed.

What does this mean for the mutual fund industry?

We might see more specialization. Each firm has to decide where its deepest bench strength is to ensure that it has scale in the areas where it excels.

What about social media—how might this affect the fund industry?

In the future, the social aspects of investing may resonate more. People talk about finance and mutual funds, and fund firms must engage investors more directly. This could also involve topics such as social responsibility, impact investing, and so on.

FEES

Alternative mutual funds are expensive. That is hardly a controversial statement, but in some ways it misses the mark.

First and foremost, fees must be seen in a portfolio context. We explore this in Chapters 15 and 18, and we assume that advisors already have access to low-cost beta, if that is what the situation requires. Even for index products, fees are just part of the fund selection process. An advisor needs to consider all of the characteristics of the product, including its factor exposures, assets under management, trading volume, bid/ask spread, tracking error, liquidity during times of market stress, and unique tax issues (such as the benefits of certain MLPs in a structure like an exchange-traded note). Advisors may also consider commission-free ETFs, which can be more cost-effective for small accounts that are rebalanced frequently. Advisors can help clients by addressing all of these considerations during the fund selection and portfolio construction process.

To add additional perspective, it also helps to consider the overall state of the mutual fund industry and advice delivery. Fee pressures are leading to all sorts of changes: ETFs are taking share from large-cap equity mutual funds, and liquid alts are taking share from traditional hedge funds. A similar dynamic is playing out in the advisory market, where some advisors are cutting fees, or are introducing streamlined forms of wealth management to compete for smaller accounts. Then there are online platforms such as Wealthfront and Betterment, which automate portfolio construction and offer fees as low as 15 to 25 basis points.

Polls of top advisors now show a lot of skepticism about online tools and automated solutions. One problem with looking at these polls is that the largest, most successful advisors are people whose success has already been established. Assets are slow to migrate, and the business models that worked in the past may not work in the future. So polling advisors is not necessarily a signal about what will work in the future, but a signal about what worked in the past.

What does the future hold? Perhaps the advisory industry will diverge into low-cost automation at one end of the market and bespoke solutions at the high end of the market. In either case, products such as liquid alternatives can enhance the value proposition of advisors by putting another tool in the tool chest.

SUMMARY

Suitability is often shortchanged in an analysis about alternatives, but it is always a critical element in the portfolio construction process. Fee pressures and technological change will continue to transform the wealth management industry, and advisors need to adapt their value propositions accordingly.

QUESTIONS

1. How can effective suitability improve investment results?
2. What is your philosophy about fees? What is your firm's perspective?
3. How do you discuss fees with your clients? Do you try to avoid the topic, or do you put fees in the context of your overall value proposition?

CHAPTER 18

Fund Selection

Synopsis

Traditional thinking has often assumed that all alternative funds are basically the same, and the investment process may lump liquid alts together and dump them into the "alts bucket." Looking ahead, it may be more useful to define liquid alts in terms of the functional roles of each fund, depending on its factor exposures and product design. So it may be time for alts to "kick the bucket" and shift to an approach such as the Micro-Endowment Model. This requires an expanded due diligence effort and a more complex portfolio construction process as advisors blend alpha, beta, and liquid alts in creative new ways. It also shifts the fee discussion from the product level to the portfolio level, allowing a wider range of fees for different investment strategies.

Liquid alternatives are often lumped into an "alts bucket" regardless of the underlying strategy. This process implies that the classifications are homogeneous and fungible, and any fund can be used as a portfolio diversifier. This approach may work with some funds, especially those funds that have a variety of underlying factor exposures. Indeed, it is time to for alternatives to kick the bucket approach and use a more robust process. We created a new framework as shown in Table 18.1—the Micro-Endowment Model (MEM). We introduced this concept in Chapter 15, and now offer additional details.

Many institutional investors use an endowment model that consists of hedge funds, private equity, and real assets. But these traditional alternatives have historically been restricted to accredited investors, and most limited partnerships have their own minimum investment requirements. So it's fair to say that traditional alternatives have been available only to the 1 percent, as they say.

The relatively recent availability of these nontraditional strategies in '40 Act wrappers has democratized access to hedge fund strategies and a few private equity strategies, and the mass affluent can now mimic some aspects

TABLE 18.1 Micro-Endowment Model

Asset Class	Allocation	Role of Asset: Type of Product
Equity		
	20% to 30%	Equity Beta: Passive Fund
	5% to 15%	Equity Complement: Liquid Alts
	5% to 15%	Diversifier: Liquid Alts
Fixed Income		
	10% to 20%	Fixed Income Beta: Passive Fund
	5% to 10%	Fixed Income Complement: Liquid Alts
	5% to 10%	Diversifier: Liquid Alts
Real Assets		
	0% to 15%	Beta Exposures: ETFs
Alternative		
	0% to 10%	Tactical Hedge: ETF/Liquid Alts
	0% to 10%	Directional Bet: ETF/Liquid Alts
	5% to 20%	Diversifier: Liquid Alts
Cash	0% to 10%	Liquidity
	100%	

of the endowment model with accounts of less than $100,000. Therefore, we created the new Micro-Endowment Model (MEM) framework. The MEM enables a broader audience to imitate aspects of the endowment model by providing a practical and feasible illustration, so that investors can understand how to use strategies that had once been exclusively restricted to hedge funds.

FIVE KEY ROLES

The first step in the process is to understand the nuances of liquid alternative strategies, and how to best incorporate these products into a portfolio. Throughout this book we assume that liquid alternatives serve five primary roles: equity complement, fixed income complement, portfolio diversifier, tactical hedge, and directional bet. We describe the factor exposures of each role next.

Portfolio Diversifier

These strategies offer noncorrelation to traditional asset classes such as stocks, bonds, cash, and real assets. We define diversification in terms of long-term returns, and the ability of the selected fund to help manage portfolio volatility. Noncorrelated means out of sync with the market, so these funds should reduce the correlations of the portfolio to the stock and bond markets, and to other asset exposures that are easily purchased in an index form (including real estate, commodities, precious metals, etc.).

Noncorrelation is a difficult concept for clients to grasp: Most investors like the idea of diversification, but they often fail to understand the implications. When stocks are up, investors want stock returns, and when stocks are down, they want cash returns. When the market is up, investors want alpha generation, and when the market is down, they want absolute returns.

Absolute Return Funds are a good representative example of a classification that serves the role of portfolio diversifier. Ideally, Absolute Return Funds have limited beta exposures to stocks and bonds and improve the diversification profile of the portfolio. Since these funds are uncorrelated to the market, they achieve low returns in bull markets, and typically outperform during bear markets. By tempering the impact of nonsystematic risk and black swan events, the addition of this strategy can reduce portfolio volatility.

Equity Complement

These strategies have a high correlation with equities and can enhance portfolio returns; they have a similar risk/return profile to long-only stock funds. Because of their equity beta, the Micro-Endowment Model places funds that act as equity complements within the equity asset allocation. Some of these funds may even be considered a form of active management with equities. In a sense, alternative strategies are creeping into the equity allocation of the portfolio. The strategy may be alternative, but the factor exposure remains firmly tied to equities. Some equity complements have far more equity beta than others.

For example, Alternative Active Extension Funds serve as an equity complement by giving the portfolio an extra dosage of equity exposure. This classification can help generate alpha, and the leverage potentially enhances returns. Bear in mind, though, that these funds amplify risk, so advisors must address suitability before using these products in client portfolios.

Most alternative strategies that serve as equity complements involve some type of downside protection. This could include shorting stocks (e.g., Alternative Long/Short Equity Funds), raising the cash allocation, using derivatives, shorting exchange-traded funds (ETFs), and so on. What these funds all have in common is nontraditional strategies for managing a fund that is primarily tied to the equity market.

Fixed Income Complement

These funds have a correlation with bonds, with a similar risk/return profile. Fixed income complements' most important feature is the active management of credit risk and duration risk. Investors are eager for enhanced income, but they want a portfolio manager to evaluate and manage the variety of risks that arise. One danger with enhanced income strategies is that they may include high-yield bonds and emerging market debt that are uncorrelated with U.S. fixed income securities in a normal market environment. When a crisis hits, correlations tend to converge, both across the globe and across the credit spectrum. Hence, these supposedly uncorrelated funds could become correlated in adverse environments.

Alternative Credit Focus Funds are the quintessential fixed income complement. These funds can be used as a bond proxy to diversify the fixed income portion of a portfolio and hedge the equity allocation. As the interest rate environment changes, this strategy's most attractive feature is its ability to hedge bond duration and credit exposures, thereby providing active management of both risks. As rates rise, investors are likely to continue to gravitate toward these funds for capital preservation, and so-called bond hawks may use them for inflation protection. For yield-hungry investors, particularly retirees, these unconstrained fixed income products provide a source of enhanced income with a reassuring overlay of active risk management.

Tactical Hedge

These alternative strategies may act as a form of insurance, with low expected returns in most environments and high expected returns during fat-tail events. For example, Alternative Currency Strategies Funds have historically had low returns and high volatility. Funds in this classification can help hedge the currency exposure of foreign stock and bond positions by making strategic bets on the direction of a currency.

Investors must always be cognizant of the cost of a hedge, since these add up over time. Since many liquid alts use forward contracts, contango can be an issue. Contango occurs when the futures price of a security exceeds the spot price. Upon expiration the price of a futures contract must converge with the spot price, and the alternative fund will lose money as the fund sells the spot contract and buys a futures contract at a higher price. This is negative roll yield, and it can sometimes make liquid alts an expensive form of insurance.

Another issue is benchmark drift, whereby a portfolio deviates from its initial allocation as underlying positions change, overexposing a portfolio to risks that cause sharp losses in the future. The costs of a hedge in liquid alternatives can be difficult to quantify, since the products use derivatives and the returns do not mirror their benchmarks. This issue occurs in dedicated short products, currency strategies, and active extension funds.

Directional Bet

Some funds provide a specific bet on an asset class or a leveraged bet on a benchmark. Some alternative strategies can be highly leveraged, and the dispersion of returns varies widely. Professional traders and investors typically take a directional bet for tactical purposes or to hedge a long exposure within a portfolio. Dedicated short funds, leveraged ETFs, and currency funds often serve this role.

For example, Dedicated Short Bias Funds aim to capture the inverse or negative multiple of an index's return. Due to the strategy's propensity to undergo sudden losses, these funds are typically employed over short time horizons. In fact, most directional bets are intended for short-term trading due to the potential for rapid erosion of capital. This classification and its respective roles are quite risky, and the advisor must have conviction in the direction, timing, and magnitude of the trade and the fund's beta exposure in order to make directional bets effectively in client portfolios.

Portfolio Illustration

Given the varying roles for liquid alts, we provide a portfolio illustration to show how funds might fit within the MEM (Table 18.2). *Please note that the funds and weightings used in Table 18.2 are illustrations, not recommendations.* The illustration uses five asset classes: equity (50 percent allocation), fixed income (30 percent), real assets (9 percent), alternative (9 percent), and cash (2 percent). Endowments typically make greater allocations to alternative and real assets, but they also have much longer time horizons. The weightings shown are simply illustrations, and the appropriate allocation will depend on client situation and the current market outlook. These weights do suggest, however, an evolution from the 60/40 mix of stocks/bonds to a 50-30-20 mix of stocks/bonds/alternatives. The past 40 years included a secular bull market in fixed income, and a stock/bond mix offered sufficient diversification for most investors. But today's environment is marked by low real yields and rising correlations among stocks and bonds. This makes it difficult to build lifetime income solutions using the usual mix of stocks and bonds.

In the equity asset class, traditional exposures typically include domestic and foreign stocks, a sprinkling of small-cap stocks, and perhaps a blend of growth and value funds. We believe that adding an equity complement, such as an Alternative Long/Short Equity Fund, will enhance the equity portion of a portfolio by providing alpha potential as well as equity beta. This would create a new efficient frontier for portfolios that use uncorrelated alternative strategies with attractive combinations of risk and return.

TABLE 18.2 Portfolio Illustration

Asset Class	Allocation	Role	Symbol	Product Name	Lipper Alternative Classification
Equity	25%	Equity Beta	VTSMX	Vanguard Total Stock Market Index Fund	
	15%	Equity Beta	SCHF	Schwab International Equity ETF	
	5%	Equity Complement	MFLDX	MainStay Marketfield Fund	Long/Short Equity
	5%	Portfolio Diversifier	DVRIX	MFS Global Alternative Strategy Fund	Global Macro
Fixed Income	20%	Fixed Income Beta	AGG	iShares Core Total U.S. Bond Market ETF	
	5%	Fixed Income Complement	JSOSX	JPMorgan Strategic Income Opportunities Fund	Credit Focus
	5%	Portfolio Diversifier	MWSTX	Metropolitan West Strategic Income Fund	Absolute Return
Real Assets	3%	Beta	VNQ	Vanguard REIT ETF	
	3%	Beta	DBC	PowerShares DB Commodity Index Tracking Fund	
	3%	Beta	AMJ	JPMorgan Alerian MLP ETN	
Alternative	3%	Tactical Hedge	PLMIX	PIMCO Emerging Markets Currency Fund	Currency
	3%	Directional Bet	PSTIX	PIMCO StocksPLUS AR Short Strategy Fund	Dedicated Short
	3%	Portfolio Diversifier	AQMIX	AQR Managed Futures Strategy Fund	Managed Futures

A portfolio diversifier such as an Alternative Global Macro Fund may also have an equity tilt, and may provide noncorrelation. Adding this type of fund would reduce the volatility drag on the portfolio. The weighting for both the equity complement and the diversifier should account for a smaller allocation than the traditional equity portion of a portfolio.

In the Micro-Endowment Model, the fixed income portion of a portfolio could include exposure to traditional long-only bond funds, along with a fixed income complement and a portfolio diversifier. A fixed income complement, such as an Alternative Credit Focus Fund, provides enhanced income, in addition to active management of interest rates. Adding a diversifier such as Absolute Return Funds with a fixed income tilt provides capital preservation and inflation protection.

The Micro-Endowment Model shown in Table 18.2 also has exposure to alternatives. This includes a tactical hedge, such as an Alternative Currency Strategies Fund, and a directional bet, such as a Dedicated Short Bias Fund. The former protects the portfolio from an unusual event such as a sharp decline in the U.S. dollar. The choice of a specific fund as a tactical hedge will depend on the risk that the portfolio manager is trying to mitigate and on the outlook for capital markets. This makes it a tactical hedge and not a portfolio diversifier (which is more strategic and protects against more general risks).

A directional bet is a speculative trade or a thematic play based on economic, political, technical, or other factors. This exposure is usually small, and is meant for short time horizons, since these funds are vulnerable to large, rapid losses. Directional bets also provide potential alpha and a way for an advisor to add value on a tactical basis.

Last, the alternative exposure might hold a position that diversifies the portfolio, such as an Alternative Managed Futures Fund that is held for extended periods of time for long-term diversification. *Alternative Managed Futures Funds are an excellent example of a portfolio diversifier, and this is one of the few liquid alt strategies that are genuinely uncorrelated with the major asset classes.* This observation is a key finding of our research, since most marketing for liquid alts promotes diversification benefits, but very few liquid alts actually deliver it.

Moreover, the allocation to real assets, while small, provides both diversification and income. Real assets typically include exposure to real estate by way of real estate investment trusts, and to commodities by way of master limited partnerships and direct commodity beta. Additionally, as in any portfolio model, holding a small reserve of cash provides a hedge, liquidity, and purchasing power during a crisis when some assets are available at fire-sale prices.

This illustration of the Micro-Endowment Model includes a small number of funds, but the framework can be used to build fully diversified portfolios for a variety of market environments. The MEM combines a core/satellite approach with traditional assets and liquid alternatives used in a variety of roles. This allows advisors to create cost-effective, transparent, and tax-efficient portfolios with optimal risk/return characteristics.

GENERAL TIPS ABOUT FUND SELECTION

The process of choosing a liquid alternative fund can seem overwhelming given the vast array of asset class exposures, fund classifications, and liquid alt strategies. Assuming that an advisor has a framework for asset allocation, the fund selection process would begin by screening historical returns and risk ratios across liquid alt classifications and portfolio roles. If the role of a liquid alt is more defensive, such as a portfolio diversifier, the screening process will put more emphasis on factors such as the maximum drawdowns and Sortino ratios. If the portfolio role is more aggressive, such as an equity complement, the screening process will put more emphasis on factors such as returns and Sharpe ratios. Once the advisor has a list of funds with attractive risk/return characteristics, the advisor can pursue a deeper dive into fund filings, marketing literature, in-house due diligence, third-party research, and in some cases direct discussions with the portfolio manager.

The complete quantitative and qualitative process of fund selection is beyond the scope of this book. But there are certain rules of thumb that due diligence teams usually follow when evaluating fund managers for each investment strategy, and evaluating alternative managers entails additional steps due to the complexity of the securities and strategies. Thus, there are certain attributes that advisors and investors should seek during the fund selection process. First and foremost, the fund documents should include a concrete description of the fund's philosophy, process, and execution. This sets expectations for exactly what the fund is, and what it is not. This should offer a clear set of expectations for the strategy, including how it performs in different market environments. One warning sign is the broad use of boiler-plate language in fund literature. Some of this is a necessary evil, but vague and sweeping claims should be minimized, especially in marketing material.

Additionally, the fund should offer monthly or quarterly updates that show accountability when explaining investment performance. Ideally, this includes performance attribution that links investment performance to the investment process, which allows the advisor to determine if the manager is executing as expected. The updates and marketing literature should illustrate a well-defined process, and should show candor when performance is poor. The fund should also have managers who are experienced with the strategy, and the firm should provide adequate resources for data, research, trading, operations, and risk management.

In terms of fees, our general philosophy treats expense ratios as secondary to risk and return. Many investors will beg to differ, and with good reason: Fees should be an investor's primary concern at the portfolio level since fees are easy to manage and the only factor known with certainty in advance. But an investor should not always make fees the primary concern at the product level, since a portfolio that blends alpha and beta will have a wide range of fees.

Thus, many investors ask if an index product can replicate liquid alternative strategies. In practice, duplicating the performance of liquid alternative strategies using a low-cost passive approach often proves difficult. After all, the fees for liquid alts often reflect the expertise and research that is necessary for complex strategies that aim for superior returns.

With that said, expense ratios merit analysis, and advisors should be cognizant of the role of the product, the appropriate expense ratio, and its overall weighting in the portfolio. Advisors must question whether the fund employs an attractive strategy that will truly improve the portfolio, and whether the fund is the most cost-effective way to receive access to the particular strategy. Depending on the account size, more cost-effective and tax-efficient forms of the strategy may exist in a separately managed account. Likewise, advisors must ascertain the inherent costs of the investment process, including the costs of the required data feeds, top-down and bottom-up analysis, and the necessary experience, technical expertise, and degree of specialization of the analysts and portfolio managers on the research team.

Advisors must also determine if a fund offers the best alpha potential for a given strategy. Simply put, if a client qualifies for a traditional hedge fund, he or she may get better returns. Some asset managers, such as AQR Capital Management, offer alternative strategies in both a limited partnership structure and a mutual fund structure.

SUMMARY

The process outlined in this chapter serves as a launching point for advisors, depending on their priorities, resources, and fund selection processes. These rules of thumb are meant to spur dialogue about fund manager due diligence and portfolio construction, and we hope that the Micro-Endowment Model is a useful tool in the process.

CHAPTER 19

Interviews

Synopsis

There are many ways to use alternatives effectively, and we offer these interviews to give a broader perspective on liquid alts, portfolio design, and the advisory business. We spoke with a thought leader at the CFA institute, two gatekeepers at major wirehouse firms, and an online advisor that aims to disrupt the business of investment advice.

We thank the participants for giving generously of their time. We hope you find thought-provoking insights that are relevant to your value proposition as a financial advisor and your investment process as a wealth manager.

STEPHEN HORAN

Managing Director, Co-Lead, Education, CFA Institute

Dr. Stephen Horan, the Managing Director and Co-Leader of Educational Activities at CFA Institute, analyzes liquid alts just like any other security: by the quality of the product. One of his primary concerns about liquid alternatives rests in bail-out risk, and reasonably so. Investors tend to panic at the bottom, undercutting the liquidity of a product that by definition is supposed to be liquid. Thus, he proposes considering a cash reserve to serve as a psychological buffer.

Dr. Horan emphasizes client goals and understanding the proper role of a liquid alternative product. Is the client seeking hedging or diversification? Understanding the difference between the two is key. The liquidity of liquid alternatives can be misleading, in his opinion, and advisors must manage client expectations; other headwinds include fees and taxes. Last, Dr. Horan warns about volatility drag. While advisors can use volatility to their advantage during the accumulation phase, it is destructive when a portfolio is in distribution—a problem many retirees now face.

The book defines liquid alts as uncorrelated strategies in a '40 Act wrapper. How do you define liquid alts?

First we must ask: What are alternatives? The industry still needs to come to terms with what we mean as an alternative. It's treated as an asset class, but it does not have the attributes of an asset class. These funds vary according to the underlying investments. Private equity is typically not purchased to diversify portfolios, but to offer higher returns.

With *liquid* alts, I get even more nervous about the definition. Does the '40 Act wrapper actually *add* liquidity? You may get liquidity when markets are quiet, but during a crisis, when everyone heads for the doors, you don't necessarily get the benefits when perhaps you want the liquidity the most.

How can advisors and investors reconcile this distinction?

Alternative strategies are heterogeneous. The investor should make a decision based on whether the product is a valuable cost-effective addition to the portfolio, and whether it fits with the Investment Policy Statement.

Personally, I'm agnostic about the use of alternatives. Some alternatives are useful tools in some situations for some clients, while others are not so useful in certain situations.

What are the proper roles of alternative asset classes in client portfolios? How do individual portfolios differ from institutional portfolios when it comes to alternatives?

It is critical to understand the difference between diversification and hedging. Diversification involves the combination of strategies that are uncorrelated; hedging involves strategies that are negatively correlated. Both of these propositions live in the alternatives space. You must understand the difference.

Dr. Andrew Lo's liquid alts fund was designed to be a hedge instrument. [This refers to the ASG Diversifying Strategies Fund.] It was designed to perform well in bear markets, and it would have performed well in bear markets. Investors headed for the door because they didn't like what hedging actually meant in a bull market.

I'd recommend a hedging tool in the right situation, but I don't think most people understand the distinction between a diversifying investment and a hedging investment.

So the issue resides in the way a fund is portrayed as opposed to the actual strategy?

Another product might be classified as a liquid alt: a market neutral fund, though this is hard to actually find in practice. This strategy is a different proposition, even in the theoretical sense, since it is designed to eliminate beta. In the alternatives space, how do you measure correlations, betas, and benchmarks? These are not trivial questions, since the wrong definition introduces a huge bias in your measurements. Poor liquidity creates a huge downward bias in volatility, correlations, and hence estimates of market risk. It creates the appearance of diversification when perhaps it does not exist. You have to be careful that you are looking at a return series that is uncorrelated with another return series.

In your view, do liquid alternatives reduce volatility?

Private equity looks like a low-volatility strategy when put in a '40 Act wrapper since the illiquidity is hidden. The wrapper does offer some benefits in terms of price discovery, since there is daily pricing. So you do discover something about the previously hidden illiquidity. But the signals from the market are a noisy form of price discovery—valuable, but noisy.

What are liquid alternatives' most pressing challenges?

Alternatives have two strong headwinds to overcome—cost structures and taxes. One thing that I know about portfolio construction is there is no single variable that drives net returns more than these: The more you pay, the less there is left over for you on average—nothing else explains returns more than that. So investors need to give the cost structure serious consideration.

Some of these structures can be replicated effectively in an ETF structure. ETFs are a wonderful tax structure. Active or passive can be done in an ETF wrapper.

Exchange-traded funds (ETFs) continue to grab share from mutual funds. Would you suggest investors opt for alternatives in an ETF wrapper rather than a mutual fund?

My biggest reservation for the private client is that intraday trading is probably not useful. The liquidity of the ETF is a blessing, but it can also encourage the wrong type of behavior, such as excessive trading.

I want to separate the wrapper from the underlying [exposure] any time I can because it helps me understand the investment more clearly. You can wind up conflating the issues and get lost in the marketing jargon.

Do you perceive volatility as a headwind for portfolios?

Volatility drag is critical. In the accumulation phase, volatility erodes accumulation. If they are disciplined via dollar cost averaging with rebalancing, investors can actually put volatility to work for them and offset the deleterious effects of volatility drag. In the distribution phase, however, periodic distributions are like reverse dollar cost averaging, which magnifies rather than offsets volatility drag.

How can advisors and investors use volatility drag to their advantage, and at what stages? How does this impact retirees?

Volatility drag *hurts* in retirement for same reason that dollar cost averaging *helps* during the accumulation phase. People can capitalize on volatility as they save [through disciplined rebalancing of asset classes]. Dollar cost averaging does this fairly well. When you are withdrawing funds, however, volatility forces you to withdraw more shares after a market decline in order to generate the same amount of income.

Volatility drag hurts retirees for reasons you just explained, but what about investors with long time horizons?

In one sense people can say, "I'm long term, and if things are more volatile between now and the end of my investment horizon, that's fine—I'm unfazed." But they *should* be fazed by volatility because they will accumulate less wealth if their average returns stay the same and volatility rises; they will accumulate less wealth over time.

Managing volatility is an important thing not just by the numbers, but also because of the behavioral overlay. If advisors/investors are not managing volatility, they are at risk of abandoning the strategy at the worst moment.

How can advisors and investors manage this "bail out" behavior?

This is the behavioral aspect: You might bail out of the strategy at the worst possible moment.... Thinking in terms of realistic investor behavior, this is why we propose the idea of a safety reserve. People should hold enough cash to cover three years of day-to-day spending, and all of their one-off five-year needs. They may think that this safety reserve takes a lot of money out of market, and it does. But the importance is that it creates a psychological buffer between the investor and market—it neutralizes deleterious market beta, and allows the investor to stay with the strategy they have laid out in their investment policy statement. It doesn't force you to liquidate at the worst possible time, and it mitigates the whole notion of volatility drag during the distribution phase, as it relates to timing.

Is it mathematically correct to have a safety reserve? No, since it will create a suboptimal asset allocation. A cash reserve creates mathematically inferior returns, but from a behavioral standpoint it promotes better decision making over time.

This approach suggests advisors should hold a cash position in client portfolios. How should they best manage cash and fees?

You have to decide what you want to be: if you want to be a wealth manager or a money manager. If you want to manage assets, then only manage assets that you will get paid to manage. Don't have excess cash. But if you want to be a wealth manager, you may have to offer advice on all of a client's assets—including cash—even though you won't get paid on the cash.

As a wealth manager, forgoing the fees on the cash may just be a cost of doing business. You are advising on the cash portion of the portfolios, but you won't be collecting a fee. This, in a microcosm, is the difference between asset management and wealth management: *Asset management focuses on assets; wealth management focuses on clients.*

How can advisors provide a robust service when portfolios are small?

Don't tell a client you are delivering something that's different than what you actually are delivering. Not everyone can afford a Ferrari, so sell the Chevy. There is nothing wrong with the Chevy, but don't sell the Chevy and tell them they're getting a Ferrari.

Conclusion

Often liquid alternatives are least liquid when liquidity is most needed—during crises—because liquidity dries up. Moreover, investors hurt themselves by panicking and bailing out at the bottom of a market. Consequently, Dr. Horan encourages cash reserves to provide a psychological buffer. While holding cash may seem like a suboptimal portfolio, he says it will enable better decision making in the long run. What does this mean for advisors? In his words, holding some cash may just be the cost of acting as a financial advisor (especially one operating under the fiduciary standard) as opposed to acting as an asset manager.

Advisors must also manage volatility during the accumulation phase unless they use it to the portfolio's advantage, by employing strategies such as dollar cost averaging and disciplined rebalancing. Managing volatility is also imperative during the distribution phase, since advisors need to sell a greater number of shares to achieve the same amount of income after a decline in the market. Dr. Horan illustrates volatility drag as follows:

There are two ways to get a 0 percent average return:

1. Two years of 0 percent in a row
2. −50 percent in year 1, and +50 percent in year 2.

Dr. Horan noted his preference for 0 percent in both years, since the second option would leave him with only 75 percent of what he started with. Advisors must manage volatility appropriately because they will need to generate greater returns to accumulate the same amount of wealth in the presence of volatility over time. Additionally, managing volatility will make the client less susceptible to bail-out risk.

Ultimately, liquid alternatives are about managing expectations. Time and time again, whether at a large institutional firm or a small Registered Investment Advisor (RIA), honesty is the best policy. As Dr. Horan put it: "Don't sell the Chevy and tell them they're getting a Ferrari." After all, both cars will get you to your destination.

ROGER PARADISO

Director of Morgan Stanley Consulting Group's Investment Solutions and Portfolio Development, Managing Director

Roger Paradiso, Managing Director at Morgan Stanley, does not view liquid alternatives as fully alternative. Rather, liquid alternatives capture the performance edge of a hedge fund in a diluted form. These '40 Act funds are new, and therefore definitions are ever changing. As the strategies become large and institutionalized, the categories will become more defined and specific. Mr. Paradiso explains how advisors can meet suitability and compliance objectives, and how they can manage expectations, both of which lead to superior investment results. Our interview with Mr. Paradiso closes with his thoughts on the future of liquid alternatives in terms of automation and smart beta.

The book defines liquid alts as uncorrelated strategies in a '40 Act wrapper. How do you define liquid alts?

These are not alternatives in the traditional sense. These are really mutual funds that are seeking something different. This is a dilution of traditional LP [limited partner] structures.

What are the advantages of hedge funds?

The LP has structural advantages that do affect performance. It's not so much compensation and incentives but about strategies that are:

- Complex
- Expensive
- Illiquid

The more esoteric and specialized the strategy, the less efficient it will probably be. These can provide a sustained performance edge.

What are the proper roles of liquid alternatives?

There is no one answer. The definitions of categories are evolving, and the roles for each product are different, and depend on the goals of the client.

If it's a REIT [real estate investment trust], MLP [master limited partnership], or a hedge-type liquid alt strategy, they may act as volatility reducers. But liquid alts are all very different, and as you build them out, they'll be recategorized.

How do advisors mitigate bail-out risk?

Whatever strategy is chosen, it is imperative to keep a client on track and in the strategy.

What are the key drivers to superior investment results?

Effective suitability screening and follow-through by the advisor have historically been done in order to prevent compliance problems. Today, some goals-based investing is done to help engage the client, build relationships, and grow assets.

But there is an equally important role that suitability plays: It actually helps generate better long-term investment results. A client who understands the strategy will stick it out. This brings us to education: An advisor who educates a client now has a more sophisticated client, and he or she is suitable for a broader spectrum of investments. Sometimes the best opportunities lie in complex investments that only hedge funds can execute. They have the resources and expertise that comes with scale and profitability.

Should advisors maintain a liquidity bucket?

The advisor should be handling liquidity events, and the ongoing suitability screening should address this. If we make tactical changes, I don't execute them through a liquidity bucket. We're always 100 percent invested [so it's up to the advisor to manage liquidity]. If I do need liquidity, I'd cut fixed income 2 percent here or there, wherever it makes sense.

Another issue that comes up is settlement. Mutual funds settle on the same day, while SMAs follow the typical settlement of T+3. Different trade settlement dates created a problem for tradition alts, which have far less liquidity. We explain these issues to clients when they choose alternatives, so they know the issues when signing on for this.

How can advisors consolidate client assets effectively?

Consolidation of client accounts is complex, and it is not easy to provide financial plans when you do not have custody of the assets. If you do not have control over the assets, there is no guarantee that your plan will be executed. [This might be the case with 401(k)s, 529 plans, annuities, and other assets that are held away.] This can be frustrating because executing a comprehensive plan over multiple custodians is inconvenient, and the client may not follow through. Then the client and the advisor may become frustrated.

Nevertheless, it is still good to look at finances holistically, so you can catch the truly egregious problems. You may not catch every wash sale across multiple custodians (because you didn't know). But if you have an elderly client with huge capital gains in a legacy position, you may be able to manage this in a tax-efficient manner.

Obviously, if you don't know, you can't help. So even if comprehensive financial planning isn't always perfectly executed, it always helps the advisor and client come closer to a better outcome.

What changes are you seeing in portfolio construction using alternatives?

The educational process continues. Hedge funds used to be about knowing someone and being comfortable with the process. Now it's more about strategies and portfolio construction. Some of the marketing and positioning of '40 Act products aimed for clones of traditional hedge funds, and that didn't work. Bad selling practices have hurt the '40 Act space, and it has not reached the expectations of traditional [products].

For example, managed futures is an uncorrelated strategy, and there are many new products that compete for shelf space with managed futures. [Managed futures performed well in 2008, leading to high expectations and disappointed clients.]

Now we're seeing '40 Act model portfolios that are more like solutions: different products for different situations. The newer descriptions are focusing on the role and the function in a portfolio.

Do the advisors and clients have the knowledge to use these products correctly? If so, we give them a list of structures and allow them to pick funds. If they don't, it may make more sense to buy a prepackaged SMA with a dozen '40 Act products. [Morgan Stanley and other wirehouse firms select the products and build model portfolios for use by advisors.]

Is the future of portfolio construction moving toward automation?

Firms that do automated portfolio construction are run by technology-driven people. They are good at tech and will likely carve out a valuable niche. This is especially true since they don't have legacy issues that prevent firms and clients from changing the value proposition quickly.

But as their business matures, the forces of the industry inevitably push people into the traditional delivery of advice. That is usually a high-touch, high-trust relationship. People want communication, and they want to know that a qualified person or team of people has their eye on the ball.

So I would argue that you need some investment advisory professionals around you. Academics and tech experts are not sufficient for success. It looks good and sounds good, and you may have high-profile names from academia and Silicon Valley. But it all depends on how you mature the relationship between the advisor and the client.

If there's anything that stands out as most important, it's contacting the client. When they don't feel loved, they leave. In a bull market, this is easy. Bear markets expose this weakness.

Nevertheless, there's a market there for automated portfolio construction. And there is an evolution there among clients who want simple, convenient, low-cost solutions. It doesn't solve every problem, but it isn't meant to.

Will liquid alternatives cross over into smart beta?

They will reclassify these funds, though it's hard to tell if the factor exposures can be replicated in smart beta mutual funds. It depends on the underlying strategy, whether the holdings are liquid or illiquid, and the process used by the manager.

Conclusion

Mr. Paradiso's comments underscore how new the liquid alternatives space is, as definitions and strategies continue to evolve. With that said, he notes the specialization of hedge fund strategies and their ability to provide a performance edge. This outperformance can now be translated into a mutual fund wrapper, albeit in a diluted manner. As one mutual fund executive put it: "You don't get the jalapeño—you get black pepper."

Advisors should focus on a goals-based approach, ongoing education, and continual communication. Keeping the client informed about complex hedge fund strategies will help the advisor and client achieve better investment results, since it mitigates bail-out risk.

Moreover, Mr. Paradiso believes automation will play some role in portfolio construction for individuals "who want simple, convenient, low-cost solutions." Traditional modes of communication may temper this trend, as investors need to know that someone credible has his or her hands on the wheel, especially during bear markets.

DARYL DEWBREY

Head of Business Development, UBS Alternative Investments

Discussions with Daryl Dewbrey of UBS covered both traditional and liquid alternatives, as well as a range of portfolio construction issues. Dewbrey uses alternatives for diversification via noncorrelation, and he sees the pros and cons of products that offer high liquidity. He refers to trying "to make the lows higher," a topic we covered in Chapter 16 when discussing volatility drag.

Dewbrey discusses the ramifications of the lack of interest in diversification, which is not easy to find in the liquid alts space. The return data for the Lipper alternative classifications show that very few liquid alt funds generate uncorrelated returns. The promise and potential are there, but the performance is not.

What is the goal of investing in alternatives?

Advisors and clients need a different mind-set for investing successfully in alternatives: It's about diversification and noncorrelation. This is very different from the expectations for a long-only manager, who rides the ups and downs of the market.

Everything in alts is about better risk-adjusted returns over time. We try to make the lows higher. So in alts, you throw as wide a net as possible for assets that are uncorrelated. The portfolio will benefit from diversification in terms of higher lows over time, and the client will be better off.

What allocation to alternatives would you recommend for a diversified portfolio?

Every client is different, but we generally recommend an allocation of 15 percent to 20 percent. At the wirehouses, very few advisors have an allocation above 5 percent to alts.

Endowments and foundations may have 40 percent to 60 percent in alts, but they have unlimited time horizons and don't have to worry about decision making by individuals. Everyone's portfolio needs diversification— clients just need the right expectations.

In aggregate, wirehouse advisors reduced their allocations to traditional alternatives in 2013. What do you attribute this to?

This reflects strong performance of equities and relative underperformance of traditional alternative strategies. Within traditional alts, we saw assets in private equity and real estate go up, but assets in hedge fund assets go down.

In hedge funds, the asset allocation data show a shift from fund-of-funds hedge funds to single-manager hedge funds. How do you see this trend?

First of all, hedge funds are not seeing a migration from fund-of-funds assets. It would be more accurate to say that funds of funds are flattish, while we are seeing an increase in single-manager hedge funds.

Point taken. What are the prospects for fund-of-funds hedge funds?

In broad brushstrokes, funds of funds are likely to see flat asset growth due to less-than-stellar returns. Fund-of-funds hedge funds are usually used for core exposure to hedge funds for diversification purposes, since you can't build core exposure with single funds. Single-manager hedge funds may complement your core exposure in hedge funds, and may add diversification, alpha, or some specific exposure. But they are complementary, not core.

People will seek core positions in funds of funds that are truly noncorrelated. As you add these types of alts, it makes your portfolio more efficient. So overall growth of hedge funds and alternatives hinges on the portfolio approach.

So in a sense, fund-of-funds hedge funds are the core, and single managers are satellite.

That's one way to say it.

Turning to specific hedge fund strategies, managed futures strategies did great in 2008, but have had weak performance since then. Some portfolio managers have cut allocations to managed futures due to performance concerns. How do you see managed futures as a strategy? Do you have any plans to change allocations?

We are a big supporter of managed futures. Yes, it has massively under-performed. But it is a wrong to say that managed futures is a hedge against market declines; it has actually been uncorrelated. There's a big difference. This strategy offers an idiosyncratic opportunity to make returns. You need exposure over time.

We use managed futures as a supplement to other alt exposures. Due to lack of knowledge, investors are apt to get in or out of managed futures—maybe they're just chasing performance.

In the environment we've had, systematic algorithm strategies aren't going to perform well. There has been a massive skew in the markets due to global monetary policy and its impact on interest rates, valuations, and investment strategies. It's a top-down market, and that's not ideal for systematic algorithms.

But the right question to ask is: What do you expect over five to seven years? If you are not willing to understand long-term diversification, then alts won't work in your portfolio. Managed futures strategies are simply noncorrelated. The strategy was originally a commodity investment, and commodities do whatever they do.

Today managed futures are much broader—they participate in every asset class. Every manager is in 50 markets or more. You need many, many markets to get returns using systematic algorithms.

As an investor who has access to both traditional and liquid alts, how do you see liquid alts?

We are big believers in seeking noncorrelated return opportunities. That means finding things that zig when other things zag. If liquid alts get the portfolio access to uncorrelated opportunities, then it works. And even if a liquid alt strategy doesn't capture *all* of the noncorrelation, it's better than nothing.

In practical terms, a client with $1 million cannot do anything other than '40 Act alts and managed futures. A client with $20 million, on the other hand, would not do a lot of '40 Act alts. Clients with $2.5 million to $10 million represent an area of overlap, with opportunities for both liquid and traditional alts.

What about the research process for liquid alts?

The '40 Act wrapper does not necessarily make the strategy less risky. Your smallest client can now get something that might be very complex. Our hedge fund research team is getting more active in the due diligence of liquid alts. These products get on the platform, and the liquid stuff sells, so we have to do the research.

Let's consider the client perspective. Is there a downside to the liquidity provided by liquid alts?

There is a massive negative to the liquidity provided by liquid alts. Although liquidity is valuable, it undermines the discipline of the investor.

Liquid alts are so easy to implement that people are not committed to them. People get skittish—they bail out in a bull market. The client will tend to bail out of the strategy at the wrong times, buying high and selling low. Using straight stock or bond ETFs is cleaner for tactical needs and liquidity needs; you would *not* use liquid alts. The biggest bang for buck is from bigger asset classes, which have a greater proportion of assets available if cash is needed. *The detriment of "liquid" is that it encourages advisors/clients to bail out at the bottom of the cycle.*

Alts are something that clients are less familiar with. They are accustomed to equities. They need a level of discipline, and there's a benefit to *not* being able to trade on daily price data.

If you look at daily moves, it's not constructive. You can't look at a portfolio over long time horizons and manage it on a daily basis. This aspect of behavior shouldn't be overlooked.

Let's shift to the portfolio management perspective. Should advisors and portfolio managers use liquid alternatives as a liquidity bucket for tactical moves and unexpected liquidity needs?

It's a bad idea to use any one asset as a liquidity buffer. You might have degrees of liquidity *within* an asset class, but it's a bad idea to designate a single asset class as a liquidity cushion. This could undermine the entire asset allocation process simply because the client needs cash. The client's need for cash has nothing to do with the strategic outlook for the portfolio or the outlook for the underlying strategies. So when you rebalance portfolios, for either tactical needs or client needs, you need to reallocate in a comprehensive manner.

This book's research of Lipper classifications found that most liquid alts are highly correlated with traditional factor exposures: stocks, bonds, credit risk, and so on. Does this reflect market demand? After all, if the mutual fund industry developed liquid alts that were truly uncorrelated, perhaps advisors and investors wouldn't buy them. How do you see it?

As more people become engaged with liquid alts they'll discover that most of these products really don't deliver the noncorrelation that people expect: Investors will eventually discover that liquid alts have excessive beta. Maybe this will happen in the next market crash. Then people will be disappointed and give up on liquid alts as a concept. But that's because the products were not designed and used for their best role: diversification through noncorrelation.

There is going to be a period of time when liquid alts will *appear* to provide value, and this will probably be a bullish market environment that's hospitable to beta strategies. People will get accustomed to the beta, and the value of a true hedge fund strategy will be overlooked.

That's a scary prospect, because it means fewer people are interested in traditional alts, and hedge funds reward skill. When the beta environment goes away, investors will miss out on the opportunity to work with the most skilled managers, and they don't rely solely on beta for returns.

Speaking of beta, how do you look at fees for alternatives?

Beta can and should be cheap. Alternatives are meant to make the lows higher, and they are tremendously helpful to limit portfolio drawdowns.

How much would an investor have paid in 2008 to have 50 percent of the portfolio in cash? How do you explain the value of *that* to a client?

Conclusion

Mr. Dewbrey confirms a few themes mentioned by Horan and Paradiso:

- Cash is the best liquidity buffer, and rebalancing should be done across asset classes.
- Liquidity of a product can undermine discipline, which is the dark side of "liquid" in liquid alts.
- Diversification through noncorrelation may be the best role for alternatives.
- Portfolio construction must be mindful of the tendency for clients to panic and to bail out during bear markets.

Mr. Dewbrey was most outspoken about managed futures, which he can speak about from experience as a former director of Ceres Managed Futures. His conviction in managed futures despite recent performance confirms his dedication to diversification as one of the best ways advisors can help clients build long-term wealth.

DANIEL EGAN

Director of Behavioral Finance and Investing, Betterment

> Technology is disrupting investment advice, as online platforms provide automated portfolio construction at lower prices and with greater transparency and tax efficiency. Betterment is one such online advisor, and we spoke with the Director of Behavioral Finance and Investing, Daniel Egan, to provide insight on this new industry. Mr. Egan outlines the ways in which an online financial advisor, like Betterment, can add value, and how it may complement traditional financial advisors.
>
> Throughout this book, our philosophy about fees emphasizes cost-effective portfolios, rather than low-cost portfolios: If the risk/return profile of a fund is attractive, it may justify a premium fee, and the client will be well served. So for contrast, we offer this perspective on portfolio construction from a firm that focuses on low costs.

What drives Betterment's advice delivery?

The advice at Betterment is strongly informed by behavioral finance, and the research from behavioral finance maps over very closely to automated advice delivery. We look at many aspects of the client's circumstances and life to advise how the client can invest holistically.

What are the things that will help investors take home the best returns after fees, taxes, and transaction costs? Expenses and taxes play a large role.

Minimizing fees and transaction costs is often accomplished by using passive strategies. How do you define passive products and passive asset allocation, and how does Betterment achieve this?

We use a market-tracking portfolio employing passive products, but we do have alpha that is specific to the investors and their circumstances. The portfolios are anchored to Black-Litterman. They aim for the highest risk-adjusted returns for each investor. We use a downside-weighted utility function that allows us to take on different levels of risk, and this gives different levels of returns, depending on the downside acceptable to each investor.

What are the ways in which an online financial advisor, like Betterment, adds value?

We add value in four key ways:

1. *Asset allocation*: We actively manage index-tracking portfolios based on a global asset allocation, and we adjust it based on how market cap weightings evolve. [See William F. Sharpe, "Adaptive Asset Allocation Policies," *Financial Analysts Journal* 66, no. 3 (May/June 2010).] We use insights from Fama and French, and overweight small-cap and value stocks.
2. *Tax management*: Many of our customers hold taxable and nontaxable accounts, and we need to optimize across both. If we have a customer who lives in California, we'll include state-specific municipal bonds to minimize the tax burden. Critically, the platform has the infrastructure to optimize across households: Being vertically integrated gives us that ability to do it. Tax loss harvesting can be very effective at deferring tax losses in the future. Monitoring of wash sales needs to be done across household accounts.
3. *Saving optimization*: We give clients advice about how much they need to save to achieve their goals. How much do you need to save to buy a house? We look at the risk-free rate now and through your time horizon, and moderate how much risk you need to take.
4. *Rebalancing algorithm*: We base rebalancing on thresholds of 5 percent drift from the client's target asset allocation. Any sort of transaction where you buy or sell rebalances your portfolio (including tax loss harvesting). *Note*: 70 percent of customers have an automatic deposit function, typically two weeks.

How do your models adjust when portfolios are in distribution?

We looked at a lot of the research and built an algorithm that looks to optimize retirement income. It is able to adapt when there are bull or bear markets in retirement; it can adjust income.

Do liquid alternatives play a role?

These may be a potential source of alternative beta. Much of the research shows that the net benefits are small if not negative. We look at returns after risk, taxes, and transaction costs. How much does it cost to access the beta? How liquid is it? Transaction costs and liquidity costs are both important.

There is a spectrum of ETFs that offer factor exposures, and these might be interesting. You are not betting on idiosyncratic manager skill. We do due diligence on all the investments that go into the portfolio. Liquid alts are not an especially attractive bet, unless held in a tax-efficient wrapper. It is difficult for us to strongly recommend them.

Is Betterment a threat to traditional advisors?

We focus on the stuff that can be done better or cheaper than the average advisor can do. We can focus on goals and investments in a way that [automates what traditionally] is time-consuming and prone to error. This allows the advisor to spend more time on understanding the client's goals, tax situation, estate planning needs, definition of risk, social security planning, and so on. We do the things that are time-consuming and quantitative, and benefit from using automation.

Some people think that so-called gamification of education can help investors learn. Any thoughts?

There are some parts of education you could gamify, but it's more effective to educate people about their individual situations. An investment game has to be customized to engage people consistently. [It has to be relevant to investors, or they lose interest: Retirees don't want to play the same games that young savers want to play.] At Betterment, every time you make a deposit, we send confirmation e-mails with encouragement. They enjoy reinvesting.

Conclusion

As online advisors attract more assets, it is important for traditional advisors to understand their value proposition. As Mr. Egan notes, the platform at Betterment aims for optimal risk-adjusted returns based on client profiles and driven by behavioral finance. By actively managing index-tracking portfolios and using algorithms to rebalance a portfolio or achieve optimal taxable accounts, the online advisor is able to provide low-cost solutions with attractive risk/return profiles in a cost-effective and tax-efficient manner.

We have no quarrel with low costs: Passive funds *are* a great complement to liquid alternatives, and a blend of ETFs and liquid alts helps create a portfolio that is flexible, transparent, tax-efficient, and fully diversified.

Many traditional financial advisors see firms like Betterment as a threat to their business model, and they denigrate automated portfolio construction as a "robo-advisor." Mr. Egan highlights how online advisors like Betterment can complement traditional advisors by emphasizing what automation can accomplish faster and more cheaply. With that said, clients also appreciate a human touch during a bear market, and this supports the value proposition of traditional investment advisors.

This approach to portfolio construction will likely appeal to younger investors who are typically tech savvy and accumulating assets. Automated portfolio construction, coupled with a gamification aspect to engage and motivate investors, gives online advice a bright future for many clients.

Conclusion

Liquid alts are making inroads on both traditional mutual funds and hedge funds, and are a disruptive force that is democratizing access to strategies that had been historically restricted to high-net-worth investors. The growth of liquid alts is likely to continue as more investors learn about the value proposition of '40 Act funds, which offer lower fees, improved liquidity, and greater transparency and tax efficiency than traditional hedge funds. Not only does the democratization of hedge fund strategies make these strategies available to mainstream investors for the first time, but the '40 Act wrapper improves the attractiveness of these strategies for many affluent investors as well. In fact, our interviews found that large institutions use liquid alts in portfolios for high-net-worth clients. Liquid alternatives empower all investors with innovative opportunities to diversify, hedge tail risks, and achieve alpha.

This newfound access to hedge fund strategies is worthless, however—or even harmful—if advisors and investors do not know how to use liquid alts effectively in portfolios. We wrote this book to help financial advisors and sophisticated investors better understand the underlying strategies of these new '40 Act products, and properly use these funds via a goals-based portfolio construction process that begins with fund screening and selection and ends with a fully diversified, cost-effective portfolio. One such framework is the Micro-Endowment Model, which enables progressive advisors and investors to run portfolios with a process that imitates the best practices of an endowment, but is feasible for individuals. In turn, we wanted to equip advisors with the appropriate tools and precise language to educate clients effectively about the roles of liquid alts in their portfolios.

It is critical for both advisors and clients to have realistic expectations for the risk/return benefits of liquid alts. Many of these products are uncorrelated with stocks and bonds, so these funds tend to underperform in bull markets and outperform in bear markets. Liquid alts may not capture market peaks, but these funds help portfolios sustain higher lows during market downturns; this volatility management enhances long-term performance.

In order to benefit fully from the noncorrelation of liquid alts, clients must maintain exposure over the long term. The market cycle for liquid alts is not correlated with equities, and this means practicing discipline when

237

the stock market is reaching record highs. You cannot have equity beta and noncorrelation, too.

With that said, alternatives can help investors sustain their equity allocations over market cycles. Equity volatility rattles investors; since uncorrelated alternative strategies are more resilient during bear markets, their inclusion in portfolios allows investors with varying risk tolerances to hold on to equities.

Therefore, liquid alts are often viewed as a form of insurance. We also perceive liquid alts as a source of psychological alpha: investments that mitigate the consequences of fear-driven and nonproductive asset reallocation that is often triggered by market volatility. Noncorrelated assets provide a sense of security, which helps abate uneasiness and reinforce discipline. As psychological alpha, liquid alts hedge the irrational behavior of investors, thereby helping them stay in the game.

About the Companion Website

This book has a companion website, which can be found at www.wiley.com/go/alts. Enter the password: rabe123.

The companion website includes:

- The authors' top ten takeaways for liquid alternatives
- A cheat sheet on Lipper's eleven classifications
- Presentation on portfolio construction
- Talking points on liquid alternatives for clients
- Answers to common client questions about liquid alternatives and its role in portfolios
- A complete list of all the exhibits in the book (full color)

About the Authors

Jessica Lynn Rabe is a research associate at ConvergEx Group, a global brokerage company based in New York. Rabe assists the firm's Chief Market Strategist in publishing the ConvergEx Morning Briefing, a daily commentary on financial markets that is distributed to 5,000 financial professionals and is frequently featured in news outlets, such as the *Wall Street Journal*, *Barron's*, the *Financial Times*, Bloomberg, and CNBC.

Rabe is a contributor for the American Enterprise Institute's *Values and Capitalism* blog, and has been published by other mediums, including the World Economic Forum's *Global Information Technology Report*, Asset International's *Strategic Insight Alternatives Quarterly*, Seeking Alpha, and the Center for Public Justice.

Previously, she was a research analyst specializing in liquid alternatives at her coauthor's firm, Right Blend Investing, LLC, a Registered Investment Advisor (RIA) in New Jersey. Her responsibilities included securities research and portfolio construction. She also helped research and write consulting reports for the asset management industry on the use of liquid and traditional alternatives by wirehouse firms, and on advisory services for the 401(k) market.

She has interned at the EMC Brazil Big Data Research and Development Center in Rio de Janeiro, and for the campaign of U.S. Congressman Rodney Frelinghuysen in New Jersey.

Rabe graduated summa cum laude from Gordon College with a BA in economics, where she participated in the Jerusalem and Athens Forum, an interdisciplinary honors program. She also founded the "Global Perspectives" column in the Gordon College newspaper, and is a member of Phi Alpha Chi, a scholastic honor society.

Robert J. Martorana, CFA, owns Right Blend Investing, LLC, a Registered Investment Advisory firm in New Jersey. Martorana manages client portfolios, analyzes alternative products, and is a consultant to the mutual fund industry. This blend of experience gives him a broad perspective on best practices in the wealth management industry.

As the founder of Right Blend, Martorana builds model portfolios and provides comprehensive, flexible, and customized wealth management for individuals. He specializes in a Micro-Endowment Model that blends a core of exchange-traded funds (ETFs) with a satellite of liquid alternatives for diversification, high potential returns, and mitigation of tail risk.

He does contract research for Lipper, Kasina, Asset International, and Dover Financial Research, which publish reports for executives in the asset management industry. Since 2011 he has been the author or coauthor of more than 500 pages of research on topics such as ETFs, alternatives, product distribution, the RIA market, portfolio construction, product innovation, and the 401(k) marketplace.

Having worked on Wall Street since 1985, Martorana began as a stock analyst at Value Line, comanaged small-cap equity funds at Schroders, and was Director of U.S. Equity Research at Barclays Private Bank in the Americas. Subsequently, he was editor of a hedge fund website at TheStreet.com, and a high-net-worth advisor at PNC Wealth Management prior to founding Right Blend Investing in 2009.

He has managed or comanaged portfolios across every major asset class, ranging from individual accounts under $1 million to pooled funds over $1 billion. Over his career, he has supervised more than 70 asset management professionals, and has published hundreds of reports in print and online.

Martorana graduated cum laude from Lehigh University with a BS in economics. He is a Chartered Financial Analyst, a member of the New York Society of Security Analysts, and contributor to Seeking Alpha. Additional details are available at www.RightBlendInvesting.com.

He supports the Sharon Children's Home in Andhra Pradesh, India, founded by Abraham Samuel. Additional information is available at www .fgcministries.org/orphans, and at www.rightblendinvesting.com/about /philanthropy.

Index